WIThOUT NOISE OF ARMS

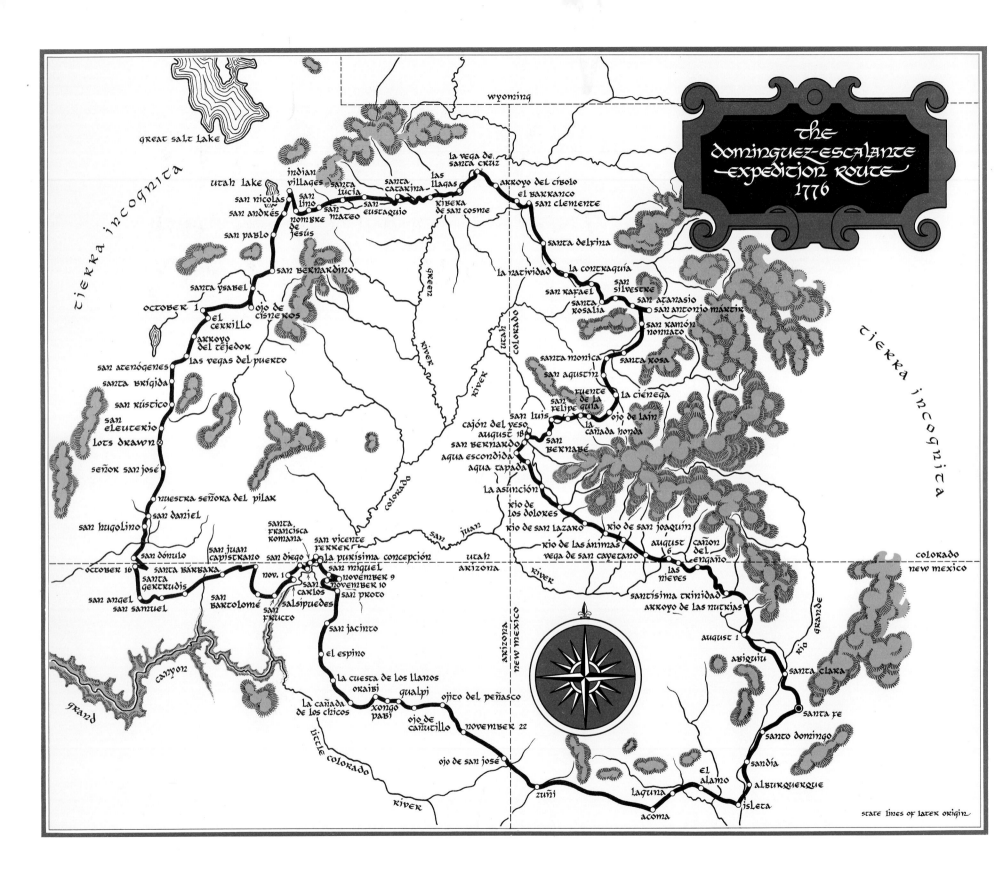

THE DOMINGUEZ-ESCALANTE EXPEDITION ROUTE 1776

wyoming

great salt lake

tierra incognita

utah lake

indian villages

santa lucia

la vega de santa cruz

arroyo del cíbolo

el barranco

san clemente

santa catarina

las llagas

ribera de san cosme

san nicolas

san lino

san mateo

san eustaquio

santa delfina

san andrés

nombre de jesús

san pablo

san bernardino

la contraguía

la natividad

san rafael

san silvestre

santa ysabel

santa rosalia

san atanasio

san antonio mártir

october 1

ojo de cisneros

el cerrillo

san ramón nonnato

arroyo del tejedor

santa monica

san agustín

santa rosa

san atenógenes

las vegas del puerto

fuente de la felipe guía

la ciénega

santa brígida

san luis

ojo de lain

san rústico

cajón del yeso

la cañada honda

august 18

san bernardo

san bernabé

san eleuterio

lots drawn

agua escondida

agua tapada

señor san josé

La asunción

rio de los dolores

nuestra señora del pilar

san daniel

rio de san lazaro

rio de san joaquín

san hugolino

santa francisca romana

san vicente ferrer

rio de las ánimas

vega de san cayetano

august 6

cañon del engaño

san dónulo

san juan capistrano

san diego

la purisima concepción

utah

arizona

colorado

new mexico

las nieves

october 16

santa barbara

nov. 1

san miguel

november 9

santisima trinidad

arroyo de las nutrias

santa gertrudis

san carlos

november 10

san proto

san angel

san samuel

san bartolomé

salsipuedes

san fructo

august 1

abiquiu

santa clara

san jacinto

el espino

arizona

new mexico

grand canyon

la cuesta de los llanos

oraibi

gualpi

ojito del peñasco

la cañada de los chicos

xongo pabi

ojo de cañutillo

november 22

santa fe

santo domingo

little colorado river

ojo de san josé

sandia

el alamo

alburquerque

zuñi

laguna

isleta

acoma

river

colorado

green river

utah river

colorado

san juan river

rio grande

state lines of later origin

WIThOUT

The 1776 Dominguez-Escalante Search

NOISE OF ARMS

for a Route from Santa Fe to Monterey

BY WALTER BRIGGS

Oil paintings by Wilson Hurley
Foreword by C. Gregory Crampton

NORTHLAND PRESS / FLAGSTAFF

CONTENTS

The Paintings

The Charts

FOREWORD

DURING THE YEAR when the war of the American Revolution opened on the Atlantic seaboard, Spain in the West staked out vast new areas, among them the western slope of the central Rockies, the intricate canyon country of the Upper Colorado River, and the endless deserts of the Great Basin. All of this was accomplished in a last outward impulse of a movement begun in 1521 when the Aztecs fell before the conquering Cortés. With great rapidity Spanish explorers ranged north from Mexico founding cities, mining, ranching, and propagating the faith. But after the occupation of New Mexico late in the sixteenth century, frontier advance was slowed until 1769, when the present State of California was colonized.

During the next decade, an historic one East and West, Spanish administrators sought to strengthen the northern frontier and members of the Order of Friars Minor — The Franciscans — volunteered to explore the lands between New Mexico and California in the hope of opening a good road to connect these outposts of empire.

To this end the most notable exploration carried out by the Franciscans was undertaken by Francisco Atanasio Domínguez and Silvestre Vélez de Escalante. During the last five months of the year 1776 the two friars, at the head of a small party unaccompanied by military escort, made a great circle tour from Santa Fe through western Colorado, central Utah (where they were turned back by weather), northern Arizona and western New Mexico.

Most of the way Domínguez and Vélez de Escalante were crossing lands altogether new to Europeans and in an entrada rivaling that of Daniel Boone, Zebulon Pike, and Lewis and Clark, they gave us the first vistas of the very heart of the North American West. In the diary of the expedition, signed by both men, we find lengthy descriptions of the complicated geography of the intermontane region, of the tribes, and the plant and animal life. Bernardo de Miera, the company cartographer, drew maps of surprising accuracy.

The Franciscans urged their king to plant settlements and missions in the newly discovered lands. Too late. In a revolutionary era Spain soon faced rebellion in her own colonies and before any further frontier expansion could be started, her own empire fell to pieces.

It is appropriate now, two hundred years after their splendid adventure, that we take the measure of these hardy Spanish pioneers, who made known so much of the American wilderness, and to appraise their indelible significance in history. In this fine work, a book written to be read, Walter Briggs has done that job for us. He has thoroughly researched the literature and, in company with artist Wilson Hurley, he has retraced the Spaniards' epic trail. Domínguez and Vélez de Escalante, and their retinue, come alive in these pages, and they are cast in the perspective of their times.

C. Gregory Crampton

La Villa de Santa Fe . . . On a July morning, 1776, the Palace of the Governors, upper left, fronting the Plaza, with the Church of St. Francis, upper right.

THE GENESIS

THE LINES OF AUTHORITY

Church

ROME
Pope Pius VI

ROME
Franciscan Minister-General

MEXICO CITY
*Provincial Fray Isidro Murillo of the Franciscan
Province of the Holy Gospel
Fray Fernando Antonio Gómez*
Secretary to the Provincial

ON THE MOVE
Commissary-visitor Fray Francisco Atanasio Domínguez

EL PASO DEL NORTE
*Custodian Fray Juan de Hinosa of the Franciscan
New Mexico Custody of the Conversion of St. Paul*

State and Military

MADRID
King Carlos III

MADRID
Council of the Indies

MEXICO CITY
Viceroy Antonio María Bucareli y Ursua

MEXICO CITY
Council of War and Royal Exchequer

SONORA
Commandant-inspector Colonel Hugo O'Conor

SANTA FE
Governor Pedro Fermín de Mendinueta

2

THEY WERE TWO young Franciscan missionaries, a retired captain, a mixed-blood guide-interpreter, six diverse others. They had mustered in Santa Fe, New Mexico, to find a way to Monterey, California. They had meant to set out on the Fourth of July, 1776, but were delayed until the twenty-ninth of this historic month and year two-thirds of a continent away.

In five months these ten men would adventure some two thousand miles, exploring more virgin territory than Daniel Boone in a contemporary lifetime, even more than Lewis and Clark in their twenty-eight-month odyssey to the Northwest three decades later.

They would rove the Great Basin without knowing it, become the first white men to fathom a crossing of Colorado River canyons, and one of them would map rivers that were to bewilder explorers until the mid-nineteenth century.

"Without noise of arms" they would treat with a dozen or so Indian tribes, some antagonistic, some friendly, some timid from never having seen their like.

They would epitomize a final spurt of Spanish colonial energy for the glory of God and in the service of their king.

Why a route from Santa Fe to Monterey? Why this vigor in 1776? Why these ten men?

Exploration of New Mexico had begun in 1539, only forty-seven years after Columbus' first voyage. Colonization began in 1598, twenty-two years before the Pilgrims landed at Plymouth. Santa Fe was settled twelve years later. In that era New Spain, today's Mexico, encompassed most of North America — a vastness none would grasp for two and a half centuries — and New Mexico comprised our Southwest and far beyond.

By 1776 the Spaniards had been talking for two and a half centuries of probing and peopling "the Californias." Indeed, the ruthless Hernán Cortés dreamed of greater glory there even as he was conquering the rich Aztecs of the Valley of Mexico in 1521.

To the north the conquistador would find the Seven Cities of Gold, a reality through European ages. Up there he would find a waterway linking the Atlantic and Pacific, the Columbus shortcut to Marco Polo's Cathay that the English called the Northwest Passage. Three commissioned voyages from New Spain's west coast did find something for Cortés, a "great island," Baja (Lower) California.

Dreams were startled into new reality in 1536 with the ghostly advent of bronzed, wayworn, near-naked Cabeza de Vaca north of the Valley of Mexico. He and three companions, survivors of a four hundred-man expedition to Florida eight years before, were the first to cross North America. He told of seeing emeralds en route, of hearing about rich cities to the north and along the Pacific.

There simply had to be another, richer land of Montezuma beneath the North Star. A final Cortés-commissioned

3

sortie up the Gulf of California was thwarted by tidal bores at the jaws of what long later could be named Colorado, the River of Red that is cast as a tantalizing yet terrifying Circe in this book's drama. Baja California was a peninsula.

New Spain's first viceroy, sent partly to curb the imperious Cortés, in 1539 dispatched Marcos de Niza, an adventurous friar, to verify the Cabeza de Vaca reports. The priest took along Esteban, a Moorish slave and one of the four transcontinental survivors. Scouting ahead, a vainglorious Esteban demanded a deity's tithe in women and turquoise. He was hacked to pieces in the domain of what would become Zuñi Pueblo in west-central New Mexico. Returning to Mexico City Fray Marcos described jeweled walls at this one of the Seven Cities of Cíbola, as Indians thereabout dulcetly called them.

A youthful Francisco Vásquez de Coronado and a cavalcade of glory-smitten gentlemen, flying royal pennons, went in search of Cíbola in 1540. Fray Marcos' Seven Cities turned out to be six *pueblos*, mere villages. After initial dismay, Coronado and his conquistadores "went in search under the Western star," as an expedition chronicler had it, all the way from the Coconino Plateau to the Rio Grande and out to the Great Plains and their Golden Cities of Quivira.

Support vessels were sent up the gulf to the Colorado, which their mariners knighted Buena Guía though this Unfailing Guide failed to guide them to Coronado. An overland adjunct dubbed it Rio del Tizón, Firebrand, because the naked Yuma Indians thereabout carried torches against the cold. Still another Coronado contingent, coming upon the Grand Canyon, couldn't find a way down to a "great river" far below. The expedition chronicler astutely deduced that this river was the Tizón "much nearer its source."

Everywhere encountered, savages gaped at crossbows and firearms, prancing horses and gilded armor. Everywhere that they were loath to furnish food and clothing, shelter and guides, they received a first lesson in white man's savagery.

The conquistadores gave up after two years. "Granted that they did not find the riches of which they had been told," the chronicler mused, they failed also to appreciate "the beginning of a good country to settle in." Coronado's career glimmered off but the Seven Cities glittered on . . . Cíbola, somewhere else, and other Eldorados shimmering in the mind's eye.

And despite Coronado's failure, gold, silver and gems kept tumbling into Spain. Firm Hapsburgs ruled the world's biggest empire. Spain prospered; arts and sciences flourished. This would be called her Golden Age.

Alta California — our expedition's goal — came into ken as early as 1542. Navigator Juan Rodríguez Cabrillo, ordered to find Cortés' trans-American strait, braved unknown Pacific waters off western Baja California. He put in at a "closed and very good" port to make his name live among San Diego schoolchildren long in the future.

In the 1560s Spanish galleons hoisted sail from New Spain's west-coast Acapulco for Magellan's Philippines, trading silver for the Columbus-sought silks and spices through middleman Manila. To recross the wide Pacific, captains rode the Japan Current northeast, then prevailing winds abeam of California.

Francis Drake and other European privateers soon were seizing galleons all along Spain's Pacific flank, Drake's *Golden Hinde* once leaking from the weight of thirty tons of silver off Alta California. This piracy impelled the

4

Spaniards to seek a harbor there for escort vessels. In 1602 Vizcaíno, a merchant-adventurer, named a bay "sheltered from all winds" for the viceroy, the Conde de Monterey.

The succeeding viceroy opted instead for a haven in the mid-Pacific. Rich in Gold and Rich in Silver, as his islands translated, surely lay out there.

Tidings from Cabrillo, Vizcaíno and others hadn't been nearly as seductive as these islands. Ores and gems, big and sedentary populations — these had attracted colonizing elsewhere. Like Fray Marcos' Cíbola, Cabeza de Vaca's coastal cities were a chimera.

Alta California was thick green forest plunging from great blue mountain to inhospitable brown coastline, but natural beauty was not a commodity on the mercantilist market.

Besides, Spain's Golden Age was tarnishing from ill-gotten treasure. Traded for foreign goods, it corroded home industry. Taxes spiraled upward as astronomical inflation set in. Farming and herding wasted from ouster of the Moors, peasant rebellion and migration to the territories. The Inquisition scarred talented Jews and scientists. The Invincible Armada was despoiled off Britain in 1588; French power shook the continent.

A decade after that naval debacle it was royally sanctioned for Don Juan de Oñate, a wealthy silver miner from the Plateau of Mexico, to begin self-financed settlement of the area north of New Spain. Oñate attracted Coronado-style conquistadores and recruited peons from neighboring mines and fields. On the stubbled highlands of future New Mexico, the peons could arise as *hidalgos*, petty gentry, their own masters in a vocation of livestock herding.

Hardly a moment after a colony was plumped down in 1598 amid obeisant Pueblo Indians on the upper Rio Grande, Oñate set about ranging even farther than had Coronado in the ceaseless quest for glory and gold. At his side rode spirited fellow adventurers, in tow rode the new hidalgos who would rather have been left to their ranching.

Six years later, on a westward swing, Oñate struck a stream he named the Colorado, today's Little Colorado, the first use of the name hereabout. He didn't realize the Little Colorado was a tributary to what, at Bill Williams Fork in our western Arizona, he named Rio Grande de Buena Esperanza.

While the Colorado was picking up a new name with each new acquaintance, Oñate did discern that his Great River of Good Hope downstream became the Tizón of Coronado's day.

Among Mojaves and Yumans along the Colorado Oñate heard volunteered the word "Copalla." The Spaniards believed that the Aztecs had migrated south from a richly-endowed lake region called Copala. A Mojave mistook a Mexican Indian in Oñate's cortege for a Copallan "because those from there," fourteen days' journey northwest, "talk thus." A Yuman pointed to a Spaniard's gold toothpick and said the Copallans wore bracelets and earrings of such metal. With such proof, the Spaniards were believers.

But Copala was left dangling, Oñate's being summoned to Mexico City after eight years longer than Coronado in the search for such treasured regions. Once in the city he was tried on complaints of hidalgos and others; convicted of mistreatment of Indians and other abuses; fined, dishonored and exiled.

Still to be capitalized on was a "new Mexico" richer than the Valley of Mexico. Being reported rich in potential converts as well, this region would be sustained by the king himself, however meagerly, as "the Kingdom of New

Mexico." In 1610 a new governor moved Oñate's hidalgos from proximity with the Indians, protecting the former from attack and the latter from molestation. On a plateau twenty-five miles south was emplaced La Villa de Santa Fe, The City of Holy Faith, as the kingdom's capital.

Oñate's successors, while supervised by the viceroys in a general way, were both governors *and* captains-general serving the king as the kingdom's ruler. Documents soon were referring to "the Kingdom and Provinces of New Mexico," the former being anciently rooted Indian pueblos and gradually dispersed Hispano settlements in the Rio Grande vicinity, the latter the territory of Apaches and other New World Visigoths along a wide rim.

The Pueblos welcomed Spanish crops, livestock and hardware but didn't take kindly to settler encroachment on their lands. Nor were they grateful for labor and tribute exacted by official and missionary alike, especially when these demands aggravated the woes of famine brought on by drouth. Nor were they adequately defended against raids by Apaches, whom the Spaniards themselves had incited by slave raids, on captured Spanish horses. Most emphatically, their powerful religious leaders balked at fanatic clerical efforts to stifle their "witchcraft" and "idolatrous" dances.

In 1680 these medicinemen led a revolt of most of the pueblos, now in league with the Apaches in mockery of the Spaniards. Some four hundred settlers were slain, the other two thousand driven south to El Paso del Norte (today's Juárez, Mexico). For thirteen years they remained in exile until the relentless Don Diego de Vargas engineered a bloody reconquest of now-divided Indian allies. Vargas is honored to this day by an annual week-long Fiesta de Santa Fe in which his *entrada* is re-enacted in pageant.

Out along the rim of New Mexico's "provinces," Oñate's Copala still beckoned. France was believed plotting an advance toward its treasures from the Mississippi. Father Posada, a former mission supervisor in New Mexico, in the 1680s wrote for the king a sort of defense paper on the region, as fair a summary of the peoples and geography known at the time as could be asked. To Posada, Oñate's Copala was Teguayo, where a Pueblo parishioner of his had been held captive beside "a large lake populated all around its borders." Though omitting reference to the Oñate-cited gold jewelry, the priest urged exploration to Copala-Teguayo. Perhaps because Posada demonstrated that reaching New Mexico would be a long haul for the French, the king ignored his advocacy of such expensive long-range reconnoitering.

While Alta California was being neglected, the Spaniards did occupy more accessible Baja California by sea, the colony supported in the main by pietistic charity. Contrary Indians were missionized step by weary step to within some two hundred fifty miles of Cabrillo's port, which Vizcaíno had named San Diego.

Meantime, on their own initiative slave raiders, miners, settlers and missionaries were pressing steadily northwest into Sonora, a huge province that intruded into future Arizona. In 1687 Tyrol-born Father Kino, a wanderer without respite, reached Pimería Alta in Sonora. After daring the deserts to the Colorado River, Kino urged an overland route to the Californias through this land of the Upper Pima Indians.

The Colorado. . . . To Kino it was the Rio Grande Colorado de los Mártires. His Great River and Martyrs would be forgotten but his Colorado took hold for its lower reaches.

From the Yumas this Jesuit "padre on horseback"

heard a curious bit of intelligence: "Toward the north and the seacoast lived clothed white men who sometimes come armed to the Rio Colorado and trade a few goods for buckskins."

These white men might be castaways from those exploratory ships sent by the early viceroys, Kino speculated. Or Japanese or Chinese. Or "foreign heretics . . . living with Indian women." Mark Kino's reference. "These are matters worthy of investigation."

Pimas and other tribes hereabout began rebelling, the Apaches raiding, in the late 1600s. During interminable punitive campaigns, thought of advancing to the Californias through Pimería Alta was never dismissed.

Three-quarters of a century after reconqueror Vargas in New Mexico and trailblazer Kino in the Pimería Alta, New Spain abruptly felt herself beset far to the unknown north.

Since those long-ago days when Spain owned almost all of North America the British, French and Dutch had gnawed away. After the Seven Years' (French and Indian) War she forfeited to Britain her major claims east of the Mississippi. In consolation France in 1763 ceded to a reluctant ally the scarcely penetrated Louisiana Territory, essentially all claims west of the Father of Waters and south of now–British Canada.

The Spaniards feared that the British would surge into Louisiana, even descend a Great River of the West to challenge their West Coast hegemony. This mighty river had joined in their minds with the saltwater Northwest Passage as a prospective continental corridor. From North America's belly flowed the St. Lawrence to the northeast, the Mississippi to the southeast, the Colorado (by whatever name) to the southwest. There had to be a comparable

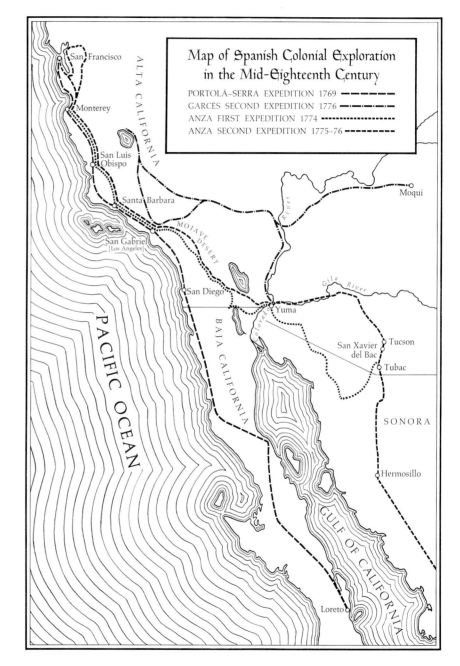

Map of Spanish Colonial Exploration in the Mid-Eighteenth Century

PORTOLÁ–SERRA EXPEDITION 1769
GARCÉS SECOND EXPEDITION 1776
ANZA FIRST EXPEDITION 1774
ANZA SECOND EXPEDITION 1775–76

river to the northwest. The logic of symmetry was irrefutable to an international coterie of cartographers.

From the northwest another threat was envisioned. The Russians had pursued fur across Siberia, then along the Aleutians. Tsarina Catherine the Great was conspiring, spies said, to exploit America from Alaska.

And more immediate peril was at hand.

Along the Rio Grande Basin nomadic warriors, painted for blood, were screaming down on the scattered and all-but-defenseless Hispano and Indian communities. Where eighty-five years earlier the settled, less militant Pueblos had grievously erupted, Comanche, Apache and Navajo, all having acquired the mobility of the horse and some the firepower of the musket, jeopardized a now more populous kingdom. In Texas newer Spanish enclaves were endangered.

Beyond this, the Comanches, Tartars of the Southwestern steppe, were driving various Apache tribes south from New Mexico and Texas. The fleeing Apaches were inflaming the stings of more southerly Apaches and desert and mountain tribes on a long thin line of presidial settlements along a fifteen hundred-mile arc between the Gulfs of Mexico and California. Should this line collapse, the colonial superstructure was doomed.

In the homeland the lassitude of the later Hapsburgs had given way to the vitality of the early Bourbons. The economy was moving, the military at the ready, the culture invigorated. The Spaniards regained pride, the Golden Age seemingly revived as if from a fountain of youth. A buoyant Carlos III sought to confront New Spain's crises, even to mining the colony of new revenue toward a mightier empire.

Equally vigorous men rose to carry out royal mandate, among them José de Gálvez, of impoverished Andalusian nobility. Through studious self-promotion Gálvez caught Carlos III's eye. He was ordered to New Spain as personal *visitador-general* with powers in part exceeding the viceroy's.

Gálvez resolved not merely to defend the borderlands but to aggrandize them. He would colonize Alta California. To obtain regal sanction he played on the Russian threat and pledged that settlement would enrich the royal treasury. He also would put down that festering rebellion in Sonora. As if he were a jinni, he would produce "a New Empire equal to, or better than," New Spain.

The visitor-general would hold Father Kino's projected overland line of advance in abeyance until Sonora was pacified. Supported by ships, he would conquer Alta California via Baja California. Sailing there in 1768, he found chaos and poverty. Unfazed, he finalized a "sacred expedition."

Put in charge of civil and military operations was a Captain Gaspar de Portolá, and directing missionary endeavor was Baja California's Franciscan father-president, Junípero Serra. Sword and cross, presidio and mission — time-honored. Old soldier Portolá was dubious. Serra, a Majorcan still vigorous in his mid-fifties, was eager. His Baja California missions would contribute settlers and some provisions.

Three leaky vessels and two overland parties, some three hundred men in all, set out early the next year for San Diego. By sea it was about twelve hundred fifty miles, for the trekkers some seven hundred. Headwinds buffeted the ships, one vanishing. Another taking 110 days was decimated by scurvy. Overland only a handful of eighty-six Baja California natives made it. With food running low, Portolá candidly related, "some of our Indians died and the rest deserted from natural necessity." By July, though just 126 men remained alive at San Diego, a presidio and a mission were thrown up.

Visitor-general Gálvez, having sailed on to Sonora, saw raid-and-run tactics defying conventional warfare — a circumstance history would duplicate down to the Vietnam War two centuries later. In "profound melancholy" he proposed importing six hundred Guatemalan apes to wipe out the Indian guerrillas. Once removed from harsh reality, he recovered sanity. The episode was hushed up.

The Sonora command, morale improved by Gálvez' departure, began to follow guerrilla example. All but the Apaches were subdued, and more presidios surely would contain them.

From San Diego duty-bound Captain Portolá at once headed farther north with sixty-two "skeletons," among them the acute Fray Juan Crespí. In veering inland to avoid coastal mountains the captain missed Vizcaíno's Monterey Bay. Scouts soon were blocked by a wild waterway. To Portolá it was simply a barrier but Father Crespí recorded: "It is a very large and fine harbor, such that not only the navy of our most Catholic majesty but those of all Europe could take shelter in." The colonizers had discovered San Francisco Bay.

"Not under compulsion from the Russians, but from keen hunger," said a cynical Portolá, the colonizers headed back. Reduced to eating "scaly" mules "like hungry lions," they staggered into San Diego "smelling frightfully" of them.

More had died despite Father Serra's ministrations. Abandonment was being talked of when, as if by Serra-bid miracle, an expedition ship hove in sight with corn, flour and rice.

Portolá set out again for Monterey. This time he found Vizcaíno's bay, small and secluded. Still, with mud and saplings he acidly saluted faraway Gálvez: "I proceeded to erect a fort to . . . defend the port from the atrocities of the Russians." Serra built a mission.

It was 1770 and Spain was present in Alta California at two isolated settlements four hundred miles apart.

Portolá himself left Monterey posthaste, "for on the return voyage one travels as fast as Sancho Panza would have liked." One would like to have met Portolá in person . . . as indeed so many of the characters in our unfurling pageant.

Couriers sped the captain's tidings from New Spain's west coast to Mexico City. The viceroy had bells rung, pennons raised, a mass celebrated, "for the dominion of our king has been extended over more than three hundred leagues of good lands." Honors went to Visitor-general Gálvez for restoring New Spain from debility to the robust, for gaining ground on his New Empire.

Portolá wrote Gálvez that it was impossible "to send aid to Monterey by sea, and still more by land, unless" he were willing "to sacrifice thousands of men and huge sums." His missing third ship had succumbed to scurvy. Settlement of Monterey couldn't prevent the Russians from digging in elsewhere. Let the Russians have California if it "by any extravagant desire be coveted" by them.

Portolá was both wrong and right. There were three more missions by 1773, among them San Gabriel in present Los Angeles . . . but just seventy-two Hispano soldiers and priests.

Bountiful though California is today, the Hispanos, 9

wanting in knowledge of irrigation, couldn't cope with the rainless coastal summers. Their scant livestock took time to reproduce. Monterey was saved from starvation only by a grizzly bear hunt.

Belying the view from early Spanish ships, Indians swarmed out of the coastal woodwork, more than in any comparable American region. From the far fewer Pueblos early New Mexico settlers had seized food. Why not call upon the coastal Indians? These hunted small game, even rattlesnakes, fished the abundant streams and collected seashore shellfish, gathered nuts, berries, roots, grass seeds. Insects they savored.

If this were a diet the soldiers couldn't altogether stomach, they were meantime alienating the barbarians with barbarities. Over vehement clerical protest, they wooed with lasso and killed for sport. (It was "the only good Indian is a dead Indian" of our Manifest Destiny which could be chivalrous as well, for even now Indian-clad colonists were infusing tea with salt water alongside British ships in Boston harbor.)

Urgent was the need, then, for provisions, livestock, farming settlers — married ones. Baja California, stripped to breed these settlements, could offer little to Alta California. Ocean hazards were too great to carry families, ships too small to carry herds. If the California outposts were to endure, a mainland route must be traced.

Visitor-general Gálvez, having left for Madrid to assume soon the powerful ministership of the Indies, spurred a dallying new viceroy, Antonio Bucareli, to wean the California settlements. Two other figures emerged to urge Bucareli on, an intrepid frontiersman, Captain Juan Bautista de Anza, and a missionary, Francisco Garcés.

Anza was of the third generation of a military aristocracy in Pimería Alta. He had had much to do with devising that triumphant counterinsurgency strategy. At thirty-seven he was commander at Tubac presidio in southernmost future Arizona.

Father Garcés, from the old Kingdom of Aragón, had been driven to New World missions by the restlessness of a Father Serra. In due course this Franciscan strayed to San Xavier del Bac, the outermost Pimería Alta mission just south of Pueblito de Tucson. San Xavier, founded by Kino, had been plundered. Garcés rebuilt the mission (the White Dove of the Desert is of later vintage), then began exploring his huge parish.

Tall and oaken, he covered desert and mountain north to the Gila River, west to the Colorado. He made do with jerky, ground meal, a little chocolate. He bore no arms and rode only with God. Fray Pedro Font, an eventual companion, would write: "He appears to be an Indian himself. . . . at night around the fire, with his legs crossed, . . . he will sit musing two or three hours or more, . . . talking with them with much serenity . . . although the foods of the Indians are as nasty and dirty as those outlandish people themselves, the father eats with them with great gusto and says they are good for the stomach. . . ."

The Indians gave the gray-garbed Franciscan the honorific "Old Man" though he had just turned thirty.

Among the Gila Pimas Garcés found cotton blankets woven by Hopis of the distant northeast and received through Indian go-betweens. He planned conversion of the Pimas with mundane complementary motives: to help check the Apaches and to open Hispano commerce with New Mexico.

From the Yumas along the Colorado River Garcés heard that they had heard of men of his skin and attire showing up "at no great distance" to the west — the

Portolá-Serra expedition a few months before. He would find a way to them. His pathfinding failed him, though, when he wandered into the Colorado's delta labyrinth. Extricating himself, he pushed northwest into the desert. From the lower Imperial Valley he sighted hazy blue mountains. Though seeing two "openings," he reluctantly turned back lest he fail to find water en route.

At his mission of San Xavier Garcés received word from Mexico City of an exploration of San Francisco Bay by Father Crespí, he who had recognized its significance. Crespí came across a delta to the northeast with twice the flow of Spain's Ebro, no mean river. He named it the Rio Grande de San Francisco. Not for Crespí to know was that the delta joined the Sacramento River, from the far north, and the San Joaquin, from the far south.

Monterey could be reached, Garcés concluded, by going north, finding Crespí's Great River of San Francisco and following it west to the Pacific. Both also could be reached by going west from faraway Santa Fe. This route might evade the torment of arid sands.

Between Garcés and Captain Anza at nearby Tubac presidio came an instant meeting of minds on opening a way between Pimería Alta and Alta California. The captain wrote Viceroy Bucareli in 1772 volunteering to lead an expedition with Garcés as companion. From the Colorado they would cross the deserts to the west (foregoing Crespí's Great River to the north for the nonce) to the Garcés "openings" in the mountains, then proceed north, bypassing the coastal missions.

Anza conveyed to the viceroy: the Yumas had told Garcés that to the north and east "were also people of our own [Spanish] kind." An echo from Father Kino.

The name Francisco Atanasio Domínguez crops up in Franciscan records in this same 1772. About thirty-two, he was making a clerical inspection in Veracruz.

Father Domínguez called Mexico City "the delightful and alluring cradle" of his birth. So sophisticated were his views, he may well have been born of the upper strata of this most regal and cultured cosmopolis of all North America. Schooled at the Convento Grande, he knew what was right and proper, and was severe with those who didn't.

Viceroy Bucareli, a bureaucrat operating by the book, submitted Captain Anza's proposition to those knowledgeable.

Father Serra thought it practical, though a better route might eventually be blazed from Santa Fe. Either way, Spanish excesses must be curbed or Indians en route, "until now gentle as sheep, will turn on us like tigers."

Captain Portolá's engineer testified he had seen "pieces of wrought silver, knives" and the like as distant as the Santa Barbara Islands. These could have come only from New Mexico. If Indians can conquer the terrain, then certainly we can also.

Proceed, Bucareli ordered Anza.

The captain meant to go north to the Gila, then follow it west to the Colorado. The Apaches just then inauspiciously raided Tubac's presidial corrals. This decreed detouring southwest to pick up extra mounts at Sonoran settlements. In January, 1774, he set out with Garcés and thirty-three men, a mule train and cattle to slaughter on the move. En route, he enlisted a Baja California Indian who had picked his way down from San Gabriel mission. At the Gila junction Anza and Garcés were greeted by Salvador Palma, Yuma chieftain and Garcés' warm friend, who helped them ford the wide, swift-running Colorado.

A Mojave from the north told them a confused story: Three days upstream a river broke off when the Colorado was in flood and wound west, yes and no, to a sea. Garcés, shuddering to face again the "horrible sand dunes" to the immediate west, opted for trying its course. Anza, with the Baja California guide at hand, chose to hew to the more southerly route.

(Anza was reporting to the viceroy by courier. Of the Mojave's riverine intimation, Bucareli wrote Madrid that "it would not be strange if it should be the one which runs to the port of San Francisco." Father Crespí and that Great River again.)

The Colorado delta still befuddled Garcés; the guide was of no help. Animals began dying. Chief Palma was sent for and agreed to hold most of them. The party turned north nearby future Mexicali-Calexico, crossed desert and passed through a Garcés "opening." Toward Monterey loomed multiple massifs. Nothing to do but revise itinerary and head west to San Gabriel. At the mission Anza at least had finally linked Sonora to a California settlement.

With six men Anza moved up a developing mission trail to Monterey to complete his assignment. A disconsolate Garcés was left to lead the others back to Palma's village. He had had in mind another project with the captain on their way back from Monterey. "I have been very sorry that advantage has not been taken of this occasion, so opportune for discovering the course of the San Francisco River, which I believe to be connected with the Colorado, and both with some very large lakes, or a water which is still, and is very large, as the Gileños have told me."

Now . . . the Great Sea of the West. By ascending the Mississippi from the east or the Great River from the west, one could find this sea at the mingling of their waters. Or it was the font only of the River of the West. Or it was an arm of the Pacific. Whichever, everyone knew the Great Sea was up there. In one vision or another, all the maps showed the Great Sea of the West.

A chief publicist for the Great Sea was the Baron de Lahontan, an able French soldier and explorer with a vivid pen. Lahontan had written of a journey he had made far to the west of the Mississippi. Villagers thereabout introduced him to "Mozeemlek" slaves. They wore clothes and were bushily bearded. He mistook the Mozeemleks for Spaniards. They came from beyond mountains that took "an infinity of Windings and Turnings" to cross. *Formidable!* From the mountains flowed west a river that emptied into a sea of salt three hundred leagues around. In a hundred towns thereabout the people, "as numerous as the Leaves of Trees," rowed galleys down canals between houses thatched with gold. *Bien!* This salt sea drained into another river two leagues wide that ran on to the Pacific. *C'est vrai!*

While Garcés was cogitating on his Great Sea and River of the West, Anza returned from Monterey, rejoining his cortege at Palma's village. A second padre there sounded like Father Serra in assessing the captain's route. If the Indians in this region "should become discontented, . . . a large force of arms would be necessary to vanquish so numerous, though so uncivilized a heathendom." He urged a presidio at Yuma.

Garcés felt no such premonition. His prelates had ordered him to look now into a route from Pimería Alta to New Mexico. Report your findings by Indian messenger to Franciscan brethren investigating from their end, he was told. North of the Gila, he roved anew.

Near Blythe, California, he asked a Yuman tribe to guide him north to the Mojaves. Their river was on his mind. These Yumans declined because the Mojaves were enemies. They would, though, see to the delivery of his letter to New Mexico via their traders. In it Garcés asked his brethren to reply by neophyte Indian courier. He would return here and accompany them back to New Mexico.

At Gila Bend, Arizona, the youthful "Old Man" wrote in his diary of a tribesman who had guided him across a chilly desert stretch. The Indian carried a firebrand in one hand, a stick to drive Garcés' now-shoeless horse in the other and a jug on his head, "enduring thirst that I might not suffer, and all this with a smiling face. . . . Who will say that this Indian is a savage?"

Captain Anza reached his Tubac presidio after four and a half months and adventuring over two thousand miles. Already he was pondering a new expedition — a whole colony to Alta California. Would the viceroy heed him anew?

The humiliation

HIS NAME WAS Silvestre Vélez de Escalante. (To contemporaries he was Vélez, as Coronado was Vásquez, but untutored Anglicism prevails.) Born in Spain's northerly Santander Mountains, Escalante crossed the Atlantic at an unrecorded early age. Why is not known. Was he tall or short, thin or stout, fair (from the north) or swarthy? All we know is that, though his body was wracked by a chronic ailment, his sinews were Toledo-tempered.

At seventeen Escalante had entered the Convento Grande, Domínguez' clerical alma mater. Now he was about twenty-four. (Like many of that era, Fray Silvestre probably didn't know exactly how old he was.)

After ordination Escalante was assigned by the Franciscan Province of the Holy Gospel to its New Mexico Cus-

tody of the Conversion of St. Paul. Shortly he was riding the hot, dusty Camino Real hundreds of miles northward. Perhaps he joined the annual trade caravan at Chihuahua for the final stretch up the King's Highway through El Paso del Norte.

Viceroy Bucareli was anticipating Captain Anza's next move. From Father Crespí's account he had decided that San Francisco Bay must be settled. The mighty San Francisco River must be explored.

The river's source might be a "great lake" — he was reading Garcés' mind as well — that the British reportedly had discovered. (A trader-explorer had penetrated to the Arctic Ocean and Great Slave Lake in 1771.) This possible Sea of the West would put the British within striking distance — from the Arctic Circle! — of both Santa Fe and the Pacific coast. And the Russian Bear was still sharpening its claws. The West must not be abandoned to foreign foes as had the East. San Francisco must become a bastion.

Just as the viceroy had questioned knowledgeable people about Anza's first proposal, he was now asking for enlightenment about the "mysterious regions" between Sonora, New Mexico and California. Through them a more direct route to San Francisco could be traced. Garcés already had been told to write his letter from Sonora to New Mexico missionaries. Among other sources, the Province of the Holy Gospel, at Bucareli's bidding, ordered her sons up north to report what they knew about these regions and to ferret out more. With geopolitical time ticking, the viceroy summoned Anza from Sonora.

In the East abandoned by the Spaniards to foreign foes, the First Continental Congress was meeting in Philadelphia. Harried by "taxation without representation" and the Coercive Acts, the colonies cut off all trade with Britain and vowed to hold out for all English liberties.

At the viceroy's pleasure, Captain Anza said in Mexico City, he would indeed lead his colony to San Francisco and go on to explore the San Francisco River. He would skirt the Colorado delta and this time find that mountain corridor to bypass San Gabriel. With women and children on his conscience, it would be more responsible than trying now to explore those mysterious regions of the Sonora–New Mexico–Monterey triangle.

From El Paso del Norte Father Escalante probably went on up the Rio Grande to Santa Fe, probably here met Don Bernardo de Miera y Pacheco, engineer, cartographer, astronomer, sculptor, painter, rancher, armorer and lately captain of militia and civil magistrate. It would become a relationship of more than ordinary acquaintance.

In December, 1774, Escalante was a missionary at Laguna Pueblo, but by January, 1775, he had moved to Zuñí, Fray Marcos' Cíbola. ". . . tranquility is not achieved . . . as it is here at this mission, for it is the best one in the kingdom," he wrote a mentor, Fray Fernando Antonio Gómez, secretary of the Franciscan mother province in Mexico City. ". . . the only disadvantage it has is being thirty leagues from the nearest one." At New Spain's two and six-tenth-mile league, that was seventy-eight miles, two to three days on horseback.

While introspective, Escalante was too young for hermitic serenity; indeed, a mind of his own was always eager to move from decision to action. He was asking for a companion. Zuñí, because of its very isolation, merited two padres from the thin Franciscan ranks.

An older friar, Damián Martínez, had left recently because of illness. Martínez hadn't shared Escalante's regard for Zuñi. He complained of "ministering to so rude a population," of "this exceedingly frigid climate and the lack of food suited to my constitution." Not all missionaries were St. Pauls in the New World wilderness.

Perhaps Fray Silvestre relished this pueblo for Zuñi élan. A meld of prehistoric peoples, the Zuñis speak a language alien to all others . . . ethnological enigmas akin to the free-spirited Basques of the Franco-Spanish region not far from Fray Silvestre's native Santander. As the first Pueblos encountered by the Spaniards, the Zuñis related what their élan had meant to Esteban the Moor: "A long time ago, when roofs lay over the walls of Kyá-ki-me, when smoke hung over the housetops, . . . then the Black Mexicans came from their abodes in Everlasting Summerland. . . . Then and thus was killed by our ancients, right where the stone stands down by the arroyo . . . one of the Black Mexicans, a large man, with chile lips. . . . Then the rest ran away, chased by our grandfathers. . . ."

Coronado was stoutly resisted in 1540. The Zuñis were vanquished with crossbow and flintlock harquebus, but the conquistador was laid low by an arrow in a foot and stones hurled from multi-storied houseblocks. Some three thousand Zuñi survivors fled to a nearby mesa, Corn Mountain.

Chastened by reality, the Zuñis in 1598 voiced submission to colonizer Don Juan de Oñate. The Franciscans took three decades to pioneer this far. Agitation by "sorcerers" fermented into the slaying of two friars. In fear of Spanish reckoning the Zuñis went up again to Corn Mountain. The day never came (so undermanned was Santa Fe's presidial garrison), and they descended after ten years to help friars build two churches. Perhaps defense was a motive in this show of compromise, but no troops could be mustered for faraway Zuñi. Apaches raided, killing many men, enslaving most women and children and executing the then lone missionary. The survivors stood their ground.

During the 1680 Pueblo Revolt the Zuñis dutifully did away with their missionary and burned their churches. They climbed to their aerie a third time with foresight that the evicted Spaniards would return with reinforcements. At the 1692–93 Reconquest they promised Don Diego de Vargas, governor and captain-general, they would submit. With eminent duplicity they then sent men to the unavailing defense of newly rebelling pueblos to the east.

When the Spaniards again failed to mount strength for reprisal, the Zunis rewove their conciliatory pattern by restoring the church at today's remaining Zuñi community. Spanish troops were finally stationed here in defense against the Apaches, who again were preying on the pueblos. These soldiers apparently provoked as much Zuñi antagonism as the Apaches; three were killed while singing in the church choir. The Zuñis withdrew to Corn Mountain for a short and final time. By 1706 they were cooperating anew at the mission.

This was Escalante's church these seven decades later. Some Zuñis had to have taken Christ into their souls by now for Fray Silvestre to find congeniality here.

In Sonora Farther Garcés received a written suggestion from Viceroy Bucareli that he travel with Anza's new expedition as far as Yuma, then work his Christianity there and among "related tribes." He accepted while demurring that "I consider it very risky" to take families over Anza's desert road and urging that the Colorado be forded farther north. In any event, a separate expedition should both track an ever more northerly road to San Francisco and explore one to New Mexico. To lead it the irrepressible Garcés recommended Sonora's Governor Crespo.

Garcés had seen Crespo not long before. A recipient of one of the viceregal inquires about the "mysterious regions," the governor already had replied in comparable tenor. As for the two-pronged complementary expedition, the San Francisco River was not many days from the Colorado; the "reduction" of the Hopis, who had not been pacified since the 1680 Pueblo Revolt, could be accomplished en route to New Mexico. To command this expedition Governor Crespo modestly volunteered. Garcés should go along because he had "won the affection of the tribes who know him."

The viceroy sent a copy of Crespo's report to New Mexico's Governor Pedro Fermín de Mendinueta for an opinion.

In seeking information on those "mysterious regions," Father Escalante's provincial in Mexico City, Fray Isidro Murillo, had further and particularly addressed certain friars in strategic locations. Fray Silvestre was so approached, specifically "to seek the opening which is projected of the route by land to California."

Before Father Martínez (Escalante's predecessor) left Zuñi he had received a collateral request from Colonel O'Conor, borderlands commandant-inspector in Sonora. Martínez was asked to exert "every means" to evaluate "flying reports I have picked up on this frontier about the existence of a settlement of Europeans on the opposite bank of the river named Tizón, which is to the northwest of New Mexico." Such reports had, as we have seen, been flying around the frontier for decades.

And not only on this frontier. Looking from the east the French and British knew about them from Baron de Lahontan and many another Quixotic writer: an isolated colony of sophisticated Welsh; white, dwarf and bearded Indians; fancy costumes, gold-studded boots, gilded pearls; opulent cities along a great river or vast sea. A French Jesuit missionary scholar had written: "I have good reason to think that there are in this continent either Spanish or some other European colonies much more to the north than what we know of New Mexico and California. . . ." All this was in print. Like the Bible, all books were gospel truth.

To Colonel O'Conor in Sonora, Martínez vouched for a baptized Navajo who had come upon "a white man on horseback with clothing and armament of the type we use" along the Colorado. When the Navajo spoke the stranger "only smiled to himself." Martínez gave even more weight to "the pagan Yutas, whose veracity and constant friendship with us is sufficiently proved." (The Spaniards had patched together a peace treaty of sorts with the Utes.) The Utes had promised to guide Spaniards to "these people." There were no enemies between. It would take about twenty days to reach them.

To find this mysterious colony, Martínez wrote O'Conor, New Mexico governors had relied on settlers incapable "of appreciating the importance of the matter in the service of both Majesties," God and king. "These unhappy wretches have been content to reach the Yutas and bring back fur pelts in exchange for trifles. . . . Let your Lordship weigh my arguments."

The Martínez "arguments" seem to verify that Euro-pean settlement, Colonel O'Conor wrote Viceroy Bucareli from Sonora. He proposed to lead an expedition the next year, 1776. Anza, Crespo, O'Conor — no want of self-assertive expedition commanders.

Bucareli, while commending O'Conor for his zeal, was somewhat skeptical. These white men out there may be those of the California presidios, he countered. He wanted more facts to justify an expedition. Still, he was so geographically naive as to believe that the California coast could be reached in twenty days from anywhere beyond.

At Zuñi Father Escalante was downright skeptical. "Long experience has shown," he would write Provincial Murillo in Mexico City, "that not only the infidel Indians, but even the Christians, in order to raise themselves in our esteem, tell us what they hope we want to hear, without being embarrassed by the falsity of their tales."

Long experience, yes. Cabeza de Vaca, Fray Marcos, Coronado, Oñate. . . .

This spring Hopi traders came to Zuñi. Escalante treated them "with affection." They invited him to visit their pueblos. This is testimony to a persuasive personality for, if the Zuñis were strong-willed, the Hopis were revolutionary. Though Hopi means Peaceful Ones, this is a verity only if defined as going to any lengths to be left in peace.

Their language is of the Uto-Aztecan branch of North American tongues. "It is no exaggeration to say that among the Hopis of today we find living traces of this great pre-Columbian culture," writes Frank Waters, an authority on both cultures. Moreover, the Hopis shared a belief of the Mayas, Toltecs and Aztecs that their cultures derived from a bearded white god-brother who would return. The Hopis' Place of Emergence, they say, was the heartland of these great interlocked civilizations. More likely fingers of their cultures crept north to our Southwest and the Hopis.

In 1539 Fray Marcos, after expressing awe over Cíbola from his hilltop vantage point, had been told by Indian camp followers that "Totoneac is much larger and better than all the Seven Cities put together, and it has so many houses and people that it has no end." Totoneac, with seven more cities, was Hopi domain to Zuñi's northwest. The Indians said of Totoneac what Spaniards wanted to hear.

Coronado dispatched troops from Zuñi the 115 miles northwest to the Hopis in 1540. These found not Totoneac but seven pueblos on terraces and atop three adjoining mesas. The Hopis believed the Spanish detachment commander to be their long-lost white god-brother, relates Waters of their oral history in his *Book of the Hopi*. They drew a line of sacred cornmeal across the trail. The Spaniards, not understanding the symbolism, took the line as a dare. As at Zuñi Spanish arms prevailed. To the Hopis, formally submissive, the Spaniards henceforth were the "dictator people."

Colonizer Don Juan de Oñate found the Hopis still outwardly submissive. Though a friar eventually was poisoned, proselyting was pushed and three churches were built. When the missionaries forced cessation of Hopi ceremonials, tradition has it, the rains stopped. Secretly the Hopis resumed their rites among their cliffs. The rains came. Christianity became the "slave church" to be shunned.

At the 1680 revolt the Hopis killed all four friars amongst them and obliterated the churches. They gave haven then and after Vargas' entrada to hundreds of Pueblo refugees from the east. Perhaps expecting reprisal, they shifted three pueblos from Mesa terraces to crags above.

(It has been suggested that possible aggression at this time variously by Utes, Paiutes, Apaches or Navajos contributed to this defensive move. The Utes alone were responsible, in the opinion of Albert H. Schroeder, National Park Service historian-archaeologist. They were "powerful and mobile" and "the traditional enemy of the Hopis." The Utes will become chief among many Indian characters in our saga.)

Reconqueror Vargas, riding out to the mesas, found the Hopis ready to fight the dictator people. He offered peace if they would swear allegiance to the crown. They did, tongue in cheek, and he left.

Shortly, a friar made inroads at one pueblo. Seeing their whole pattern of ceremonialism again threatened by the slave church, other Hopis slew most of the pueblo's population and left it a smoking ruin. This violence left guilt, says Waters, that scars the Peaceful Ones to this day.

A Hopi delegation to Santa Fe proposed a permanent peace under which each nation would eschew trying to convert the other. A new governor summarily snubbed what later came to be called religious freedom.

From then on it was granitic resistance. After the Hopis had twice repelled Spanish attacks, another governor led a force to retrieve the Pueblo refugees. Storm their mesa and take them, the Hopis dared. The governor turned tail.

Franciscans came and left with pulse-beat regularity. Only a small minority of Hopis heeded them, even when offered gifts. The Hopis did, though, permit departure of some Pueblo refugees and a few Hopi Christians under priestly persuasion during a leadership wrangle. Descendants of remaining refugees inhabit Hopi's Hano Pueblo to this day.

17

In 1747 Santa Fe launched a campaign against the Apaches south of Zuñi with an accompanying detachment assigned to subdue the Hopis. Hearing of this, Hopi leaders rushed to Zuñi. They "prostrated themselves" before priests and commanders, Escalante would write, pledging to accept Christianity and "assuring that they were already subject as before the [1680] rebellion." The detachment withdrew to other business. The Hopis went on about their own apostate, nonsubservient business, another skirmish won.

Seven years later the Havasupais to the Hopis' west decided to seek Christianity and Spanish sovereignty. Protection against Yavapais and other marauders was their aim. In their remoteness the Havasupais didn't realize what Spanish missions and authority entailed or that any defense was problematic. Six spokesmen were sent off to Santa Fe. These were killed either by the Hopis, as hazy history has it, or by unidentified "Christians" at Hopi incitement, as Escalante would state. The Peaceful Ones couldn't abide the dictator people crossing their soil.

Such was the temper of the Hopis when Father Escalante agreed with the visitors to Zuñi to go to their pueblos a few weeks hence. He was "particularly pleased" to accept for cogent reasons:

As directed by his Mexico City superior, he should learn more about Indians along any possible route to Monterey. Similarly, he could inquire about a way to Sonora. And he would have the opportunity to raise questions about that mysterious European colony.

From there, it would be convenient to visit the Havasupais, seeking the same answers and preaching to them.

Finally, that Hopi apostasy. To reconvert and regain obeisance where so many had failed. What a coup!

Escalante took the initiative for the trip, though he informed Governor Mendinueta and received written permission from New Mexico's Franciscan vice-custodian. Let no sagebrush grow under his feet.

Sometime in early 1775 Fray Francisco Atanasio Domínguez, he who knew what was right and proper, was ordered by Provincial Murillo to go from Mexico City as commissary visitor — one to whom a special task was committed — to inspect New Mexico's missions. Also he was to advance the search for those routes to connect New Mexico with Sonora and Monterey.

What Mexico City knew about neglected New Mexico could be put in a primer. Anything Domínguez learned of it would help not only to promote spiritual welfare but to fashion frontier civil and military policy. Viceroy Bucareli provided letters "in my favor" to this end. Domínguez was ordered to report on the kingdom's lands and waters, farming and industry, Indian customs and languages, the kingdom's caste composition. He was to be an ethnographer long before such a discipline existed, a geographer as well.

The office of commissary visitor was entrusted only to clergymen of the highest caliber. Domínguez obviously enjoyed Murillo's utmost regard for keen observation. Yet he must be "prudent and pacific" with respect to "defects of his brethren." The provincial knew his envoy.

As for those new routes, Domínguez specifically was to learn whether any missionary had received the letter that Father Garcés had sent via the Yumans in an effort to open communications between Sonora and New Mexico. If so, "this news will be most welcome" in view of the viceroy's current interests. If not, Domínguez was to seek out an Indian convert to "take the risk" of carrying one to Garcés and bringing back a reply.

Father Escalante had thought to go to the Hopis with only a guide and an interpreter, a Hopi convert from Sandia Pueblo, but Don Juan Pedro de Cisneros, Zuñi's *alcalde mayor,* and "my Zuñi sons" protested. Though the Hopis "made a howl of affection, they were heathens and might take my life." Escalante perforce was to be escorted as well by the Hispano magistrate — who would be a companion on another, epic adventure — and seventeen Zuñis bent on trade. Escalante would keep a journal, a portent of an even more historic diary.

The party left in June, 1775. It is of later moment that Escalante carried a "needle to determine the direction," though this compass was rendered useless, he inferred, because of lodestones nearby. His Zuñi companions being well-acquainted with the route, they scaled First Mesa to Walpi Pueblo three days later.

Escalante received a "very affectionate welcome" from officials, including the cacique, or ritual headman, of adjacent Hano, the refugee Pueblos' pueblo. (Also here was a third, smaller and unnamed, village.) Lodgings had been readied for him "with order and cleanliness."

Next day a Walpi resident came to warn that over one hundred Navajos were plotting an ambush for the party's homeward trip. Escalante replied that, trusting in all-powerful God, he was not worried. The Walpi was "astounded."

Two days later Escalante proceeded four and a half leagues to Third Mesa and Oraibi, its sole pueblo, "which is like a provincial capital." Oraibi was "larger than any known in the Interior Provinces," with eleven two-story houseblocks "arranged like a chessboard." It held "nearly four thousand souls" out of a total Hopi population,

"without exaggeration," of 7,494. How could Fray Silvestre project that Oraibi, built about A.D. 1150, would still be standing in the late twentieth century as the oldest continuously inhabited community in a country called the United States?

Rain and melted snow were collected in six large cisterns since there was "only a little spring water, distant more than a *milla* [mile]" — an aridity common to this land. With "good horse herds, droves of sheep and some cattle," Oraibi was somewhat more plutocratic than the six other pueblos. (All such livestock had been Spanish-introduced, the Indians having domesticated only dog and turkey.) The Hopis raised corn, beans and squash (the basic Pueblo prehistoric diet), chile (a Spanish import from the Valley of Mexico) and peaches and watermelon (from Europe). They wove "very fine textiles in their style" of both wool and native cotton.

While the "Moquis are very civilized" there were "no manifestations of courtesy" at Oraibi. Escalante and the Spaniards generally didn't realize they were uncivilized and discourteous in using "Moquis" for the Hopis. They had picked it up from the eastern Pueblos, who called them *Mochis,* "Awl People," for their bone needles, according to Frank Waters. They distorted this into *Moquis,* "Dead People" in Hopi.

When no Oraibis came to a house that had been cleared for Escalante, he sent for the pueblo's leaders. The cacique avoided him but his subordinate chief captain and a few elders entered. As Fray Silvestre began to preach he was told by the captain not to "weary myself" further "for none would give ear to me."

Escalante seethed as the leaders, while begging the interpreter to calm him, contended that, "although being Christian is repugnant to them, they wanted to remain on friendly terms with the Spaniards." He regained composure. He had exploded, he explained, in "profound sorrow" at "seeing so great a multitude of souls lost."

As to what Hopi souls favored above the repugnant, Escalante observed: "The religion of the Moquis today is the same as before they heard about the Gospel. The chief god they worship is the sun. . . . they have a multitude of innumerable idols, which are no more than petrified and painted pieces of wood. In Gualpi [Walpi] especially they keep some snakes, which become tame with handling. They take them out of the estufas for most solemn dances and perform many idolatrous ceremonies with them."

(Those "painted pieces" were *kachinas*, doll-like representations of supernatural spirits. *Estufa* is Spanish for *kiva*, a Hopi term used by modern Pueblos for their esoteric ceremonial chambers. The snake dance is still a major Hopi rite for calling down rain.)

Few of the lesser Oraibis dared approach Escalante, none openly, to discuss Christianity. Fray Silvestre was uplifted, though, to hear his interpreter's uncle whisper, "If the father could bring Spanish people, . . . I and most of the pueblo would become Christians."

Oraibi's chief captain sent word to the other Hopi pueblos, Escalante would learn, that his "aim was to subject them to the Spaniards." A prophet, this captain. His warning was carried to the three Second Mesa pueblos. While Escalante was received more politely here, he wasn't allowed to preach.

He began to suffer from a chronic urinary ailment. Though it became so painful he couldn't walk, he rode back to Walpi the next day. On this second sojourn he faced defiance . . . but here his whole trip was made worthwhile. A Havasupai sought him out.

Escalante "lit a cigarette, . . . then gave it to him." After a second one had passed from mouth to mouth, the Havasupai was "serene and happy."

They expressed mutual esteem and, of note, esteem also for the Utes, who lived to the north. The Havasupai then underwent a two-hour grilling. Finally he drew a "rough but clear map" with charcoal on a cotton saddle blanket. Again of note: "I do not reproduce this map now because I hope that God is going to allow me to do so after I have already seen all this."

The Havasupai said, "Father, now my heart is at ease. . . ." When Escalante's party first had come to Walpi, he explained, two fellow tribesmen were here. They hastened to the nearest Havasupai settlement. Its men galloped to Oraibi. The Spaniards had left and couldn't be overtaken — a Hopi falsehood. Crushed, the Havasupai captain sent him, a petty captain, to try to catch up. He was to say the Havasupais were "very fond" of Spaniards.

Escalante would have gone at once with the petty captain to visit those "whom I already loved as my sons" but was simply too ill. He gave the Havasupai tobacco for his people to smoke "as if I were present."

He now knew "everything" about the Havasupais, Escalante would write. He did know more than any other Spaniard. From dint of scholarship we know somewhat more.

The Havasupais are Yuman-speakers who sought refuge from enemies at the bottom of Havasu Canyon, a tributary to the Grand Canyon, in about the thirteenth century. Of communication with their netherland, ethnologist Frank H. Cushing wrote in 1882: "At times, so impossible does it seem for any living thing to pass further that nowhere can a trail be traced; when a turn to some crack in the rock, almost hidden by intervening boulders, and hewn down with stone hammers to give precarious footing, shows where it goes up or descends." Because of delightful streamside groves below, Cushing called the Havasupais the Nation of the Willows. Actually, their name means

Blue and Green Water People. *Cosninas,* the Spanish for them, came from their Hopi name, *Coconino.*

The Havasupais lived in the canyon only in spring and summer to farm tiny plots. Winter there being dark and dank, they ascended in autumn to "rancherías" — Escalante's usage — on the adjoining plateau to hunt deer, antelope, mountain sheep. (The term *ranchería,* for clusters of tipis and wikiups of nomadic tribes, evolved from *rancho,* a Spanish troop encampment on expedition.) In time some Havasupais apparently made their rancherías semi-permanent, though the abyss remained their heartland.

The Havasupais acquired livestock from the Hopis and bartered buckskins, salt and red ocher paint for textiles, pottery and turquoise as well. That six emissaries to Santa Fe were killed with Hopi involvement hadn't severed intercourse, though Escalante would hold that the Havasupais were "ill-contented" with the Hopis' "specious conduct."

(In our day some four hundred Havasupais live mainly on a canyon-floor reservation. Trails have been improved since Cushing's day but it still is a zigzag eight-mile hike or ride the half a mile up to the canyon rim and another world.)

At Walpi the next day, Escalante, hearing a "great noise and disturbance," rushed outside to be confronted by dancing men. "The frightful and gloomy painting of their masks and the height of indecency with which they ran in view of many people of both sexes were very clear signs of the foul spirit who has their hearts in his power. The only part of their bodies that was covered was the face, and at the end of the member it is not modest to name they wore a small and delicate feather subtly attached."

"This horrifying spectacle" — which probably was coincidental with his presence — "saddened me." Escalante's reaction, plausibly intensified by his physical pain, was so traumatic that he resolved to leave Walpi early next day. So recently out of the cloister, he perhaps didn't realize that brother Franciscans had made reluctant peace with Pueblo religion after the trauma of the 1680 rebellion. At New Mexico pueblos church and plaza were now a stewpan of theism and animism — after mass, ritual dancing. Had Escalante reached Zuñi in time for the annual Shalako of late fall he would have known what lascivious dancing, as judged thorough some Western eyes, could truly be.

Walpi's captain insisted on an escort of forty armed men to scout out whether "some smokes" were of the reported Navajo ambushers. Escalante both "tried to avoid" this and was "most grateful." On a beeline this time, the party followed a road made "dangerous" because it was "the nearest to the Gila and Mescalero Apaches." No encounters, "God be forever blessed."

Anza, promoted to lieutenant colonel, found recruitment of settlers for San Francisco no problem, "submerged in the direst poverty" as were inhabitants north from Guadalajara. To discourage gambling and other prodigality, supplies were issued in lieu of money, including petticoats for wives, colored ribbons for men's hats and hair. All male civilians became auxiliaries with issuance of thick cuirasses and carbines, swords and lances.

From Zuñi Father Escalante began to write a series of reports on his two-week Hopi investigation. In an initial letter to his friend Father Gómez, Provincial Murillo's secretary in Mexico City, he wrote that "the land where the

Cosninas dwell" — likely the chasm — was "six days of bad road" west of Oraibi. Directly north was the Rio Grande (de los Misterios), a mingling of "several rivers that come down from the Yutas" that "I judge to be the Colorado." Escalante seems to have been the first to make this connection since Coronado's chronicler over two centuries before.

The river thereabout is "impassable" and the Havasupais have seen no signs of people on the other side. In this Escalante must have misunderstood his Havasupai informant, for Paiutes, with whom the Havasupais traded, were accessible directly across the Colorado.

Beyond the Havasupais lived warlike tribes, one nation so savage that "they eat the human flesh of those they kill." Besides conveying a message to Garcés, Escalante's Franciscan provincial headquarters had urged that, to initiate contact from New Mexico, friendly Indians be asked to carry a letter to Monterey. None could be found "who will dare" this route since "the majority of the infidel nations are enemies." Escalante didn't know that Garcés was making friends of several.

Also, along this route were over one hundred leagues of "impassable road, . . . pebble and flint, and water and pasturage is scarce."

In view of the savage humanity and geography "the way to Monterey" was not via the Hopis but through the Utes to the north. "The method, if I am not mistaken, which would be suitable would be for his Majesty to bear the expenses of twenty men, or a few more, giving the same amount daily as the soldiers of this land for three months at least, in order that, led by some intelligent person who would take the enterprise to heart, they might reach said Monterey and reconnoiter the intervening provinces."

Escalante judged the distance from New Mexico to be

four hundred leagues — only slightly more, remarkably, than its nine hundred twenty crow-flight miles from Santa Fe. All the more remarkable in that the English, at the time, were accepting an explorer's thesis of only half a day's travel from the Mississippi's headwaters to "the South Sea [the Pacific] stretching from America to Japan and China."

"There are men of valor [in New Mexico] who would undertake the journey for the said daily wages alone. There is also a *paisano* [fellow countryman as distinguished from local Hispano] here [in Santa Fe] called Don Bernardo Miera [y Pacheco], clever enough for the affair, and even I would sacrifice myself" — doubtless an allusion to his ailment — "for such an undertaking."

As for a route to Sonora, Escalante had gained intelligence from Miera and the Zuñis, among others. Via the local San Francisco and the Gila rivers, a Sonora presidio could be easily reached in about eight days "if one succeeds in clearing away the [Apache] enemies."

Escalante now noted that in New Mexico "it is believed that the Spaniards or white people whom the Yutas say they have seen many times may be descendants from those three hundred soldiers whom Captain Alvarado left when he entered by the Rio Colorado at the beginning of the conquest." He was speaking of Hernando de Alvarado of the Coronado expedition though he may have meant Alarcón, who had named the river the Buena Guía in 1540. There is no evidence either that Alvarado saw the Colorado or that Spanish soldiers were left anywhere. Of that mysterious colony, "I do not give great weight to this opinion, but if it were true, this discovery would be of the utmost utility . . . to both Majesties."

As to the Hopis, Escalante informed Gómez they are "obstinate in their foolish libertinism, especially those who govern, who impede with terrible threats the conversion of their inferiors . . . because they fear . . . that they will be abused and almost enslaved by the Spaniards if they submit. A falsehood in which the demon succeeds in holding them by some sadly undeniable truths . . . I achieved only the sorrow of leaving them in their obstinancy. . . ."

Escalante's "undeniable truths" were an inference that Spanish rule had been abused. It reflected a Franciscan will, especially in the previous century, to contend with New Mexico governors over uncivil treatment of Indian mission wards.

Escalante closed his letter to Gómez by asking for an "exact account of Monterey and its limits and of the Indians who are known on [its] east and south." This would be "very useful to me." Fray Silvestre was beginning to think four hundred leagues away.

Anza, following in large part Coronado's road north toward Cíbola, carried out royal rights of requisition in rounding up horses and mules en route. The rest would be had at Tubac. Two weeks south of there he learned that the Apaches had struck his presidio again, making off with five hundred mounts. There was delay to acquire replacements hereabout.

Father Domínguez, having traced Escalante's hoofprints, arrived at El Paso del Norte, the New Mexico custodial headquarters, in September, 1775, to find "a state of miserable panic" because of Apache attacks "on this whole New Kingdom." Travelers were being slain, children kidnaped, horses and mules stolen. He and two companion padres were still at El Paso two months later because the vice-

custodian had written from upriver that it would be "foolhardy" to try to enter New Mexico now, so sweeping was the siege by Comanches and other tribes there.

While the prelate stationed here saw his New Mexico custody "on the point of suffering its last agony," Domínguez held hope. A double-barreled "general campaign" was under way against the Apaches from El Paso's vicinity and by Colonel O'Conor in Sonora; New Mexico's Governor Méndinueta was waging one against the Comanches.

"But if when they seek them in one place, they are already in another, how are we going to grapple with them?" It was all the more urgent for him to get on up the Rio Grande to render a trustworthy eyewitness report. He hoped that, armed with the viceroy's letters, he would soon be granted an escort by the local military.

Lieutenant-colonel Anza, greeted by Father Garcés nearby, reached Tubac presidio in mid-October 1775. With more recruits here, his company numbered 240, including 155 women and children. Fray Pedro Font, who would go along, compared the endeavor with "the journey of the children of Israel through the Red Sea to the Promised Land" in a sermon.

New Mexico's Governor Mendinueta received Sonora Governor Crespo's report from Viceroy Bucareli and sent a copy to Escalante because of his now-special knowledge. Comment at once, the governor ordered. "Notwithstanding the little knowledge that I have of these regions and the paucity of my abilities," Fray Silvestre was as forthright as his order's beloved St. Francis in his convictions.

The proposed Crespo expedition, attaining Monterey, should proceed due east to "Payuchi" territory along the Colorado. Once the river is forded, the Paiutes "may serve as guides . . . to come down in a straight line" to New Mexico.

In reiterating the feasibility of a road to Sonora, Escalante especially credited Miera y Pacheco, "a settler of this villa," an indication that Fray Silvestre traveled to Santa Fe to submit oral thoughts to Governor Mendinueta. Miera probably drew for Escalante a map of Hopi country that was submitted with his report.

(It may have been at this time that Escalante commissioned Miera to create a new altar screen and carve *bultos* of saints for his Zuñi church, for both are identified by the late authority E. Boyd as the captain's work. Miss Boyd characterizes Miera paintings and carvings, which both before and after this time were placed in several mission churches, as having in common "ambitious compositions, theatrical poses, a quality of human naturalism, athletic muscularity and realistic details." Whether Miera sent his Zuñi work from Santa Fe or executed it at the pueblo church, we don't know.)

Escalante now augmented his proposal for a twenty-man, three-month expedition from Santa Fe. It should be "well-armed and prepared to go as far as might be convenient. . . ."

And he hedged on the expedition's goal. "This means I held and hold as sufficient" to look for those mysterious Europeans but "but not to reach as far as Monterey." Was he absent-minded? He renewed his offer to go along, specifically as chaplain and diarist.

Fray Silvestre hedged also on his skepticism. Indians had reported such an isolated colony to a missionary in Baja California long before, he recalled. This predated the Alta California settlements, so more recent Ute and Yuma reports probably didn't refer to them either. Another echo from Father Kino, he supposed that these colonists were descendants of castaways.

(Elsewhere Escalante would state that the "heathen" described these Europeans as "a nation similar to the Spaniards, wearing long beards, armor, like our ancient kind, with breastplate, iron helmet and shoulder-piece.")

Whatever, "Their discovery would be very useful to religion and the Crown both to prevent any attack upon this kingdom, if they are foreigners, and to incorporate them with ourselves if they are, as they say, Spaniards."

Did Escalante believe all this? Or was he toying with the colony, as Gálvez had played upon the Russian threat, in an ambition for personal action?

In this report to the governor Escalante turned to the Hopis. (His "sorrow of leaving them in their obstinancy" was gnawing at him. Priests are human; his ego was involved.) The Hopis once had accepted Christ and king, he stressed. Despite the "suave exhortations" of many visiting priests, their leaders continued to rebuff both through "terrible threats to their people." And they harbored refugee apostates. Though rebels, the Hopis were still vassals.

Escalante proposed that the Hopis be "subdued by arms" of the Crespo expedition and be "brought down from the pueblos to a plain and proper site." Reduce and relocate. Yes, a prophet, that Oraibi captain.

While "at first view the pueblos present themselves as almost impregnable," the Hopis depended on waterholes below. By Crespo's seizing these, they "will be forced to surrender without great fatigue to ourselves" for "by pretense they are lions on a road on which there are no more than traces of wily but weak vixen foxes."

To sustain conversions and prevent new revolt, Escalante recommended a presidio at a Hopi resettlement site. From this presidio the pacified Hopis could join Spanish campaigns against the Apaches. The presidio would "render less dangerous" a route to Sonora. It would open the way, now barred by the Hopis, to conversion and allegiance of the Havasupais.

Escalante dangled still more bait: Spanish interest already was "piqued by the mineral resources" on Havasupai land. He doubtless was alluding to Sierra Azul, a Blue Mountain of silver known to be out there. A century and a half earlier a Franciscan had heard of "deposits of silver [in Zuñi] of so fine a blue that they use it for paint" and, having "bought some stones to show," was told by Mexico City painters that it was the "best blue in the world." A New Mexico governor later proclaimed Sierra Azul to be west of the Hopi pueblos. Don Diego de Vargas cited the exploitation of Sierra Azul, by this time thought to be a virtually bottomless deposit of quicksilver, as justification to reconquer New Mexico. Vargas eventually obtained specimens from the Hopis. Though Mexico City assayers found they contained no quicksilver, Sierra Azul did not erode away. In Sonora a missionary said that an Indian showed him some of it, liquid, oily and so heavy that a hatful "could not be lifted." Another priest cited a "tradition that this mountain is the richest in all New Spain."

Reduce the Hopis and on to Sierra Azul, Escalante implied.

Just as he had become a vigorous defendant in the case of the mysterious colony he was now a fighting prosecutor building a case against the Hopis.

Governor Mendinueta relayed summaries of Escalante's report, with his own comments, to Bucareli in Mexico City and Colonel O'Conor in Sonora. While describing Fray Silvestre as a "religious of exemplary life and unusual talent," Mendinueta told O'Conor that the Utes and Navajos would regard Hopi reduction as "unjustly declaring war on Indians who were living at peace with us and were giving no cause for complaint." They might form an alliance with the Hopis that "would very soon finish off this kingdom."

Let us send three or four zealous missionaries to the Hopis, the governor urged instead, with "some goods of small value" to sway their chieftains into permitting the friars "to teach the mysteries of our religion."

This so soon after Escalante had contended that "suave exhortations" wouldn't work with the Hopis. Ironic, a priest avowing force, a chief civil and military authority avowing religious conversion.

Anza's second expedition moved north down the Santa Cruz River and west down the Gila to the Colorado. At Yuma Chief Salvador Palma begged Anza to permit this contingent to remain and Christianize his people. Other Spaniards would soon settle here, Anza replied. Meantime he was leaving Palma's friend Garcés with the Yumas. And for their fealty his people were presented glass beads and tobacco. Palma received a fancy costume with a black-velvet cap adorned with imitation jewels. Again they helped Anza and company cross the turbulent river.

Anza avoided the delta entrapment but cold and snow forced him to divert once again to San Gabriel. He reached the mission with 242 persons, an increase of 2, after three births and a death en route. Garcés meantime was interpreting the catechizing of those "related tribes" in the broadest sense. He headed up the Colorado to Mojave country.

25

"I was the first Spaniard to enter their land, at which they rejoiced greatly on account of their desire to know us." Though he didn't know that Don Juan de Oñate had beaten him to it 172 years before, thus did Farther Garcés demolish Escalante's presumed peril of the warlike Mojaves. To Garcés the "very obliging" Mojaves provided guides. After stepping onto what was to be Nevada soil north of Needles, California, Garcés swung west from the Colorado to what would become the Mojave River and surmounted Cajon Pass to San Gabriel mission. Almost casually he had established the more northerly route that had daunted Anza. He looped north through California's San Joaquin Valley, then returned to the Mojaves along the Colorado.

The CABAL

FATHER DOMINGUEZ JOURNEYED three weeks up the Rio Grande from El Paso to Santa Fe in March, 1776. He apparently rode without personal military escort though he may have accompanied an armed government train. Governor Mendinueta's campaign had abated for a time the Comanche peril to New Mexico, for Fray Francisco wrote Provincial Murillo from the kingdom's capital of "the impetuous manner in which the Spanish population is now leaving for El Paso because of minor risk."

Fray Francisco had gone "directly to the house of the lord governor," today's Palace of the Governors, where he was accorded "the favor of his table and conversation." Those "mysterious regions" presumably were much on their minds.

To Escalante in Zuñi the visiting inspector sent an order that Murillo wanted to see a copy of his complete report to Mendinueta. Then Domínguez left for a formal visitation to the missions of Rio Arriba, upstream from Santa Fe. That journey would include observations, as will be seen, on their defenses against the nomads.

His expedition having reached Monterey, Anza and a vanguard sighted the Golden Gate in March, 1776. After choosing presidio and mission sites, he and Father Font set out to explore Father Crespí's San Francisco River. They pushed up the San Joaquin Valley to present Suisun Bay, which receives the combined flow of the Sacramento and San Joaquin rivers. Its water was fresh and blue and there was no discernible current. Crespi's river was not that but an inland sea, Font concluded.

From Zuñi Escalante sent Provincial Murillo a copy of his official Hopi report as Domínguez had requested. He blamed his delay on the "constant affliction of my chronic ailment and certain unavoidable occupations," then got to the truth of the matter: "The knowledge that my sins were responsible for [my visit's] failure causes me great chagrin . . . when I speak of it." You "can send more effective workers than I or devise more efficacious means to convert" the Hopis. His wound was festering. By his "efficacious means" he doubtless was seeking to make his reduce-and-relocate passion Murillo's own.

Domínguez spent a week in Santa Fe before visiting the downstream missions of the Rio Abajo. The kingdom's capital was beautifully located beneath the Sierra Madre, he reported. But the "Villa" — sarcasm in the designation — was "a rough stone set in fine metal."

Domínguez contrasted Santa Fe with a Mexico City suburb of "streets, well-planned houses, shops, fountains; . . . something to lift the spirits by appealing to the senses." Santa Fe was "mournful": adobe houses, only one "quasi-street," scattered farms and corrals. "The government palace is like everything else here, and enough said."

Turning to other business, Domínguez responded to Escalante's request of the year before and assigned one of his traveling companions to Zuñi. This friar carried orders for Fray Silvestre to report as soon as possible to Santa Fe "to discuss some matters" regarding Provincial Murillo's separate instructions to both of them. Those "mysterious regions."

Perhaps Escalante's new companion friar brought copies of Governor Mendinueta's comments on his Hopi report that had been sent to Viceroy Bucareli and Colonel O'Conor. In any event Fray Silvestre apparently had just become aware of their contents, for he now elaborated to Provincial Murillo why "I hold as imperative" the reduction and relocation of the Hopis "notwithstanding others to the contrary." In resentment he was a Tom Paine ready to take on the highest lay authority.

Priestly "kindness and persuasion only" could not bring to pass reconversion and resubjugation, Escalante insisted. Gifts were likely only to incite "the malice of the rebellious." As to Mendinueta's reference to the Hopis' "living at peace with us," they still were vassals.

Use of force "only is directed to remove the barriers" of obstinate chiefs. It did not contravene Laws of the Indies forbidding such force against "nations who maintain themselves quiet and neutral" for the Hopis' "is a very improper neutrality." Nor did it contravene pontifical injunctions against "excessive zeal" brought about by "the indiscreet ardor with which others have tried to convert Indians and infidels with the sword before preaching."

As for the Utes' and Navajos' joining the Hopis in a "general league" against the Spaniards, these nomads were quite aware that the Hopis had long been vassals who, unlike other Pueblos, never resubmitted. Hence "they will never conclude themselves may suffer the same." What's more, "These Indians have no concern in what molests their neighbors."

Escalante well may have underestimated obstacles to the Hopi reduction. Probably unbeknownst to him Mendinueta had repeatedly called on Bucareli for men, weapons and horses for New Mexico's very defense. His presidial garrison numbered only 80, his militia 250, his Indian auxiliaries 250, armed mainly with bows and arrows. It simply "is not possible to guard so many and such distant settlements" throughout the kingdom. After Indian raids many a retaliatory strike had been aborted, the governor complained, because "to follow the enemy requires three or four horses" for each soldier. There were ample horses to be had in New Mexico but the kingdom's treasury lacked the wherewithal to buy them, it would seem.

From the Colorado Father Garcés headed east, his eyes on New Mexico. After passing among friendly Hualapais, he was urged by equally friendly Havasupais to visit their heartland. The trail was "some three handbreadths wide"

along a "hideous abyss" with a final descent by wooden ladder. Garcés had now done what Escalante had vowed to do . . . and become as well the first Spaniard known to have visited the Blue and Green Water People in Havasu Canyon.

Domínguez returned to Santa Fe after finding some Rio Abajo missions in a state of beleaguerment. Perhaps deviously, his itinerary had omitted the three westernmost of New Mexico's twenty-one (today nineteen) pueblos: Laguna, Acoma and Zuñi. In the relatively secure capital he cast his eye upon the populace, which he put precisely at 1,338.

There were no schools to speak of. He heard little music. The art was horrible. As historian Fray Angelico Chavez has it in *My Penitente Land,* "Accustomed to the urbane manners of his much more civilized native land, he look patronizingly upon the native folk here as a strangely rustic species of Spaniards."

There were a few Spaniards and other Europeans, Domínguez allowed, "educated in speaking with courtly polish." Most residents, though, spoke Castilian "according to their own fashion." Domínguez didn't realize that, so isolated had they been, they were speaking the simple, Cervantes-flavored tongue of his ancestors. Spanish had "progressed" meantime to the Gongorism of his own sometime floridity, involved phrasing, bigger Latin words.

A goodly number of New Mexicans, after all these isolated generations, were *castas,* "mixed bloods." Among them were the *genízaros,* "who, after being ransomed from the pagans by our people, are then emancipated to work out their account under them." *Genízaro* was a term from Spain for those of mixed Spanish and foreign blood. It was

derived not, as is often written, from the Turkish *yenicheri* (English "janizary") for "enslaved troops," but from the Greek *xenogenesis* for the fancied product of an organism unlike either of its parents.

Almost a third of New Mexico's Spanish-speaking population was genízaro, Domínguez reckoned. The nomads commonly captured one another's young women and children for slaves, selling them at New Mexico trading *ferias* held under truce at outlying pueblos and settlements. Other genízaros-to-be were seized in battle or picked up at random. However much exposed to Castilian, said Domínguez, they could neither wholly understand nor speak "without twisting it somewhat."

Genízaros were obtained to be beneficed with Christianity as well as to become unpaid servants and herders. They were not considered slaves. Having acquired baptismal names and their adopters' surnames, they were, as Fray Angelico puts it, "on their own around marriage time." Most genízaros, though, were a people apart, not to be wholly integrated for generations. In the capital they lived in a barrio south across the Santa Fe River near San Miguel chapel.

While making his observations on the populace, Domínguez relayed a letter from Provincial Murillo to Escalante in Zuñi. This letter, which has not been found, obviously dealt in some part with the "mysterious regions." "From that time I began to gather information," Domínguez himself wrote Murillo. "This will mean considerable work, for the people" — a reaction shared with Escalante — "are very light in their speech and there is no rhyme or reason to what they say." Superb reporter that Domínguez was, anything dispatched to the provincial "must first be tested by the fire of close investigation (if possible), reason, and actual proof."

Governor Mendinueta now received a letter from Viceroy Bucareli asking for elaboration from Escalante's detailed report. The viceroy understood Escalante to have "promised to discover the route to Monterey with twenty men," Mendinueta told Domínguez. This had been extracted from Fray Silvestre's initial letter to Murillo's secretary, Gómez.

"I am expecting him hourly," Domínguez wrote Murillo.

As Escalante prepared to leave Zuñi for Santa Fe he received the Domínguez-forwarded letter from Provincial Murillo. He apparently had infringed the chain of command by addressing his earliest communications to Gómez, to which he now pled "ignorance" of protocol and promised to mend his ways. He added that, as requested, Murillo's secretary "has furnished all the relevant information he has been able to acquire" about the Monterey region. Archivists have yet to discover what could be yet another intriguing document or perhaps a small treasure of documents.

Escalante's disagreement with Mendinueta over how to handle the Hopis may have caused Murillo to conclude that friction had arisen, for Fray Silvestre replied that he was trying to retain a "close friendship" with the governor. He deplored "lack of talent . . . to marry politics with the religious state," adding that "it usually deprives me of the peace I thought I should find in this out-of-the-way place."

Fray Silvestre didn't concede he had brought this disquiet on himself as he proceeded to take exception to Mendinueta's omission from his own reports of the Escalante rationale for reducing the Hopis with arms. The friar feared that the viceroy would indeed order their reduction solely by missionary effort, which could be achieved "only if we expect miracles."

Though the governor praised "my expedition in hyperboles," he had impugned the many missionaries who "labored to this end before" among the Hopis, Escalante complained to Murillo. Civil authorities had long derided missionaries in official reports. "If we are silent now," what judgment will be made by the viceroy, the Royal Tribunal, the Council of the Indies? "What our Catholic Monarch?"

While awaiting Escalante, Domínguez made his formal visitation to Santa Fe's churches.

St. Francis (its adobe remnants to be incorporated in a stone cathedral in the next century) was "carefully covered with planks," sufficient to note in that packed earth "is the usual floor throughout these regions." Its three bells "are cracked (like many in most of these missions because of the extreme cold)." Its *viga* roof beams typically were covered with wattle and mud. Above an ornate governor's chair hung an oil canvas of Carlos III "breaking out in scabs like smallpox." Hanging from a side altar were paintings of saints on buffalo skin, a practice to which he everywhere took exception as he did to most *santos*, New Mexico-crafted bultos and paintings on wood.

Across Santa Fe's plaza from the governor's palace was the Chapel of Our Lady of Light. Domínguez did appreciate its huge stone altar screen, which "resembles a copy of the façades which are now used in famous Mexico." This majestic 225-ton reredos is nowadays in Santa Fe's Cristo Rey, the world's largest adobe church.

Finally there was the Chapel of San Miguel, which ministered in part to the genízaro colony. Billed in our day as the "Oldest Church in the United States," San Miguel, rebuilt from the ground up about 1710, is almost a century younger than two churches that will figure on these pages.

Escalante reported to Domínguez in Santa Fe in early June, 1776. Asked at once whether he had received the letter from Father Garcés, he replied that he had not . . . but that "his own strong wishes" and the fulfillment of Provincial Murillo's desire for information "had led him to decide to make a journey to Monterey . . . during the present summer if [Domínguez] considered it fitting." Just like that! (We don't know if Fray Francisco ever tried to send his prescribed letter to Garcés.)

Escalante may have known and begun to respect Fray Francisco from his seminary days in Mexico City. Domínguez obviously respected Fray Silvestre, for he would write Murillo a year later that he "is the only person who can carry out my just plans and decisions." Many another Franciscan he would cite by name for such infractions as living with a woman, being a "notorious drunkard," or "trading at the cost of the Indians' sweat."

Domínguez saw eye to eye with his junior. They would travel together. "In my judgment it was so necessary and proper," he now wrote Murillo, "that from that very night we made a pact for the two of us to undertake to seek out persons who might be useful to us in the enterprise."

Domínguez and Escalante thus would make a *fait accompli* of one prong of Sonora Governor Crespo's projected expedition, the exploration to California. Fray Francisco apparently didn't even consider waiting the weeks that Murillo's approval would require (though it is conceivable that one or both had been authorized in advance to undertake such an expedition). Even Crespo had sought

Viceroy Bucareli's sanction. The two friars did communicate "our intention and decision to the lord governor."

Mendinueta, said Domínguez, "not only applauded our plan, but also opened his heart and his hands, giving us supplies and everything we might need for the journey." Perhaps it was in his enthusiasm for the expedition that the governor may have dispelled suspicions of hard feelings over Escalante's difference of opinion on how to handle the Hopis.

Mendinueta opened the government archives to Escalante, though he said they contained "nothing but old fragments" and recommended the captaincy-general files. In one or the other did Escalante unearth the Rivera diary?

We know nothing of Juan María de Rivera other than that he was of sufficient stature to have been commissioned by an earlier governor to lead an expedition north in 1765. How large his cavalcade was is not recorded. Rivera got as far as the Gunnison River, some two hundred fifty air miles from Santa Fe, in what probably was the first Hispano penetration of west-central Colorado. His diary is lost to history but we shall learn something of its contents from Escalante's references in his own journal.

Why was Rivera so commissioned? He may have prospected for silver in southwestern Colorado's La Plata Mountains. Also, recalling Father Martínez' letter to Colonel O'Conor, he and his companions probably were those "unhappy wretches" sent to find that mysterious European colony — they who had returned only with furs traded for trifles.

From Escalante's and other fragmentary references we know also that traders meantime had gone among the Utes for two to four months at a time. They engaged in "the vile commerce in skins even in violation of just prohibitions," Escalante would write, "that no Indian, genízaro, or citizen shall enter the lands of the heathen without having obtained a license for it from the governor." When such ventures were private it was of advantage to cover their traces.

These excursions were banned primarily to prevent cheating and mistreatment that would inflame Indians against the Hispanos. Even at controlled fairs, Domínguez would say, "our people ordinarily play infamous tricks on them." The illicit traders, precursors of our fabled Mountain Men, lived with friendly Indians, savored generously offered sex and saw what there was to see — while, not incidentally, pioneering provinces unknown to the kingdom.

In all events the Rivera diary proved to be the proverbial gold mine. It gave Domínguez and Escalante a word-map and, it may be inferred, a roster of potential guides and interpreters.

Among first recruits of "people who voluntarily accompany us" doubtless was Andrés Muñíz, who not only had gone with Rivera but had traveled among the Utes as recently as the year before and perhaps had made other trips between. Muñíz, a resident of Bernalillo near Albuquerque, was enlisted as chief guide-interpreter. Church records of a 1758 marriage list him as a *mulato*, his wife as a *coyota* (from a mestizo and Indian union). He is recorded of *vecino*, or "citizen" status. Though there were no true mulattoes (half-white, half-black) among citizens of this era, Fray Angelico Chavez says, a few padres had the habit of designating those of extra-dark visage as such. Muñíz probably was of mixed Hispano and Indian blood, not a genízaro as some historians have deduced. He was likely

about Domínguez' age, hence about ten years older than Escalante. With Andrés would go his brother Antonio Lucrecio Muñíz, citizen of Embudo near Santa Cruz, who had jaunted among the Utes at least once.

Of considerably more social consequence was Don Bernardo de Miera y Pacheco, the Santa Fean who had provided Escalante with the Hopi map and the religious art for Zuñi. Miera was born in the mountain of Burgos, year unknown, scion of a distinguished military family, his grandfather having been governor of Navarra. He was a captain in the Cavalry of Cantabria before emigrating. From a record of a son's birth we know he was in Chihuahua in 1742. By 1776 he would have been at least in his mid-fifties, twice Escalante's age.

Meantime Don Bernardo had been an engineer and captain of militia at El Paso del Norte, fighting Apaches and those fringe tribes of northern New Spain. He was with that 1747 campaign out of Zuñi that prescribed a route to Sonora, Escalante has told us. In the mid-1750s he was magistrate and captain at Galisteo and Pecos, southeast of Santa Fe on Coronado's trail to Quivira, from which he campaigned against Comanches to the northeast. Next he held these concurrent posts in the capital itself.

All the while Miera was drawing maps: among others, of the Gila Apache domain, the Rio Grande–Rio Concho vicinity (for which he declined an eight-peso-a-day salary, an inference that he was then relatively well-off), Comanche territory on the Buffalo Plains, the Navajo country to the northwest.

Domínguez, in his visitation to San Felipe Pueblo north of Albuquerque, had noted that Don Bernardo sold to the Indians there, "at a high price in proportion to those of the land," a bulto of their apostle saint. "Although it is not at all prepossessing, it serves the purpose and stands on the high altar at this mission." Fray Francisco may have written this before he met Miera, though he was not reticent about saying almost anything to almost anyone's face.

As a further jack-of-all-trades, Miera tried in Santa Fe to recast some ordnance pieces, probably of bronze. He failed.

Don Bernardo was not at all humble, as we shall learn. The flourish of his signature would have done proud his contemporary, John Hancock. Yet he was as capable a man as there was around. He was signed on as the expedition's astronomer and cartographer.

There were two others titled *don*, men of some substance or holding an office such as magistrate. Don Juan Pedro de Cisneros, Escalante's friend, the Zuñi magistrate, may have accompanied him to Santa Fe. All we know of Cisneros is that he probably was born in Rio Arriba of a couple wed there in 1714; he could have been about sixty, older even than Miera. (With him was a servant, Simón Lucero, who perhaps was of considerable Indian blood.) Don Joaquín Laín, a Santa Fe resident, had been born in Spain thirty years before; later records would add Herrero to his name, indicating he was a blacksmith.

Juan de Aguilar was a citizen of Bernalillo, Andrés Muñíz' residence; records shows he was not married until 1781, so he may have been about twenty and the youngest expedition member. Of Lorenzo de Olivares we know nothing except that he was a citizen of El Paso del Norte.

There were not "twenty men, or a few more" that Escalante had recommended. That there were only ten points up a lack, not of able bodies, but of funds to equip more.

Father Garcés, led by Havasupais, took a two-day side trip to where "a deep passage was cut, steep-sided like a man-made trough, through which the Colorado River enters these lands." He was the first Spaniard to have seen the Grand Canyon since that Coronado party 236 years before.

All expedition members were warned not to "carry any kind of merchandise, and that those who would not agree to this must stay at home." All promised, vowing that their sole purpose was "glory to God and the salvation of souls." They then were given "whatever they requested for their equipment and to leave for their families."

We don't know whether such amounts were deducted from the soldier pay Escalante had suggested or even that they received it. Miera would write in another context that soldiers received six and a half *reales* a day. A real was one-eighth of a *peso*. A peso would buy two chickens, half a pound of chocolate, a string of chile.

Of the "everything" that Governor Mendinueta was providing it is likely that horses could be acquired for only ten men. These horses were the Spanish mustang, from *mesteño* for "horse gone astray." The mustang was of two strains, the Andalusian and the barb, the latter brought to Spain by Hannibal two centuries before Christ and in time blooded with the Celtic garron and Germanic horses of successive invaders. Small, wiry and hot-blooded, writes authority John L. Sinclair of mustangs generally, "No other breed was better qualified or could have contributed so gallantly" to the conquest of the New World.

Escalante originally had proposed, we recall, a three-month trip. From figures proportionate to those available for Anza's first expedition, it has been estimated that the expedition set out with thirty horses, ten mules for provisions and twenty head of cattle for fresh meat en route.

These animals and "all the other things," Domínguez

said he acquired 'by my own efforts" — most from the governor, some with resources from a priest with a surplus at hand. They almost certainly were obtained by barter, which "is customary everywhere" as pesos are such "in name only, for actual coins do not exist." Parenthetically, merchants gouged in an "iniquitous manner."

There being no inventory of those "other things," we know what some of them were only from Escalante's diary entries as the expedition proceeded. These included sugar, flour, corn, chocolate and tobacco, ropes, adz, chisel, axes and crowbars, a "little barrel" for water. Miera would be responsible for an astrolabe, an instrument for reckoning latitude through measuring altitudes of sun and stars. For gifts to Indians: white glass beads, woolen cloaks, woolen cloth, red ribbon, hatchets, hunting knives.

They would carry at least one musket and possibly a lance. Something had happened to Escalante's recommended "well-armed" men, another measure of the kingdom's poverty.

Would they take, as had Anza, beans and brandy? His iron frying pans and copper camp kettles? There is no hint that they carried even one of Anza's military tents. Crude tools doubtless were packed for Laín the blacksmith. There must have been a compass. And they had to have either or both flint and steel and Anza's "glass for making fire."

The cavalcade was scheduled to leave on July 4, as we know, but Comanches slew ten persons in a raid on La Ciénega, about fifteen miles southwest of Santa Fe on June 20. With only one other priest in the capital, Domínguez felt compelled to send Escalante "to exhort and confess" presidial troops pursuing the warriors. Whether a ten-day "scouting expedition" quarried them is not known.

Accompanied by eight Havasupais, Father Garcés, who had belied the enmity of Escalante's Indians en route, now belied the impassability of his southern road by reaching Oraibi on the Hopis' Third Mesa. Sullenly the Hopis denied him entry into any house and refused him corn even for payment of tobacco and seashells. On a street he lit a fire of cornstalk litter, cooked a little gruel and made ready to spend the night.

A Spanish-speaking Indian from Zuñi came up and offered to lead Garcés there next day with two Zuñi companions. The Havasupais, intimidated by the Hopis, refused to go with him to Zuñi. He felt he could not relinquish the services of these guides should he have to retrace his steps through Hopi country. "Better the known evil of the present than the uncertain good of the future," he wrote in his diary. But he did send a letter via the Spanish-speaker to the priest at Zuñi.

On July 4, even as the Liberty Bell was pealing in Philadelphia, dancers swarmed onto Oraibi streets "with feather ornaments . . . and other finery, making a din with small sticks . . . in company with flutes." Unlike Escalante, old Indian hand Garcés expressed not the slightest disapproval of this — but it did make him "fear for [his] life" when a tall dancer accosted him: "For what hast thou come here? Get thee gone without delay — back to thy land!" Garcés: "I mounted and, with a smile on my face . . . I left."

"Worn out" though Escalante was, Domínguez now had to send him north to Taos "on urgent business" while he himself had "to finish other business that summoned me" to Isleta Pueblo, seventy-five miles south. The crisis at Taos apparently had to do with the validation of an annulment and the approval of suspect marriage proceedings because the parties "love each other and are mostly Indian." At Isleta it seems to have involved the replacement of a priest "so ill and feeble" that he couldn't handle his duties.

Escalante was seized with an "acute pain in his side," perhaps related to his urinary ailment, that necessitated Domínguez' riding the seventy miles to Taos to aid him. Fray Silvestre by then was "out of danger" but a week's rest was required.

The delays would mean a three-month expedition would last through October. In weighing the urgency of these delaying trips, nowhere was the weather of the future taken into recorded account. Otherwise, the postponement was fortuitous.

That Spanish-speaking man, an Acoma Puebloan named Lázaro, had hurried Father Garcés' letter from Oraibi to the priest at Zuñi. Escalante's subordinate there had questioned Lázaro, written of what more he had learned, then sped him on to Santa Fe.

Garcés' letter was as laconic as his life was pithy. "I have come to this pueblo of Moqui. Here they have shown me no courtesy . . . I would gladly have gone that way [to Santa Fe], but . . . it would be necessary to return with troops." A few comments about other tribes and trade with Sonora, and that was all, three short paragraphs of it.

From the Zuñi missionary's interrogation of Lázaro, he learned that Oraibi's cacique had proclaimed: "The father wants to deceive us by bringing us gifts, and therefore let no one accept anything." Thus was confirmed Escalante's

premise as to the Hopis' attitude toward priestly bribery.

To test Lázaro's veracity, the missionary had asked him to describe the father's habit. "He replied that it was gray." This was a telling point in that, while gray was customary in Franciscan Sonora, priests of the New Mexico custody wore blue in honor of the Immaculate Conception of Mary, a belief especially hallowed in this isolated kingdom.

Governor Mendinueta, Domínguez and Escalante now "examined [Lázaro] with special care." They were convinced. Father Garcés had, in effect, opened a trail from the coast through the Hopis to Santa Fe. Not incidentally he attained the major goal (though the Hopis remained unsubdued) of the other wing of Sonora Governor Crespo's proposed expedition, the exploration from Pimería Alta to Santa Fe.

Reviewing their plans, the friars still considered "useful" the search for a more northerly route to Monterey. This, after all, has been Escalante's stated aim from his earliest interest in the "mysterious regions."

"Even if we should not attain our end" in this respect, Domínguez wrote Provincial Murillo, the "knowledge we could acquire . . . would represent a great step forward." In his precise fashion he enumerated their goals.

First, they could learn what nations besides the Utes "inhabit the regions between," though this investigation *"may involve a roundabout route"* because to visit them "it is necessary to go down to reach said port." In other words, they would likely travel latitudinally north of Monterey while en route. It will be of future moment that Santa Fe stands at 35° 41' north latitude, less than a degree south of Monterey's 36° 35'.

Again, returning by a more southerly route, they could learn more about "the tribes who dwell from west to east" as far as the Havasupais.

Third, they intended to confirm the Havasupais' "good intention to become Christians." Also they would investigate Havasupai sites "convenient for settlements." The lure of the silver-laden Sierra Azul.

Finally, "if no insuperable obstacle intervenes" — an allusion to treatment accorded Escalante, then Garcés — they would explore Hopi territory for sites "to which the Moqui pueblos can be moved." Escalante apparently had infected Domínguez with the virus of his Hopi compulsion.

Governor Mendinueta startled Domínguez "on one occasion when we were speaking of sending friars into the interior to discover lands and win souls." The governor asked: "If there are not enough fathers for those already conquered, how can there be any for those that may be newly conquered?" He was speaking of missionary vacancies at three New Mexico pueblos. Domínguez described this to Provincial Murillo as an "expression of opinion which can chill a spirit ardently burning to win souls" . . . but he recorded no rebuttal.

Were there reasons for the two friars' taking the expedition upon themselves beyond those itemized by Domínguez in such a prosaic manner? Was there in them the wanderlust of a Kino, a Serra, a Garcés? Escalante already had demonstrated a lust for adventure. Maybe Domínguez, having filled thick folios with reports on his visitations to known land, was so exhausted by tedium as to seek freedom of spirit on the open road. Did they not welcome going "in search" of whatever, to paraphrase Coronado's chronicler, "under the Western star"?

Escalante may have worked into the night before departure on a letter to Provincial Murillo seeking to clear up questions that Viceroy Bucareli had put to Governor Mendi-

nueta about Fray Silvestre's original proposal for an expedition. "The direction in which the intervening territory can be crossed [to Monterey] is not known . . . although there is some information about the country the Yutas occupy as far as the Rio del Tizón . . . the character and number of the intervening tribes are unknown."

They had enough men to seek out the mysterious colony, Fray Silvestre believed. And, "although I say that [reaching Monterey] has never seemed possible of attainment with so few men, I do feel that there is enough probability of success in the latter to risk expense of the royal treasury. . . ."

A word before departure. What follows has long been known as the Escalante Expedition because its diary is in Fray Silvestre's handwriting. Indeed, *the Escalante Expedition* is part of the very subtitle of Dr. Herbert E. Bolton's *Pageant in the Wilderness*. It is an impression compounded by writers before and since the publication of the late, great historian's study of the expedition in 1950.

Let there be no mistake: Domínguez, not Escalante, led the expedition. It has been so put by Eleanor B. Adams and her colleague Fray Angelico Chavez in their annotated translation of Domínguez' visitation, *The Missions of New Mexico, 1776*, in itself an unparalleled sourcebook on eighteenth-century American life. While paying tribute to Dr. Bolton for retracing much of the route, adding "immeasurably to the enduring value" of the diary, Miss Adams and Fray Angelico state:

We feel obliged to emphasize the fact that Fray Francisco Atanasio Domínguez was not only a full partner, but the senior partner, in the "Splendid Wayfaring" for which Vélez de Escalante has long received the lion's share of the credit. We have no desire to detract from Fray Silvestre's achievements. . . . It is high time, however, that Father Domínguez received a just meed of appreciation. . . . Domínguez was a perfectionist . . . this very trait of his character, his habit of meticulous attention to the most minor details, and his strong personal sense of duty make it incredible that he could ever have delegated to a younger man, his subordinate, however much he respected and trusted him, full responsibility for recording the observations that they made during explorations of major importance. Father Vélez de Escalante would have been the first to deplore this time-worn misconception. He himself never referred to their account of the expedition except as *our* diary. . . . It is greatly to the credit of both men that they recognized each other's qualities, that they were willing to cooperate wholeheartedly in a cause for which they had received separate instructions, and that they remained fast friends under conditions calculated to mar the best of human relationships.

This writer's own study of the diary and his retracing of the route elicit one demurral. It may be assumed that Escalante made daily notes upon which the final journal was based. It is to be wished otherwise for, as fine as Escalante's contribution was, a Domínguez account could have provided us with far more in light of his "meticulous attention to the most minor details." Doubtless Domínguez was too preoccupied with leadership to have taken closer charge of daily entries. Be that as it may, his failure to do so raised many whys and why nots about events en route that probably never will be answered.

THE EXODUS

The WAYFARERS

Fray Francisco Atanasio Domínguez

senior leader of the expedition — born in Mexico City and about thirty-six at the time of the wayfaring — sent by the Franciscan provincial in 1775 as *commissary visitor* to inspect the missions of New Mexico and to advance the search for routes to connect them with Sonora and Monterey

Fray Silvestre Vélez de Escalante

co-leader of the expedition and keeper of the daily notes from which the diary was later constructed — about twenty-five and a native of Spain, he was the Franciscan missionary at Zuñi in 1775 and a veteran of extensive encounters with both the Zuñis and the Hopis prior to the expedition

Andre Muñíz

chief guide and interpreter — probably of mixed Hispano-Indian blood — a resident of Bernalillo, he had traveled among the Utes as recently as a year prior to the expedition

Don Bernardo de Miera y Pacheco

cartographer and astronomer — a captain in the Cavalry of Cantabria before emigrating, he was in Chihuahua by 1742 and held numerous civil and military posts throughout the northern part of New Spain — in his mid-fifties at the time of the expedition

Don Juan Pedro de Cisneros

magistrate at Zuñi and friend of Escalante — may have been about sixty at the time of the expedition

Simón Lucero

servant of Cisneros — perhaps of considerable Indian blood

Don Joaquín Laín

thirty years old — the expedition blacksmith — a resident of Santa Fe

Juan de Aguilar

citizen of Bernalillo — about twenty and probably the youngest member of the expedition

Lorenzo de Olivares

a citizen of El Paso del Norte

Antonio Lucrecio Muñíz

brother of Andrés Muñíz

July 29, 1776

DOMÍNGUEZ AND ESCALANTE likely rose at the cock's crowing to finish long letters of this date to Provincial Murillo in Mexico City.

Escalante was still reckoning the odds on reaching Monterey: "In going without noise of arms (which usually terrifies the tribes encountered on the way, and therefore must be a sufficient force or none at all) I [hold] some probable hope that God will facilitate our passage as far as befits His honor, glory, and the fulfillment of the will of the All High that all men be saved." Without weapons their progress would be a gamble governed by the Almighty.

Domínguez, reminiscent of Father Font's sermon on the Anza passage to the Promised Land, asked for prayers as wandering Elishas "clothed in the spirit" of the provincial's Elijah.

With their companions they celebrated mass, imploring the protection of their chosen sponsors the Virgin Mary and the Patriarch Joseph. All then presumably assembled for their historic adventure in historic Santa Fe Plaza.

Against the wear and thorns of the road the blue-cassocked friars probably wore not their order's penitential sandals but the stiff-soled, ankle-high leather moccasins and knee-high, soft-leather leggings of the day. And it is probable that they covered their tonsures not with their priestly shovel hats but with the common stiff-leather, broad-brimmed sombreros against the journey's sun and rain.

Their companions presumably wore sleeveless, knee-length leather jackets over blouses, the customary breeches and the same footgear. Economic status doubtless was reflected in ornamentation and quality. The more affluent no doubt wore breeches of wool, and the others leather. If there were any plumed hats, we don't know about them.

The horses almost certainly were shod for the rough terrain. Saddletrees were wooden though some saddles surely were leather; trappings of the likes of Miera and Cisneros may have been adorned with silver. There were leather saddlebags

39

SCALE: 50 MILES ▭━━━━━━━━━

for tobacco, jerky, personal effects. Poncho-blankets of coarse local wool were packed behind.

One wonders if bells were rung, if residents were out to see them off at this early hour, if relatives and *enamoradas* wept. Governor Mendinueta doubtless was there with an adios.

At Santa Fe's 6,990-foot elevation were all those low-slung evergreens — most had sprung up long before our wayfarers were born and would linger long after them in a seemingly timeless environment. Those with sprays and blue berries were juniper; the needled ones were piñon, their nuts a food staple in prehistoric times and favored to this day. Juniper and piñon would be with them much of the way.

At a rise the Sierra Madre stood toe to tip to the east. This Mother Range eventually would be named Sangre de Cristo, though not for its scarlet at sunset, as many have written, but from a stream, pass, peak and military post near the Colorado border. A stripling as mountains go, the Blood of Christ, pushing from earthen clefts, has lifted some seven thousand feet to over thirteen thousand. This growth alone is higher than North Carolina's Black Mountains, highest east of the Mississippi, and it would be far higher but for the erosion of rain, grit-laden wind and temperature extremes cracking the rock. Our travelers had no way to know it is still inching up.

A Spanish lieutenant in the 1760s had drawn a map of Santa Fe inscribed: "To the east of the Villa, . . . there is a chain of very high forested mountains which reach so far from south to north that its limits are unknown even to the Comanches, who came from the north, ever along the base of said sierra during their entire migration, which they say was very long." The Sangre de Cristo is an extremity of the Rocky Mountains. The limited Comanche contribution to knowledge of them is to be respected. The Rockies, along with the Great Basin, would be the last of our nation's geography below Alaska to be explored and comprehended.

Draining the southern Sangre de Cristo during the spring snowmelt and when the rain pours is Tesuque Creek. Trailing their cattle, pack mules and extra mounts, the rovers probably tracked its summer-dry bed to Tesuque Pueblo, Dry Spotted Place. Tesuque was among New Mexico's six remaining Tewa-speaking pueblos, all to be visited or skirted this day and the next (and all extant to this day).

40

Though the Tewas may have been here as far back as A.D. 1050, they were by no means the first to inhabit these lands. From unearthed spear points we know that perhaps twelve centuries ago Stone Age wanderers hereabout hunted camel, mammoth, saber-toothed tiger. The Desert Culture flourished here as early as six thousand years ago. These people were gatherers of wild plants and hunters of deer, elk, bear and smaller game. They lived in caves, rude huts, eventually pit-houses. The Tewas, farmers who erect adobe houseblocks, are cultural descendants of the Anasazi (Navajo for Ancient Ones), Pueblo peoples who lived along the San Juan River drainage to the northwest.

To cover this first day's distance our travelers didn't tarry at Tesuque. They turned west along the Pojoaque River, bypassing Pojoaque and Nambe pueblos and cutting through San Ildefonso Pueblo downstream.

Miera would depict San Ildefonso's 550-foot Black Mesa on a map. Perhaps the more sophisticated of our travelers were aware that its inhabitants and those of eight other pueblos once had made Black Mesa a bastion. After the Reconquest the Spaniards assaulted the aerie four times during a nine-month siege. In one attack they "were surrounded by Indians like hungry lions," complained reconqueror Don Diego de Vargas. "I'm cutting off your corn and water down here," he finally thundered. The rebels came down after talking with Vargas.

Probably none of our travelers knew of Black Mesa's being a sacred aerie as well. The Tewas' origin myth has it that, while living beneath Sandy Place Lake far to the north, their ancestors sent up four pairs of brothers, *Towa é*, to explore the outer world. The Towa é threw mud in the four cardinal directions, creating four mesas. Eventually the Towa é led the Tewas out of their subterrane. As the Tewas became worldly beings, the mesas became hallowed. The Towa é watch over San Ildefonso from atop Black Mesa to this day.

Mission priests disdained such "superstition" while preaching of Adam and Eve. Domínguez, in a mass of detail about San Ildefonso from his northern visitation, mentioned that La Mesilla stood to the north — only this.

Lapping to within a few score feet of Black Mesa was the Rio del Norte. The expedition's River of the North, today's Rio Grande, came into being from the San Juan Mountains as waning regional glaciers, along with others in the Sangre de Cristo, unleashed torrents after one Ice Age. Domínguez wrote that Hispano settlers, though going "very far north," hadn't traced the river's beginnings: "Moreover, the heathens in these regions, like the great wanderers they are, have gone

41

even farther in than the settlers, and in spite of this give no account of its source." The Rio Grande slithers and tumbles some eighteen hundred miles to the Gulf of Mexico, our nation's second longest river after the Missouri-Mississippi system.

The caravan forded the Rio Grande along here. To the west rose its Sierra de Santa Clara, northern crags of today's Jémez Mountains named for Indians whose pueblo sits to their southwest. The Jémez range, even younger than the Sangre de Cristo, was sired by volcanoes that still were spewing ash as far away as Kansas in the geological yesterday of twelve millennia ago.

The first night was spent at Santa Clara Pueblo. Escalante wrote little of the first two days' journey — here merely "Today nine leagues," about twenty-three miles — obviously because the region was known so well. Domínguez, who had visited Santa Clara only four months earlier, described a *convento* of six rooms. Some or all of the ten men doubtless ate and slept in this rectory.

A first church here, built in the 1620s, had been razed in the Pueblo Revolt. Santa Clarans, be it noted, were among those rebels besieged atop Black Mesa after the Reconquest. Some then went to the Hopis as refugees; most had returned. The 1776 church, the pueblo's third, was so narrow that it "resembles a wine cellar," Domínguez said, and "its adornment is so soulless that I consider it unnecessary to describe anything so dead." Still in character, he faulted the resident missionary for an inventory description of a vestment as purple when it was blue. "This affirmation is made because there is no other color that can serve for purple."

The clerical inspector also was caustic about the Indians here and Hispanos settled nearby. Granting that they had built most of the church on a voluntary basis, he added that a previous padre had needed to complete the roofing from his alms. The workmen, besides being well-paid, ate, drank and lived in the convento "in the winter when the [work] days are very short in this region." What's more, New Mexican workers "want a thousand delicacies, and in their homes they eat filth," so "the gravy cost the father more than the meat (as the saying goes)." Domínguez didn't specify the delicacies; other than chile, if it be deemed such, none was recorded among the mission's provisions. So much for the dignity of labor to the Hispano upper class.

Parishioners tended the mission's several small garden plots. As such donated labor was customary, Fray Francisco perhaps felt it unnecessary to add that they also tended the mission's ten sheep.

The church had "very thick walls. . . . The pueblo consists of a plaza which

42

La Mesilla . . . As Domínguez termed Black Mesa, in San Ildefonso Pueblo, New Mexico, facing east
to near where the expedition crossed the Rio Grande, foreground, on July 29, 1776.

lies to the south of the convento and church, and it is composed of four small blocks with two passageways on opposite corners. There is a fortified tower on one corner. . . .''

Miera, in a map description of the pueblos generally, would point up that "all the houses [have] portable ladders which they pull up in time of invasion, . . . the roofs and upper and lower terraces with embrasures in the parapets for defense against the enemy."

Only two years earlier a reported one thousand Comanches had rampaged through the Santa Clara region, killing seven and kidnaping three boys. Troops hadn't the horses to pursue them, Governor Mendinueta lamented to the viceroy. The Santa Clarans presumably were barricaded within their plaza at the time.

Shades of present-day Americans stationed abroad, few Spaniards, even few priests, bothered to learn Indian languages. Let the Indians learn Spanish. They spoke "in such a disfigured fashion," Domínguez observed, "that it is easier for our people to adjust to their manner of speaking [Spanish] than for them to attempt ours." Pidgin Spanish.

Santa Clarans were (and are) master potters. The Pueblos never have used the potter's wheel, instead molding coil upon coil of damp clay. Our wayfarers probably dined from Santa Clara pottery on this July 1776 evening. The Spaniards, little given to pottery-making, acquired almost all their tableware from the Pueblos.

July 30-31, 1776

THE CORTEGE CUT NORTHWESTERLY from the Rio Grande through four Hispano communities, each with its own name, "but this is nothing but a whim, for it all continues without even a middling break." Domínguez should have lived to see suburbia.

The Chama River, which flows about a hundred miles south from Colorado mountain meadows, was reached about a league north of where cottonwoods along its banks merge with those watered by the Rio Grande at their San Juan Pueblo junction to the east. Don Juan de Oñate and his original settlers had moved in on San Juan 178 years before. There could have been talk now of Oñate's bravado, his ruthlessness, his failure.

A "rough road," hilly, sandy and ravine-cut, led along the Chama, "red earth throughout its course," to the Shrine of Santa Rosa de Lima. "The settlers built it and provided the set of vestments, which is mother-of-pearl satin, but it is so old [in 1776!] that even to look at it is indecorous." An adobe wall fragment still stands seventy-five feet north of U.S. 84.

About thirty-five years earlier the authorities had tried to implant a buffer settlement here between the nomads and the Rio Grande communities. Who would buffer the buffers? Ute and Comanche raids forced abandonment at least twice.

Two miles west our travelers climbed a mesa to Santa Rosa de Abiquiu. Timber Point in Tewa, for whatever reason, Abiquiu was the utmost Spanish outpost to the northwest. Beneath jagged red and gray cliffs, "from all points there is a view of everything [except to the south]. . . . The pueblo consists of a large square plaza with a single entrance to the north. . . ."

A colony of genízaros had been emplaced on the Abiquiu mesa two decades before. Domínguez saw them as "weak, gamblers, liars, cheats, and petty thieves." And "sterile in their labor," they "are always dying." Little wonder. The nomads "keep the settlers in such a state of terror that they sow their [outlying] lands like transients and keep coming to this place where they can live in less fear." Abiquiu itself, later numbering some Hispanos, probably had been temporarily evacuated as recently as the late 1760s.

The church was of the usual adobe and dirt floor. While wrought vigas were pleasingly supported by multiple corbels, "there is no substitute for the vaulted arch."

Thirteen years earlier witchcraft had created a cause célèbre here. A genízaro girl accused a genízaro man of having brought on the death of Abiquiu's first priest by *maleficio*, malevolent occult practices. The next priest, suffering stomachaches, feared he might be a second hex victim. He joined the girl in pressing charges — echoing Salem of the 1690s — at Santa Cruz district headquarters. Unlike Salem, no stoning or garroting occurred, though death for witchcraft was not unknown in New Mexico. The magistrate ruled that the defendant and seven other Abiquiu genízaros be bound over as servants of selected Hispano families to be closely watched and better Christianized.

The present priest, Asturias-born Sebastián Fernández, was one of a few exceptions to Domínguez' critical efficiency ratings. Fernández was "punctilious" at his apostolic tasks, fed the poor and "doses everyone who needs it." Then this one-sentence statement: "Fridays of Lent, . . . after dark, discipline [is] attended by those who come voluntarily, because the father merely proposes it to them, and,

. . . after dark, discipline [is] attended by those who come voluntarily, because the father merely proposes it to them, . . .

45

following his good example, there is a crowd of Indians and citizens." Discipline? The word is freighted with historical connotation. This "discipline" means flagellation. Was this a harbinger of the Penitente movement that came almost half a century later?

More nonsense has been written about the Penitentes than about any other New Mexico institution: that Oñate was a member, that it witnessed sacrifice on the cross, that Mafia is an apt metaphor. If the Penitentes existed in Domínguez' time such an acute observer would know it. No other friars practiced Fernández' discipline. Fray Francisco was suitably impressed that Fernández inspired this body-chastizing commiseration with the suffering Christ in view of all the other scourges — drouth, epidemic, Indian raids — endured at this time.

The record is set straight by historian Fray Angelico Chavez: "The Penitentes are a lay society of flagellants that came to New Mexico shortly after 1800. Someone introduced the movement from Mexico or points farther south. Its history is much older, going back to sixteenth-century Spain. It was a revival in Spain of similar practices common all over Europe in the Middle Ages, but distinct in spirit and motivation.

"When the movement came to New Mexico the Mexican bishop of Durango tried in vain to suppress it, and more so the American bishops who succeeded him. Not because it was altogether wrong but because it was something outmoded. In our more tolerant age a former archbishop of Santa Fe gave his approval, provided the penitential practices were greatly toned down and done only in private."

"Because of various circumstances," Escalante wrote tersely, the wayfarers laid over on the thirty-first. These circumstances probably included a briefing by Father Fernández on the Utes, whom they expected to see much of on their way.

While sometimes attacking hereabout, the Utes ironically came to Abiquiu, Domínguez reported, to "celebrate their fair" with the settlers. A captive female of twelve to twenty was worth two good horses and "some trifles" such as a short coat, a horse cloth, a red lapel; a male was worth less by some no doubt interesting but unstated amount.

The captives became new genízaros. That horses sorely needed by the kingdom went to the Utes seems a travesty, but the Utes had something valuable to offer for them, the government nothing at all.

A "good race" tested a horse. One "much to the taste" also brought fifteen to twenty deerskins. ("To the taste" is an appropriate double-entendre, for many

Indians ate their ridden-out horses.) Traded as well were deer and buffalo meat for cornmeal and hunting knives.

In the next century Abiquiu would serve as a U.S. Army encampment against recalcitrant Navajos, then as an Indian Agency to dole out rations and blankets in what amounted to bribes to keep Utes and Jicarilla Apaches quiet on less-than-luxuriant reservations.

Again it may be assumed that our travelers enjoyed the hospitality of the convento. Perhaps here was their last taste of bread for a long time. Perhaps, from one of the mission's two jugs of sacramental wine, Father Fernández lifted cups with them in *salud* to their expedition's success. There being no beds on inventory, they doubtless slept on pallets atop fireplaces or on the floor. This might be their most comfortable night until late November.

August 1-4, 1776

"AFTER HAVING CELEBRATED the holy sacrifice of the Mass," recorded Escalante, "we set forth." A mass was in order. This region had long been a battleground; seven years earlier the kingdom's lieutenant governor had been killed by Comanches six leagues north of Abiquiu, Domínguez recalled.

Our travelers headed up the Chama. Along here they met two Indians. Though nothing would be said of them until weeks later, they probably were Utes coming to barter at Abiquiu.

The Cerro de Pedernal commands the western horizon two leagues along, Escalante observed. Beneath this flat-topped 9,857-foot Peak of Flint, the Chama makes a sharp S. The rovers scrambled up an embankment a few hundred yards west of one of present-day New Mexico's most photographed escarpments.

The guides were well-advised. Though continuing along the Chama would pare distance, the caravan soon would have faced a narrow canyon that, say today's river-runners, offers some of the nation's wildest, if relatively unknown, white water.

They halted for their daily siesta near Arroyo Seco, Dry Stream, in the alum-studded valley of La Piedra Alumbre, applying already-given place names to both. In fact, modern maps give most sites the same names through here, though time has elided Alumbre to Piedra Lumbre, Rock of Fire.

Since the science of geology was yet to emerge, our travelers didn't know that

47

these semi-arid vistas had been covered with water repeatedly through the eons. Some four hundred million years ago swamps bred horsetail rushes and spiked-leaf trees. Later came the first fish, primitive amphibians and reptiles, the dinosaur. Around ninety million years ago the seas rolled back for the last time. As far back as fifteen million years horses, elephants, giant sloths and other such mammals roamed these parts. Some forty of these species disappeared from North America about ten thousand years ago.

Recession of the latest Ice Age from Montana and farther north wrought changes down here from wet and cool to dry and hot. This probably killed off some of the mammals. Others emigrated across the Bering Strait to Asia. Still others may have been exterminated by those Stone Age wanderers' driving them into bogs and box canyons. (No endangered species concept among America's first colonists, who came in surges from Asia many thousands of years ago.)

Our cavalcade, noting gypsum deposits nearby, passed east of Echo Amphitheater, then returned to Arroyo Seco near where it empties into Arroyo del Canjilón, Deer Antler. The Dry Stream probably was dry at this season but "Today a good [heavy] shower fell upon us." Escalante's "good" means welcome as well. Anywhere in the Southwest's lower elevations rain generally is a benefaction, so much so that contest for its runoff would pit man against man and community against community, sometimes in bloody feuds, then state against state, even nation against nation. Rio Grande and Colorado River water is a recurring source of dispute with Mexico.

As the country became less known Escalante became more articulate about the route. His diary obviously was meant to point the way for successor missionaries. We see him now, sitting on a fallen tree, as he inscribes his lines. His ink may be from a wetted block such as the Chinese use even now, though Miera's decorative signature shows us a bottle beside his quill pen. Domínguez had brought plenty of paper from Mexico City so as not to cut into meager supplies at his visitation missions.

With their trail today parting from the Canjilón for a stretch, our travelers lost it, themselves and "track of four animals" in a scrub oak thicket. A word about such a trail. Nature's building and erosion created it. Animals trekked it to waterholes.

48

Indians traced animal tracks and explorers would take up from there — as, in many cases, would highway engineers.

Having rediscovered the trail and animals:

We came to a small plain of abundant pasturage which is very pleasing to the sight, because it produces some flowers whose color is between purple and white and which, if they are not carnations, are very much like carnations of that color [probably the pink]. Here there are also groves of *lemitas* [skunkbush or squawbush], a red fruit the size of the blackthorn. In freshness and taste it is very similar to the lemon, so that in this country it is used as a substitute for lemons in making refreshing drinks. Besides these fruits there is the choke-cherry, much smaller than the Mexican variety, and another berry which they call manzanita ["little apple," bearberry], whose tree resembles the lemita though the leaf is more like that of celery and the size of the berry is that of ordinary chick-peas. Some are white and others black, the taste being bitter-sweet and piquant but agreeable.

Those dense oaks are still to be seen; the meadow, alas, has been plowed under. Escalante would glory in nature's wonderment again but nowhere with such sustained eloquence. Perhaps it was that, as fatigue compounded and conflicts arose, he was not up to it after long marches.

From "where these flowers begin" our caravan veered northwest to the Rio de la Cebolla, Wild Onion, then camped along the Rio de las Nutrias, Beavers, for their numerous ponds. Beavers, it is a pleasure to relate, still dam the Nutrias' upper reaches.

Descent today to the familiar Chama. "Its pretty meadow . . . is of good land for crops with opportunities for irrigation. It produces much flax [for linen and cordage] and good and abundant pasturage, and there are also the other advantages necessary for the founding and maintenance of a settlement."

Near the ford were "large hidden sinks" in which Cisneros' horse was "completely submerged." Diarist Escalante, lacking the Attic salt of observer Domínguez, made nothing of the raillery doubtless directed at the unlucky Don Juan Pedro for his misadventures in pebble-covered quicksand.

Our travelers entered a small valley they called Santo Domingo, perhaps because tomorrow would be this saint's feast day. Though no longer known as such, it was the first of scores of places they would christen.

Three pine-covered mesas, fronted by three small hills to the north, curved around the valley toward the Chama. They are landmarks to this day near Los Ojos village. The guides told of two lagunas behind the mesas, today's Stone and Stinking lakes on the Jicarilla Apache Reservation. Escalante took their word that land thereabout was "very suitable for raising large and small stock." He was, as we shall see, ever the land-developer.

Riding between the two more northerly mesas, our journeyers came to a third lake also on the Jicarilla reservation. They named it for companion Olivares. "Although its water has not a very pleasant taste it is fit to drink." Today it is Horse Lake but its water is still brackish.

They wound through a troublesome *chamiza* thicket (from *chamuscar*, "to singe"). Early Spaniards gave this name to several kinds of low silvery bushes they brushed through, annalist Chavez tells us. One reason is that the greasewood and creosote species had blackened stems as if scorched by the sun. A second is that the prettier sagebrush varieties looked from a distance like rushes of this name in Spain. What we know as the flower *chamisa*, sometimes used interchangeably with its bush *chamiso*, is the rabbit brush, gray-green and topped with yellow in late summer. Our wayfarers would encounter chamiza, by whatever name, as profusely as piñon and juniper.

At some 7,760 feet they crossed the Continental Divide, of course without knowing it, and emerged at the Arroyo del Belduque, Hunting Knife, perhaps for its sharply eroded defiles. They descended what is now the Amargo (Bitter) River through Dulce, Jicarilla reservation headquarters, to Cañon del Engaño. Escalante gave no clue to why the canyon had been called Deceit.

He wrote of plentiful water in pools here. Perhaps these were springs from which Dulce got its name, Sweet. (For potable water Spaniards say "sweet" instead of "fresh.") Water. In every account of Southwestern exploration, before and since, water is of constant moment. Man can carry enough for several days but man's animals need new sources daily to carry on.

The closest Jicarilla Apaches then were centered northeast of Taos. The Jicarillas, Little Baskets for their pitch-lined water jugs, were not among the Apache tribes posing a life-or-death threat to northern New Spain, though they provided a persistent measure of trouble even into U.S. territorial times. They were moved no less than seven times before the present reservation was assigned in 1887. Though almost as big as Yosemite National Park, it is in large part as barren a place as could be found for them. How could U.S. officials have anticipated the oil and natural gas beneath lands inherited by today's some two thousand Jicarillas?

August 5-6, 1776

GUSHING DOWN from the northeast and crooking an elbow here is the Navajo River. It rose in the Sierra de la Grulla, the Crane, Escalante noted — our San Juan Mountains. The cavalcade forewent following the Navajo, perhaps because its canyon was deemed too narrow for the cattle, and clambered up a mesa to the west. "We continued . . . through canyons, over hills, and through very difficult brush. The guides lost the trail and even seemed to have forgotten the slight knowledge which they appeared to have of the country."

Escalante's petulance is to be appreciated. This writer, while searching out landmarks of the mesa route, led friends astray several times over. Though the trail was known generally, it was no Camino Real deepened by two-wheeled *carretas*. Perhaps Juan María de Rivera in 1765 and those succeeding traders had not been burdened with cattle. If not, they could have ridden directly along the Navajo's banks. There's a reservation road this way in our day, some of it over the bed of long-since-dismantled narrow-gauge tracks of the Denver and Rio Grande Western.

The lost ones finally spied a river below and descended, crossing into a Colorado-to-be and Southern Ute Reservation-to-come just short of a ford. "This stream is called Rio Grande de Navajó because it separates the province of this name from the Yuta nation." It was our San Juan River. Their San Juan, though Escalante correctly stated it to be the larger of the two, hence had lost its identity upstream to the tributary Navajo. United they formed "a river as large as the Rio del Norte" in July.

Camp was named Nuestra Señora de las Nieves, Our Lady of the Snows. Such San Juan peaks to the northeast as Conejos (Rabbit), 13,280 feet, and Summit, 13,172 feet, may have been snow-capped even at this time of the year. August 5

The guides lost the trail and even seemed to have forgotten the slight knowledge which they appeared to have of the country.

51

was the feast day of Our Lady of the Snow, singular. As Catholic legend has it, a childless Roman couple of the fourth century promised their wealth to the Virgin Mary. Her approval of the vow came with a miraculous midsummer snowfall on Esquiline Hill and a dream of Pope Liberius confirming dreams of theirs to build a chapel on the site.

A century after our expedition's sojourn here Las Nieves would be Coraque, possibly a Ute word, then Carracas in a misspelling of the Venezuelan capital. It was a speakeasy of a Hispano town in lively bootleg trade with the Utes. Hardly a trace remains of Las Nieves by any name.

Though the cavalcade had covered eight tortuous leagues, Escalante rode upstream "three leagues as the crow flies" to examine the confluence of the Navajo with the San Juan. A long day for a man so recently ailing. "Right at the junction, there were good advantages for a fair-sized settlement." These days there's a charming ghostly settlement here, Juanita, started about 1890.

Today departure was held up to "observe the latitude . . . by the meridian of the sun," perhaps the first such Hispano observation made north of present New Mexico. Miera and his astrolabe put it at 37° 51', about fifty-one minutes too high. Some of Miera's later sightings would give the expedition pause.

They descended the San Juan amidst shale and limestone built up in lakes and rivers in eons past. An ancestral river, carving its canyons, had left gravel on benches and hilltops. Closer to the river's basin, Escalante found that "there is good land, with facilities for irrigation and everything else necessary for three or four settlements, even though they might be large ones. . . . there are dense and shady groves of white cottonwood [poplar], dwarf oak, chokecherry, manzanita, lemita, and garambullo [gooseberry]. There is also some sarsaparilla, and a tree which looked to us like the walnut [which it undoubtedly was]."

Why *was* Escalante the incessant tract salesman?

Missionaries had had only to move in among the Pueblos and preach, baptize, supervise. The nomads could be brought under control and Christianized only by assembling them into sedentary communities. Communes, in effect, were envisioned. Here the nomads would cultivate the soil and tend livestock for themselves and the missions. Here they would be taught such crafts as carpentry and black-

. . . there is good land, with facilities for irrigation and everything else necessary for three or four settlements . . .

52

smithing and adopt Spanish-style government, with its own panoply of officials. Here they would dedicate themselves to Christ.

So it was hoped.

Our trekkers reined in after only two and a half leagues because Miera had a stomachache. They gave no name to tonight's camp. Nameless it is in our day beneath man-made Navajo Lake.

Hereabout they were close to the foothills of the San Juan Mountains, like the Sangre de Cristo a relative newcomer to the land. Gray granite peaks up there, fourteen of them over fourteen thousand feet, are broken by sharp pinnacles and deep crevasses, erosion having yet to do its polishing. As with several ranges en route, the San Juans rise from a semidesert base to arctic above timberline, lacking only the tropical of nature's seven life zones.

The NORThING

August 7, 1776

"GOD WILLED" Miera's mending so our journeyers rode on west to the confluence of the Rio de la Piedra Parada, Standing Peak. Here they left the San Juan River. They knew it flowed west to the Colorado, which they eventually had to cross. Had not Escalante recommended that Governor Crespo's projected expedition proceed due east from Monterey to the lands of the Paiutes who roamed due west of here? He had stated from maritime data, in fact, that Monterey stood between thirty-seven and thirty-eight degrees latitude (since it is actually at 36° 35′, they were already north of their stated objective). Though our leaders may not have known of the rugged San Juan canyons farther down, they logically should have considered following the river's descent. They apparently didn't. Why not?

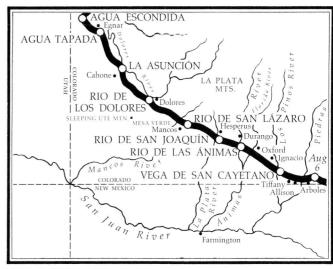

Perhaps because they had guides who knew the next stretch of another, if longer, trail. Then there had been Domínguez' speculating to Provincial Murillo on their taking a "roundabout" route. They could see what could be seen to the north as well as to the west — the Great River, the Great Sea, strange Indians, that mysterious colony, those opulent cities. For whatever reason, they now headed on a continuing course to the northwest.

SCALE: 50 MILES

Camp was made along a river called Los Pinos "because some pines grow along its banks." It was just south of the future reservation headquarters town of Ignacio, named for a conciliatory chief. In the expedition's time Utes roamed a homeland stretching from Great Salt Lake southeast to the Four Corners (New Mexico, Colorado, Utah and Arizona — the only place where four states meet) and encompassing much of Colorado and some of northern New Mexico.

As with the Jicarillas the United States broke a series of treaties that progressively whittled away the Utes' vast territory. An ailing Kit Carson hastened his 1868 death by accompanying a delegation to Washington that same year to assure them of fifteen million acres of hunting grounds west of the Continental Divide. With Carson's passing, Colorado clamor wanted rid of them altogether. The United States "compromised" by forcing them onto this and the adjacent Ute Mountain Reservation, a total of eight hundred fifty-seven thousand acres that, at perhaps five acres to a cow, are equivalent to only about half a dozen respectable-sized Anglo-American ranches for their some two thousand people. (There is another reservation for about fifteen hundred Utes in northeastern Utah.)

August 8, 1776

HAVING CROSSED the Rio Florido, Full of Flowers, our cavalcade plunged to the Rio de las Ánimas, forded it and made camp. This River of the Departed flows through a canyon here "but farther down they say it has good meadows."

Miera would have something to say of these meadows to his "Sacred Royal Catholic Majesty" next year. He would submit an unsolicited "brief report" based on his accompanying the present expedition "with such risk of my life" and further guided by the many years' "service which I have rendered your Majesty." Fortunately not brief, the report is a valuable historical document despite Don Bernardo's braggadocio.

Miera would urge three presidios and adjacent settlements of one hundred Spanish families each plus Indian converts by means of which "the door will be opened to a New Empire." Visitor-general Gálvez' very term. These should be at Yuma, beside Utah Lake and "along the beautiful and extensive meadows" near the confluence of the Ánimas with the San Juan. Baedeker couldn't have described the site better.

This juncture is about forty-five miles south of our expedition's route. Nor is

54

Miera known to have visited it, though he had drawn that map of the Navajo nation thereabout. His information perhaps came from among those present companions who had traded with the Navajos.

Miera would speak of "vestiges of irrigation ditches, ruins of many large and ancient settlements . . . and furnaces where apparently they smelted metals." Among his ruins are those of Aztec National Monument. His "metals" doubtless were a promotional come-on. He probably mistook descriptions of burned-out kivas for European-style smelters without realizing there had been no smelting in all of prehistoric North America.

Miera's presidio there would be a way station between New Mexico and Monterey. In hindsight he seemed to be thinking of a far more southerly northern route than the expedition took. Fifty-three years later one Antonio Armijo would inaugurate such a trade trail out of Abiquiu. With thirty men and a pack train, Armijo headed west-northwest and forded the San Juan near Miera's junction with the Ánimas. He recrossed the San Juan at the Four Corners to avoid its downstream canyons and traversed northeastern Arizona to ford the Colorado at a point we shall hear much about in these pages.

Most pointedly, Miera's presidio also would provide a site to which "to transplant" the obdurate Hopis. The Hopis "should be brought down by force from their cliffs." They would surrender in less than a week "without the shedding of blood" if soldiers were stationed at their waterholes below. "Within a few years there would be in that place [the river junction] a rich and strong province adjoining New Mexico and expanding toward these [other] new settlements."

Did Escalante indoctrinate Miera on the Hopis as he apparently had gotten to Domínguez?

Miera's linking presidios with missions — time-honored, yes, but with clerical ambivalence. The friars were ever fearful that garrisons would corrupt their neophytes, even prey upon them as we have seen of California. But most friars felt they couldn't do without the troops both to protect their missions against other nomads and to protect themselves against such assassinations as have been described herein. Besides, troops were useful to confine the settled nomads, to keep them from returning to wild ways. (The United States would emulate such concentration camps long hereafter.)

The Hopis *should be brought down by force from their cliffs.*

55

MOVING EVER NORTHWEST our wayfarers climbed to a high valley (Ridge's Basin). "The land is very moist, for because of the nearness of the sierra it rains very frequently. For this reason, in the forests, which consist of very tall straight pines [ponderosa], small oaks and several kinds of wild fruits [plum, for one], as well as in its valleys, there are the finest of pastures. The climate here is excessively cold even in the months of July and August. Among the fruits there is a little one, black in color, of agreeable taste [probably the golden currant], and very much like the medlar [a crab apple-like Eurasian tree], although not so sweet."

Descending to the Rio de la Plata (about a mile south of Hesperus), they held the day's journey to a little over four leagues because their animals were weak from not having eaten well on the Ánimas' sandy banks and because it rained long and hard. Many times they might wish for that rain.

The La Plata rises in the La Plata Mountains. "[It] flows through the canyon in which they say there are veins and outcroppings of metal. But, although years ago several persons came from New Mexico to examine them by order of the Governor, . . . and carried away ore, it was not learned with certainty what metal it was. The opinion formed previously by some persons from the accounts of various Indians and of some citizens of this kingdom that they were silver mines, caused the mountains to be called Sierra de la Plata."

Had Rivera carried away the ore after another, unrecorded Hispano saw its glint? Why was it not assayed? Silver there was aplenty hereabout, as a breed of Anglo prospectors would find, along with gold, lead and other minerals.

Domínguez awoke with severe sinus trouble. Both he and Miera had now fallen ill en route yet the ailing Escalante remained sound. Had Fray Silvestre steeled himself in the obverse of the psychosomatic?

The caravan would have stayed on at the La Plata but continuing rain and the "great dampness of the place forced us to leave it." Perhaps spirits were lifted by "beautiful" roses Escalante remarked upon along a trail winding through successive valleys. Though he failed to record it, ever present to the west from some forty miles away rises Sleeping Ute Mountain, for all the world a comatose giant with

The La Plata flows through the canyon in which they say there are veins and outcroppings of metal.

La Sierra de la Plata . . . Looking northwest toward the La Plata Mountains from two miles
southeast of Hesperus, Colorado, near where the party camped on August 9, 1776.

arms folded on his chest. (The Sleeping Ute would give the Ute Mountain Reservation its name.)

Another downpour. Domínguez' pain was growing sharper; the road was "impassable." Camp again was made early, along the Rio de los Mancos (near Mancos). *Mancos* meaning "one-handed, faulty, crippled," historian Bolton suggests that "Indians or skeletons with hands cut off had been seen or heard of in the vicinity, but this may be a bad guess."

Domínguez was too weak for our travelers to move on. "For this reason, we were not able to go to see the veins and metallic stones of the sierra, although they were nearby, as we were assured by a companion who had seen them on another occasion." This companion may have been guide-interpreter Andrés Muñíz while with Rivera or on another sally. Why, leaving Domínguez in camp, did not some of them go to the ore site?

Here also they were within twenty-five miles of Mesa Verde and its huge cliff dwellings. Escalante made no mention of them.

And from here they again conveniently could have cut west, descending the Mancos River to its junction with the San Juan at the Four Corners. Though this would have put them roughly at Monterey's latitude, no service station maps were at hand to pinpoint a route. Besides, adventure called to the north.

With Domínguez better and "to change terrain and climate rather than to make progress," our expedition traversed an easy eight and a half leagues. Did the departure reflect the guides' eagerness to leave the Mesa Verde vicinity? Bolton asks. "With all its wonders, Mesa Verde is mighty spooky."

There is no record that the Hispanos knew of the cliff dwellings, hidden on highlands of what would become a major national park. Not until 1887, in fact, would a few of Mesa Verde's hundreds of ruins be discovered by latter-day Americans. And the Hispanos were not superstitious about Indian ruins. "They had no qualms about living in or building on prehistoric sites," says David H. Snow, a Museum of New Mexico archaeologist. "In general these were favorably situated for water and farmlands."

Camp was where the Rio de Nuestra Señora de los Dolores, dropping off the La Platas from the northeast, turns sharply north (near Dolores townsite).

Our travelers stopped here another day, partly to give Domínguez a chance to improve, partly to observe the latitude. That Miera's sighting was almost three-fourths of a degree too high Bolton lays to "primitive apparatus" and says that such inaccuracies were true of most Spanish expedition diaries to the end of the eighteenth century. Perhaps taking this into account, cartographic historian Carl I. Wheat says, "The remarkable quality of Miera's achievement is best appreciated when his map is compared with a modern map of the same area."

While here Escalante observed that, "On an elevation on the south bank of the river in ancient times there was a small settlement of the same form as those of the Indians of New Mexico, as is shown by the ruins which we purposely examined." Our diarist implies that this expedition was not the first to have visited the ruins. Amid trees and ground cover they can't be seen from below. A good guess is that Rivera had climbed the hill's some three hundred feet to survey the route ahead. One can see far down Our Lady of Sorrows up here.

The Spanish colonizers were not much given to inspection of or introspection on Indian ruins. Their voluminous archives are archaeologically taciturn. Miera's interest was in metallurgy. Escalante's may have reflected his own innate curiosity.

These pueblo vestiges are known these two centuries later as the Escalante Ruin rather than for Domínguez, which proves anew that the pen is mightier . . . A visitor center here is a bicentennial project of the U.S. Bureau of Land Management.

As a matter of fact, the Escalante Ruin, tiny and isolated though it may be, was "discovered" long before Mesa Verde's awesome archaeological treasure, by Captain John N. Macomb's 1859 expedition to explore the Grand Canyon. Perhaps Macomb, of the Topographical Corps, had read of the site in a copy of Escalante's diary that was available in Washington. Or perhaps the captain found it as presumably had the Spaniards: to scout out the landscape. His geologist, John S. Newberry, wrote: "From the summit . . . we obtained a magnificent view of a wide extent of the country lying on every side . . . stretching far off southward, the green slopes and lofty battlements of Mesa Verde beetling over the plain like some high and rock-bound coast above the level ocean. . . ."

How could Newberry have guessed what beetled on that plateau? As to his "magnificent view," Dr. Bertha Dutton, the eminent archaeologist, tells this writer that "I've never seen an Indian ruin that was not placed in a beautiful setting." And often on an eminence for defense, drainage and climate comfort as well.

Newberry described the pueblo as "once substantially built of dressed stone, now a shapeless heap in which the plan of the original structure can, however, be traced." Like Escalante he compared it to New Mexico pueblos, its rooms being like "cells in a beehive." He found depressions that had been kivas, pottery sherds strewed everywhere.

In the 1910s the ruin was visited anew by J. Walter Fewkes of the Smithsonian Institution, who took note of Escalante's diary for being "valuable to students of archaeology, as it contains the first reference to a prehistoric ruins in the confines of the present State of Colorado." In Escalante's time, be it noted, there was no "archaeology."

The Escalante Ruin was built by the Anasazi, those Ancient Ones, who occupied the San Juan drainage from about 100 B.C. About the time of Christ came a transition from the hunting and gathering Desert Culture to that of the mainly agricultural Basket Maker. The Escalante Ruin was occupied from about A.D. 900, a University of Colorado survey has determined, after a further transition from Basket Maker to Pueblo Culture.

Multi-roomed houses had arisen. Basketry increasingly was supplemented by pottery (introduced from the Valley of Mexico?), which gradually became more refined. Kivas, circular and underground, appeared as religious and social systems gradually became more complex. Cotton began to be woven, turquoise to be prized.

The Escalante Ruin was abandoned about 1300 along with Mesa Verde and all adjacent communities. Nomadic (Ute?) attacks, climatic changes and deforestation and erosion are among possible causes; a quarter-century drouth probably was the primary reason. The evacuees from here and elsewhere moved generally south, many to sites near and along the Rio Grande to become Keres and other Pueblos. In time Utes and other nomads filled the vacuum, hunters and gatherers here anew.

60

Apparently deterred by thickets along a Dolores that flows through a gentle valley here, our sojourners climbed a ridge to the west only to face other thickets and a "deep and broken canyon." But for their cattle they could have avoided this and other digressions. Trailing cattle had become a custom for expeditions in game-scarce Sonora, though Father Garcés did without beef. The Mountain Men, sharp-shooters, would also do without. Though game abounded over much of their route, our rovers seem not to have been much on hunting.

This afternoon they were overtaken by a coyote, Felipe, and a genízaro, Juan Domingo, from faraway Abiquiu. (Though "coyotes" properly were products of combined mestizo and pure Indian blood, the term often was used loosely to denote mestizos and even genízaros. What Felipe actually was is unknown. He remained, inconsiderately, a man without a surname) Our leaders were not overjoyed. "To wander among the heathen, they had fled from that pueblo without the permission of their superiors, protesting that they wished to accompany us. We did not need them, but to prevent the mischief which either through ignorance or malice they might commit by traveling alone any longer among the Yutas if we tried to send them back, we accepted them as companions." Had Domínguez imparted to Escalante his class bias, deserved or not, as the party now grew from ten men to twelve?

The wayfarers descended again to the Dolores, camping at a "small meadow of good pasturage" that they named La Asunción de Nuestra Señora, The Assumption of Our Lady. Attesting to Escalante's assessment, one finds a verdant, canyon-walled ranch here, east of Cahone town.

The guides knew what they were doing as the caravan now broke away from the Dolores anew. East of Dove Creek town is a Forest Service overlook where the Dolores makes a V within V-shaped walls of butte-sized slabs of reddish rocks that are artistically seared by nature's acid. If none is clamoring nearby, the music of rushing waters fifteen hundred feet below is heard in counterpoint to the hoot of an unseen owl. To climb out of this canyon would take mountaineer gear, it seemed to your writer.

A siesta halt was made at an arroyo (possibly Dove Creek) that the guides had "thought had water, though we found it entirely dry." Scouts were sent ahead. They found a hole sufficient only for the men. "It was covered with stones and logs, apparently on purpose. Perhaps this was done by the Yutas because of some mis-fortune that they had suffered at this place, for, according to what was told us by

. . . to prevent the mischief which either through ignorance or malice they might commit by traveling alone any longer among the Yutas if we tried to send them back, we accepted them as companions.

61

some companions who had been among them, they are accustomed to do this in such cases." Camp was called Agua Tapada, Covered Pool, a reflection of this ethnological insight.

Crazed for water, over half of the animals had strayed during the night. Several companions, surely cursing when out of earshot of the padres, retraced about half of yesterday's long trek to find them at a water source of an undescribed nature.

"For this reason we did not leave Agua Tapada until half past ten." Here is indication both that there was a timepiece among them and that camp usually was broken early to start marching in the coolness of a sun low in the sky.

Their course, which had been northwest since leaving the San Juan, shortly turned north in a hope to get back to the vagrant Dolores. They lost a trail in loose, washed-out soil. Perhaps it was asking too much of the guides, even of one who had made two round trips, to recognize every landmark over hundreds of miles.

A "much-used" trail eventually was found that led into a canyon (Summit, northwest of Egnar) and to a waterhole hidden in dense piñon and juniper. "More specific directions . . . are not given because the trail goes right to it" — an indicator that for future travelers Escalante was trying to make up for where Rivera's diary and the guides had failed their own expedition.

Fray Silvestre's own directions aren't all that helpful in places, this being one such. If one were to follow the diarist's bearings and distances on this day's march, he would wind up in Utah. The terrain dictates against it. Perhaps lodestones, such as Escalante had predicated en route to Zuñi, betrayed their compass.

Their leagues en route varied from one and one-half to four and two-tenths miles, a Bureau of Land Management study shows. "It seems that the easier the going," the study says, "the longer the league becomes." Along with some other aficionados, I hold that Escalante was somewhat closer to the mark. The Spaniards sometimes used human pacers to determine more exactly a distance covered, according to historian-archaeologist Schroeder. In all events, such a task apparently wasn't assigned for our mounted expedition.

Here they dug two shallow wells for the animals and called their camp Agua Escondida, Hidden Pool. "Don Bernardo went on alone through this canyon without our seeing him. . . . we . . . sent another companion to tell him to return before

We . . . sent another companion to tell him to return before he got lost. But he got so far ahead that they did not return until after midnight . . .

he got lost. But he got so far ahead that they did not return until after midnight to the place where the rest of us were waiting, greatly worried on account of their tardiness. They said that going through the canyon they had reached the Rio de los Dolores, and that on the way there was only one stretch that was difficult to get through, and that it could be improved.''

With a route now known, the worry the impulsive Miera had caused was worth it. Worth, that is, the expedition's being prepared to turn in the opposite longitudinal direction from Monterey. Since leaving Santa Fe it had traveled about two hundred twenty air miles yet, because of its northing, advanced only some one hundred ninety-five toward Monterey. Be it said in extenuation that no adequate longitudinal reckonings were available. At that time these could be made only during eclipses. Lack of them explains some foreshortening of certain east-west distances on Miera's maps.

To have turned due west here would have plunged our journeyers into Utah's horrendous south-central canyonlands. Had they but known, they could have veered northwest, crossed the Colorado at present-day Moab and skirted the more tortuous Utah terrain by proceeding to Castle Dale. A satellite topographical map could have told them that! The fact is that traders and trappers a few decades later would hit upon this as the preferred of several routes to be known collectively as the Old Spanish Trail to California.

Our rovers had watered at the covered pool and trod the much-used trail, evidence that Indians were about. To the best of their knowledge the nearest were to the east. One of their self-assigned missions was to learn more about the Indians of the mysterious regions. This apparently was the immediate motive for a pivotal decision.

The EASTING

August 17-20, 1776

THEY THREADED THE CANYON. "Because of the varied and agreeable appearance of the rocks on either side, which being so high and rugged at the turns, make it appear that the farther one goes the more difficult it is to get out, and because Don

We saw very recent tracks
of Yutas. . . . We thought
one of their rancherías must
be nearby, . . .

64

Bernardo Miera was the first one who traveled it, we called this canyon Laberinto de Miera.'' Miera's Labyrinth, amid huge chunks of limestone tilting away from foundations of red rock, covered seven leagues, "although by a straight line it would be four or five at most," to a third meeting with the Dolores, again in a pleasant valley (at Slick Rock).

"We saw very recent tracks of Yutas. . . . We thought one of their rancherías must be nearby, and that if they had seen us and we did not seek them they might fear some harm from us and be alarmed." The evaluation of the tracks attests perhaps to the guides' Indian blood. But, since the pathfinders still seemed to be in a quandary, our leaders wanted to enlist Utes as guides, "enabling us to continue our journey with less difficulty and labor than we were now suffering because none of the companions knew the waterholes and terrain ahead."

To meet the Utes Domínguez chose to employ his own tact. He, Cisneros and Andrés Muñíz followed their tracks upstream three leagues to where the Rio de las Paralíticas emptied into the Dolores. They found no Indians though it was determined, presumably by Muñíz, that the tracks were of a Tabehuache band. Determined from moccasin prints, tree slashes, litter? When questions such as this one arise, it is indeed aggravating that Domínguez, with his eye for enlightening detail, didn't take more of a hand in the diary.

"They say that this Rio de las Paralíticas is so called because the first of our people who saw it found in a ranchería on its banks three Yuta women suffering from paralysis." Here is evidence that Rivera passed this way, which makes Muñíz' ignorance of the route hereabout the more mystifying.

Escalante noted further that the Paralíticas (which now bears the equally dejected name Disappointment Creek) divided Moache territory to the south from the Tabehuaches. For Ute bands to pass from one territory to another provoked no imperative, ethnologists tell us. Our travelers had seen no Moaches (whose descendants are among those on the Southern Ute Reservation) unless the two they met the first day out of Abiquiu were of that band.

From a camp called Don Bernardo, doubtless again for Miera's exploratory exploit, scouts were sent out early to find a means of getting away from the Dolores that began to be hemmed in again by "high and very stony mesas." None could be found that would keep them on a northeasterly course, so they had to proceed by the bed in which, because of rocky stumbling blocks, it was feared the animals would bruise their hoofs.

So harsh was the way, they traveled only a league, their shortest distance yet, before camping (near the mouth of McIntyre Canyon). Scouts again were dispatched. "About eight o'clock at night they returned saying that only by the bed of the river would we be able to emerge from this impassable network of mesas and that only with difficulty."

Your writer seconds the scouts' estimate. Driving along a rutted mining road on mesas above the east bank, I got stuck in the sand. While ranch houses could be seen far below, it would have taken a parachute to reach them for help. Nothing to do but leg it back. What's more, it was not trodding the packed sand of a beach, I found, but picking them up and laying them down as in wet snow . . . an appreciation of our travelers' travails with the terrain. After a few miles, a uranium mine. A congenial miner rousted out a trio of husky sons from nearby Slick Rock to heave a city slicker's car back onto firm surface.

Two leagues along, the Dolores bed itself was "impassable" and a scout found a parallel northerly trail also to be "impassable." Escalante was addicted to this adjective. Another trail, backtracking to the southwest, offered immediate prospect for getting out of their predicament but "we did not dare follow it because . . . we could see high mesas and deep canyons in which we might again be surrounded and find ourselves forced to turn back."

There remained another possibility, a trail that "goes to the Yutas Sabuaganas." Though the route to the Sabuaganas headed immediately southeast, this Ute band roamed far to the northeast. Why should they not have continued to seek out Tabehuaches hereabout? There is a clue in a diary entry of four days later: "A Sabuagana chief [is] said by our interpreter and others to be very friendly toward the Spaniards and to know a great deal about the country." The "others" probably included the stowaways Felipe and Juan Domingo. "Everyone had a differing opinion. So, finding ourselves in a state of confusion, . . . we put our trust in God and our will in that of His Most Holy Majesty. . . . we cast lots between the two roads and drew the one leading to the Sabuaganas, which we decided to follow

About eight o'clock at night they returned saying that only by the bed of the river would we be able to emerge from this impassable network of mesas and that only with difficulty.

65

until we reached them." In an extremity, God, grandee and gamble. Were the lots of paper, twigs, stones?

After long fencing with the Dolores, our travelers bid it a final goodbye in taking a "very well-beaten trail" at the foot of a high mesa (along Big Gypsum Creek) to the "east-northeast." Escalante was about sixty-seven and one-half degrees off. Mental fatigue or more lodestones?

Soon Miera "did not wish to follow this road," perhaps because it was off-course. Therefore "the interpreter, Andrés, led us up a very high and rugged hill having so many stones that we expected to be forced to go back when halfway up, because it was so hard on the animals that many of them left their tracks on the stones with the blood from their feet." It took "several hours" to climb about one-fourth league.

Up here they saw that the road they had been on ran along the base of the opposite side of the mesa "over good and entirely level terrain." If Miera had been patient for another couple of leagues they would have spared the bloodstained climb by rounding the foot of the mesa. Escalante's sarcasm was implicit. He took no written notice of what must have been Miera's chagrin or the others extreme displeasure.

For that matter, our leaders could have felt chagrin. By continuing east from the Paralíticas junction with the Dolores (across Disappointment and Big Gypsum valleys and Dry Creek Basin) they would have spared four or five days' muddled wandering. But was there water thereabout in this season? Oh, for a backpacker's guidebook!

After an easy descent to the north they encountered (in upper Dry Creek Basin) "much small cactus," perhaps the clusters of small prickly knobs commonly called *huevos de Indio*, "Indian eggs." To shun further hardship for the animals, they took to a nearby arroyo that led to a focal point: a small spring, the road they had seen from the mesa top, a convergence of other trails and ruins of huts they judged to be a Ute campsite. They had to be elated at being so hot on Ute presence as they lit the night's fires at what they called Fuente (Fountain) de San Bernabé on the feast day of Barnabas, Paul's companion. After such a difficult day rest must have been well received that night.

THEY ASCENDED A CANYON (Dry Creek) to a level pocket (southeast of Paradox Valley). Had they been so minded, they could have swung northwest up Paradox Valley to shorten their distance to Monterey. But no, not even a recorded contemplation of it. They rode on through a lesser canyon (below Sawtooth Ridge) to the Rio de San Pedro.

This is the expedition's first major stream, aside from the convolution of the San Juan and Navajo, that in time would bear another name, the San Miguel. It "rises in a spur of the Sierra de las Grullas," Escalante now making it Cranes, plural.

On one of his maps Miera would attach the San Juan Mountains to the Rockies proper and inscribe: "This mountain range is the backbone of North America, since the many rivers that are born in it empty into the two seas, the South Sea [Gulf of California] and the Gulf of Mexico." Miera possessed extrasensory perception in drawing this "backbone" conclusion. It would take Anglo explorers decades to realize it. Miera's rivers, with their tributaries, were of course the Rio Grande and the Colorado.

Their San Pedro joined the Dolores "near the small range which they call Sierra de la Sal because close to it there are salt beds where, according to what we are told, the Yutas who live hereabouts get their salt," Escalante added. Salt is a necessity almost on the order of water and food; Indians often had to travel long distances for it. Fifty miles west of here across the Utah line the La Sal peaks are conspicuous, Mt. Peale chief among them at 12,721 feet. They are laccoliths, masses of igneous rock that pushed up domes of overlying strata and over the eons were exposed by erosion.

Fording the San Miguel (northwest of Naturita), our men climbed to a "wide mesa which looks like a remnant of the Sierra de los Tabehuaches." Escalante's remnant was a fringe of what would become the Uncompahgre Plateau. They "went down from the mesa by another rugged but short slope . . . the one which Don Juan Mariá de Rivera in his diary describes as being very difficult." The party must have regained confidence in their orientation at hitting this landmark on the 1765 explorer's trail. Here they rejoined the San Miguel.

67

Moving ever eastward, they left the San Miguel at a creek (the Cottonwood) that led to a lush valley. "There is a sort of ledge upon which there are ruins of a small and ancient pueblo whose houses appear to have been of stone, with which the Yutas Tabehuaches have made a weak and crude fortification." Fortification against the far-ranging Comanches?

"We again have found good pasturage . . . which had been very scarce from the camp of La Asunción [on the Dolores ten days ago] until today, because the country was so scorched and dry that it appeared not to have rained during this whole summer."

It rained, so fickle is Southwestern precipitation, this very afternoon. Afterward they climbed, "rugged in places," to the Uncompahgre Plateau and: "We were overtaken by a Yuta Tabehuache, who is the first Indian we have seen in all the distance traveled to here since the first day's march from the pueblo of Abiquiu. . . ." After all their eagerness to find Utes, no emotion. Yet twenty-three days! So much, quips historian Bolton, for "any notion that everywhere in primitive America the woods were full of Indians."

It is possible that the Ute was mounted to have caught up with them, though many Indians were of marathon stamina. "To talk at leisure" they camped and gave the Tabehuache "something to eat and smoke."

"At first he appeared ignorant of everything, even of the country in which he lived," but in time "he recovered somewhat from the fear and suspicion." Why the apprehension? The Tabehuache's instigation of their encounter probably meant he had met Spaniards before. Perhaps it was a dozen pairs of eyes pressing intently on him.

Presently he forecast that they would soon meet the Sabuaganas to the northeast. As to orientation: "All the rivers from the San Pedro [San Miguel] to the San Rafael [still another name for the Colorado] inclusive, flow into the Dolores, which, in turn, joins the Rio de Navajó [San Juan]." He erred doubly, for both the Dolores and the San Juan are tributary to the Colorado.

Our leaders asked him to guide them to the ranchería of that friendly and knowledgeable Sabuagana chief. "He consented on condition that we wait for him until the afternoon of the next day. We agreed to this, partly so that he might

. . . the country was so scorched and dry that it appeared not to have rained during this whole summer.

68

guide us, and partly that he might not suspect us of anything which might disturb him and the rest."

Camp was called La Fuente de la Guía, The Guide's Fountain, perhaps for this Ute who had given welcome news.

Before noon the Ute reappeared, along with his family, two other women and five children, "two at the breast." All were "good-looking and very agreeable." Though the Utes comprised small bands, these in turn comprised even smaller kinship groups, as this occasion attests. They had brought tanned deerskins, dried manzanita "grapes" and "other articles for barter." Told that "we did not bring goods to trade," they were "not fully convinced."

The friars worried that they might "regard us as explorers whose purpose was to conquer their land after seeing it" and thus "impede our progress." A non sequitur nonpareil, attention was turned to the safety of Father Garcés after he had dispatched his report to Zuñi from amidst the Hopis. The friars suggested that word "of our brother" could have spread from the Havasupais to the Paiutes to Utes hereabout.

"Thereupon they were entirely quieted, sympathized with us in our trouble, and said they had not heard anything about the Padre." It often appears to be a universal trait to switch a subject to one's commiserative concern when at oral loggerheads. As in this confrontation, it often works.

The Hispanos now gave "food to all of them," probably including fresh beef, and paid the guide's wife in flour for some dried venison and their "tasty" dried bearberries. Like latter-day C rations, their own diet may have begun to pall.

Next was presented what the male Ute had "requested for guiding us": two hunting knives and sixteen strings of glass beads. These he handed to his wife, who left at once with the others. Had the Ute delayed the expedition to skim choice trade goods before other Utes got their pick?

Our men set forth with him "whom we now began to call Atanasio" and followed a tortuous route that Escalante logged at five leagues but credited only two actually covered. Where's he taking us? they surely asked themselves. The day ended in a "very steep" descent into a valley (apparently of a tributary to Horsefly Creek). Camp was called La Cañada Honda.

69

There are stags, fallow deer
and other animals, and some
fowls of a size and form
similar to the ordinary
domestic hens . . .

Out of The Deep Gulch they began to cross the Uncompahgre Plateau, "without any difficult slopes," toward the northeast. Escalante found the crest "of agreeable appearance on account of the [fern?] brakes and the beautiful groves of cottonwood which here grow close together." In those days the Spaniards lumped aspen, poplar and cottonwood into the term *alamo*, which Bolton invariably translates as "cottonwood." Here Escalante assuredly meant aspen.

Many such groves hereabout stand in meadows that were laid flat by Ice Age glaciers. Cliffsides were quarried by the glaciers, the fragments dragged along to bulldoze the landscape under behemothic pressure. These meadows often are amphitheater-shaped — "cirques" to geologists.

At this elevation our travelers also were amid ponderosa pine, Engelmann's spruce, Douglas fir. Escalante, neglecting these stately trees, again spoke of "several kinds of wild fruits." And "there are stags, fallow deer and other animals, and some fowls of a size and form similar to the ordinary domestic hens, from which they differ in not having combs. Their flesh is very savory."

Among those other animals Escalante could have mentioned the scampering deer or the swift antelope, elk, bighorn sheep, black bear. His fowl probably were grouse. There were no shotguns in those days. How were they obtained for eating?

Up here are the brilliant broad-tailed hummingbird, the violet green swallow, the red-naped sapsucker. Perhaps it was from weariness that Escalante failed to write of these or of such wildflowers in bloom at this season as the showy columbine, the blue gentian, the Indian paintbrush. Somewhere about was "the place [Rivera] called El Purgatorio." Why had the 1765 explorer termed this Garden of Eden a place of fiery purgation?

Camp was named Ojo de Laín, perhaps because it was the Santa Fean who had stumbled upon one of the numerous springs in this vicinity (west of Log Hill Mesa). At about nine thousand feet this would be the expedition's loftiest night. "Before it was possible to prepare any food, of which we were in great need, a heavy shower fell," dampening any possibility for a campfire. Probably they settled for jerky and even in August were shivering . . . recalling those hot meals and comfortable nights at the Abiquiu mission.

At this elevation clouds are beckoned. Most of the moisture blowing off the

Pacific is captured by the California mountains that were seen in hazy blue by those early Spanish mariners. Of that which escapes, a minute part falls in the hot, dry Great Basin, the rest to be blown to the Colorado Plateau. Here it rises, cools and drops on peaks and high slopes. Were it not for the runoff, far more of this region would be semidesert, indeed "the Great American Desert" that it would erroneously be called.

An easy descent from the Uncompahgre Plateau led to the Rio de San Francisco, "by the Yutas called Ancapagari (which according to the intrepreter, means Laguna Colorado) because near its source there is a spring of red water, hot and tasting bad." These days it is the Uncompahgre River. Our rovers camped at what they called La Ciénega (Marsh) de San Francisco (south of Montrose).

Escalante penned another pitch for a settlement site. It was as if for a vacation-land advertisement that he added, "North of this meadow there is a chain of little hills and lead-colored knolls crowned with yellow earth" — handsome, as Montrose residents will attest.

Near the campsite nowadays are the Chief Ouray State Historical Monument and Ute Indian Museum in Chipeta Park. Ouray was a Ute advocate of amity with the Anglo conquerors, Chipeta his wife. The museum, operated by the Colorado Historical Society, exhibits a splendid collection of Ute garments, utensils, weapons and arts and crafts as well as maps, dioramas and photographs. To visit it is to get a feel for the Utes our expedition will continue to greet.

Downstream our travelers met a Ute called El Zurdo, The Left-handed, whom Escalante implies was known to some expedition members. "In a lengthy conversation we learned nothing useful except to have suffered from the heat of the sun" — the difference three thousand feet make.

Nothing useful? In his diary tomorrow Escalante would note that "yesterday we learned" of Sabuagana rancherías nearby and "that in them were some of the Timpanogotzi or Laguna Indians." And two days hence he would write that "the Yutas told us that the Lagunas lived in pueblos like those of New Mexico." This

71

intelligence, coming in dribbles, was portentous. Escalante's phrasing implies that the Timpanogotzi were not unknown, though there is no earlier historical record of them. That they also were called Lagunas meant that they lived near a lake or lakes. And that they inhabited pueblos . . . a malleable sedentary population! Might not their homeland border the Great Sea of the West? Might not it be Cíbola, Copala, Teguayo?

We have seen that the Utes ranged a vast domain. Divided into about ten bands, they were without a central authority. Their language was of the Shoshonean branch of the widespread Uto-Aztecan phylum, a branch of which their sometimes enemies the Hopis were a part. Their cultures were as dissimilar as Chinese, say, and Chilean.

About A.D. 1000 Shoshonean speakers, Utes among them, had fanned out eastward from the Death Valley region, linguists postulate. By 1150 they had reached this region from the northwest, overrunning agricultural peoples of the Frémont culture. The latter is named for ruins in which this culture was identified by archaeologists along a Utah river named for the nineteenth-century explorer John C. Frémont.

Our men forded the Uncompahgre and camped at what they called San Agustín (north of Olathe). Escalante here entered an aside. About four leagues north the river joined "another and larger one which is called by our people Rio de San Javier." The San Javier is today's Gunnison. At the junction Rivera had carved a cross, his name and the year on a poplar, Andrés Muñiz related. Muñiz himself stopped three days short of the junction at that time, he said, but last year he had gone all the way there with two companions of the Rivera expedition and found the tree. "These two were the only ones who crossed [the Gunnison], having been sent by the said Don Juan María to look for Yutas on the bank opposite the meadow where they were camped and from where they turned back." This junction then was the farthest known limit of Hispano exploration. Ahead was the unknown and hopefully a route to connect Spanish settlements in North America. A mystery river and the question — whither Monterey?

"And so," added Escalante, "this was the river they then thought was the great Rio del Tizón," the Firebrand Colorado. How, when and by whom it had been decided that the Gunnison was not the Colorado are among our many unsolved questions.

These two were the only ones who crossed [the Gunnison], having been sent by the said Don Juan María to look for Yutas on the bank opposite the meadow . . .

72

THE DETOUR

LEAVING THE UNCOMPAHGRE RIVER, our travelers reached the Gunnison (near Austin). Escalante put the junction (about eight miles west) at the western point of the Sierra del Venado Alazán, into which he lumped Grand Mesa ahead and the latter-day Elk Mountains to the east. Venado Alazán, literally "roan deer," is New Mexican for elk.

This is a historic moment. From here they would leave known country — though it sometimes may have seemed otherwise in view of their guides' failings. Now they were trailblazers. After the animals and the Indians, that is.

At a bend of the Gunnison, which they named Santa Monica, our explorers called a halt. To go upstream toward the Sabuagana rancherías would mean a "detour," Escalante's word. This seems implicit recognition that it would take them father east from Monterey, though without further recognition that their northerly trend was taking them farther above Monterey's latitude. (They were losing ground: while advancing about two hundred seventy-five air miles from Santa Fe, they had gained only some one hundred forty-five now on Monterey.) In any case, this was their first sign of perturbation. Taking into account that a detour would "consume many supplies," they sent Andrés Muñíz with the Ute Atanasio "to summon [the Sabuaganas] and see if any of them or any of the Lagunas would guide us for pay as far as he knew the way."

SCALE: 50 MILES

While awaiting the pair's return, our men this morning noticed "five Yutas Sabuaganas on a hill on the [north] side shouting loudly." These, crossing the Gunnison, were given "something to eat and smoke." This smoking, as between Escalante and his Havasupai amigo at the Hopi pueblo of Walpi, seems to have been a peace rite that perhaps was akin to the Plains Indians' smoking peace pipes. "After a long conversation, whose subject was the disputes which they had this summer with the Cumanches Yamparicas, we were unable to get out of them a single thing useful to us, because their aim was to frighten us by setting forth the danger of being killed

73

by the Cumanches to which we would expose ourselves if we continued on our way. We refuted the force of the arguments with which they tried to prevent us from going forward, by telling them that our God, Who is the God of everybody, would defend us in case of encounters with these enemies."

The Yamparicas were named for "yampa," a carrotlike root found in the Yampa River drainage to the northwest. Those Ute "disputes" with the Comanches were perhaps an understatement. God's defense against enemies might be good enough for the Spaniards but the Utes, as with the Hopis about Escalante's homeward trip through Navajo country to Zuñi, didn't see it that way.

This morning Andrés Muñíz and the Ute Atanasio returned with five Sabuaganas and a Laguna. The visitors were served "plenty of food" and there was the ritualistic smoking. The Utes were told that the party definitely sought "to go to the pueblo or pueblos of the Lagunas" — a fateful decision. Since "they were our friends," they were asked to provide a good guide.

But the Utes flung back at them, the Comanches! "We should turn back from here." Besides, "none of them knew the country between here and the Lagunas."

Our explorers wouldn't accept the implication that the Laguna didn't know how to return to his own homeland. (Why had he come here was not stated: perhaps to obtain horses.) "We tried to convince them, first with arguments, then with flattery, in order not to displease them."

Finally the Laguna was offered a woolen cloak, hunting knife and white glass beads. He took the payment. He would guide them.

The Sabuaganas now "confessed that they know the road [but] insisted that we should go to their ranchería. . . . We knew very well that this was a new excuse to detain us and to enjoy for a longer time the favors [food and tobacco] we were conferring upon them . . . But in order not to give them any occasion to be displeased, and not to lose so good a guide as the one we had obtained, we consented to go."

They had to make Escalante's "detour" after all. This afternoon they forded the Gunnison, "in which the water reached above the shoulder blades of the horses," and paralleled it to a campsite (probably where Leroux Creek joins the North Fork of the Gunnison just west of Hotchkiss) they called Santa Rosa de Lima for her feast day. They would continue to resanctify saints across the landscape.

We knew very well that this was a new excuse to detain us and to enjoy for a longer time the favors [food and tobacco] we were conferring upon them . . .

74

Following the Utes, who had spent the night with them, they twice had to ford the North Fork where its canyon edges close before climbing a "very deep valley" (of Hubbard Creek). At camp a Ute "gorged himself so barbarously and with such brutish manners that we thought he would die of overeating. . . . he said that the Spaniards had done him an injury. This foolish notion caused us great anxiety, because we knew that these barbarians, if by chance they become ill after eating what another person gives them, even though it may be one of their own people, think this person has done him harm, and try to avenge an injury they have never received."

As to this bit of ethnology, "God was pleased that he should be relieved by vomiting some of the great quantity he could not digest." Withal, Escalante knew something of what he was talking about. Seventy-six years later a U.S. Indian agent in Santa Fe would report the following incident:

A Ute war captain had a beautiful wife who took sick. A medicine man was called in. "Either the disease or the medicine was the death of the woman." The war captain "paid off the doctor bill by putting a bullet through" the medicine man, "leaving another vacancy in the medical department among the Eutaws."

Such gorging had another serious side. It was eating into the expedition's supplies, including cattle. "It was necessary for us to use a great deal among the Yutas, especially among the Sabuaganas," Domínguez would write later. A few mouths here and there added up to a feast.

Had the companions known it, they would have had one cause for satisfaction here. This was the farthest they would ride east in their projected effort to go west. Their advance toward Monterey had now been reduced to one hundred twenty air miles after thirty-four days' travel, the proverbial one step forward and two steps back.

Perhaps it was here that our leaders learned that some in the party were "secretly carrying" trade goods, for Escalante would write tomorrow that "we did not discover [this] until we were near the Sabuaganas." How naive he had been in predicting to Father Gómez, Provincial Murillo's secretary, the availability of volunteers at "daily wages only." The goods, to have remained hidden all this while, must have been such compact items as beads and knives. "Here we charged and

. . . a Ute gorged himself so barbarously and with such brutish manners that we thought he would die of overeating. . . .

75

entreated everybody not to trade, in order that the heathen might understand that another and higher motive than this had brought us through these lands."

September 1-2, 1776

THEY WERE MET EARLY by "about eighty Yutas all on good horses," it was noted. Moments of high drama rarely elicited emotion from a stoic Escalante.

Indian use of the horse had begun in the early 1600s with Apache acquisition, mainly by ill means, from New Mexico colonists. Southern Utes began to seize horses in raids on New Mexico settlements in the 1630s. During on-and-off peace agreements, they began to trade for them as well.

Horses spread from the Southern Utes north to the Tabehuaches and Sabuaganas while Plains tribes also were getting their hands on them from New Mexicans. The mobility of horse culture enabled both Southern and these Northern Utes to sally out of their mountainlands onto the Plains to hunt buffalo and steal horses from Indian lodges.

In clashes with both New Mexicans and Plains Indians, some of the latter of whom had been armed by the French far to the east, they also seized muskets. Thus at least some of the eighty Utes met here surely carried firearms. "They told us they were going to hunt, but we concluded that they traveled together in this way partly to make a show of their large force and partly to find out whether any more Spanish people were following us. . . ." An alertness to Spanish aggression?

The Sabuaganas rode off, leaving the Laguna with the expedition. He was named Silvestre, Escalante's turn for a namesake. The Tabehuache guide Atanasio meantime had faded. Maybe it was from Silvestre that the men learned the Sabuaganas also called his people the equivalent of *Come Pescados*, "Fish Eaters," Spanish for their lakeside diet.

Along a "small river" (probably Cow Creek) was "an extensive grove of very tall and straight royal pines [the regal blue spruce], among them being some cottonwoods [aspens] which seem to emulate the straightness and height of the pines."

They came to the Sabuagana ranchería, "which was populous . . . about thirty tents," and camped about a mile below. This sentence evidences the revolution worked by the horse. Bands had grown larger as the Utes could roam farther for the food required for more people. Tipis, a concept acquired from the Plains Indians, supplemented brush wikiups with horses available to carry their heavy hide covers.

They told us they were going to hunt, but we concluded that they traveled together in this way partly to make a show of their large force and partly to find out whether any more Spanish people were following us. . . .

76

Besides this, these Utes probably wore full animal-skin clothing since, their hunting range extended by the horse, they had surplus deerskins to trade.

At once Domínguez — another index of his leadership — went with Andrés Muñíz to visit the Sabuaganas. He entered the tipi of the chief (the one said to be amiable and knowing?), embraced him and his sons, number not given, and asked that his people be assembled.

When many of both sexes were gathered, the guide Silvestre warned that "they must believe whatever the Father told them because it was all true." All heeded "with pleasure, especially six Lagunas . . . amongst whom our guide and another Laguna were conspicuous."

Domínguez held up a crucifix. A hard-of-hearing Sabuagana asked what he was saying. The "conspicuous" other Laguna spoke out: "The Father says that what he is showing us is the one Lord of all, who lives in the highest part of the heavens, and that in order to please Him and to see Him, it is necessary to be baptized and to beg His pardon."

The Laguna demonstrated by touching his breast, "an action admirable in him, because he had never seen either the Father or the interpreter." Was this tentative sign of the cross not instinctive?

Domínguez asked the Laguna's name.

"Oso Colorado." Red Bear.

At this the friar expounded "the difference between men and beasts" and the "purpose for which each was created." It was "evil" to name themselves "after wild beasts, making themselves thereby equal and even inferior to them." (Yet Spaniards themselves stood proud of such names as León, Lion, and Cabeza de Vaca, Cow's Head.)

This Laguna Domínguez named Francisco, doubtless after himself.

Francisco was delighted when the crowd iterated Francisco, "although with difficulty."

Domínguez next gave the chief the name Captain.

Captain replied that the real chief was, as Escalante would describe him, "a youth, a good-looking fellow who was present." This seems to have been merely a compliment, the young man's being a brother of another, "very much venerated" Sabuagana chief.

Fray Francisco asked if the young "chief" were "already married."

He has two wives, Captain replied.

77

This "mortified the youth," who "tried to convince them that he had only one wife."

"... from which," Escalante wrote, "it is inferred that these barbarians have information ... of the repugnance we feel for a multiplicity of wives at one time." Such information probably had been acquired on raiding-trading trips to New Mexico. There was a certain amount of duplicity in it. While the Spaniards definitely didn't contenance bigamy, concubinage was more than tolerated. Reconqueror Don Diego de Vargas, having left a wife in Spain, had proudly brought to New Mexico two sons born of an honorable woman in Mexico City.

Domínguez proposed to Captain that, if his people would accept Christianity, "we would come to instruct them and arrange for a mode of living to prepare them for baptism." Translate "mode of living" as "sedentary settlement."

I'll ask my people, Captain replied.

Domínguez now bought some dried buffalo meat with glass beads. Will you trade fresh horses for some lame ones?

We'll trade this afternoon.

Domínguez returned to camp. While waiting, he and Escalante may well have reflected on the Utes' willingness to consider Christianity as contrasted with Hopi opposition to the Spanish religion.

The Utes had adapted their culture to the land about them, as had the California Indians. Roaming arid flats, sunburned plateaus, forested mountains, and lately the Plains, they lived in transient quarters and sustained themselves on roots, insects, small game, later buffalo — almost anything edible beyond a porcupine tabu. They shared relatively simple customs and beliefs. They were "strongly individualistic with the extended family as the basic and only permanent social unit," ethnographer Anne M. Smith writes; so fluid were Ute bands, in fact, that a family often moved from one to another. They were animists, with shamans, basically healers, encouraging good health through their people's "thinking good thoughts."

The Hopis, on the other hand, were stable farmers and herders, living in towns of considerable architectural sophistication and organized into an elaborate social and religious structure. Beyond this, the Hopis knew from experience what accompanied Spanish Christianity.

While our friars may not have appreciated the origins of the Ute-Hopi contrast, they must surely at some time have asked themselves the cause of it.

"... during the whole afternoon," though, the chief failed to come with a reply

... it is inferred that these barbarians have information ... of the repugnance we feel for a multiplicity of wives at one time.

78

to their "well-founded hope" for Christianization. Just before sunset, he and others finally appeared . . . but not to talk of conversion.

Turn back, these Utes urged. The Comanches won't let you through. We tell you this not to deter you from your goal, but because we esteem you greatly.

We esteem you too, the Hispanos countered. God will defend us. His Majesty also is on our side. We have no fears. That's why we bear no arms, bring no soldiers.

God still carried no weight with the Utes. If you insist on going forward, you must write the Great Captain of the Spaniards, "as they call the Señor Governor," that you have passed through our territory. If there is "any mishap" the Great Captain won't blame us for your deaths. (Escalante: "This was the idea of some of our companions who desired to go back or remain with them.")

We'll write the letter, the Spaniards said. Any of you going to New Mexico may carry it.

You must send it with one of your men.

None can go or remain here.

We won't trade for your lame horses.

Trade or not, we must go forward. "Under no circumstances" will we turn back — again that remote allusion — "without knowing the whereabouts of our brother, the Father who had been among the Moquis and Cosninas and might be wandering about lost." Our priests here appear to be dissembling. Father Garcés had proved more than competent at making his way among strange Indians and, though he had lost himself more than once, at finding his way across strange terrain. But Domínguez and Escalante may not have been sufficiently aware of their brother's competence.

The father can't get lost, the Utes rejoined, because "the Fathers . . . had painted on paper all the lands and roads." (Escalante: The Utes were "inspired by those of our men who understood their language and were secretly conspiring against us.")

The Utes finally relented. They would trade horses tomorrow morning, they said before filing off after nightfall.

Why should these Utes have so feared the Great Captain's reprisal if the expedition were wiped out? The New Mexican military record against nomads generally had been singularly unimpressive. Perhaps the Utes were being honest with themselves: they were not as well-organized, as well-disciplined, as the all-powerful Comanches to take on Spanish retaliation.

79

We have seen the Comanche peril to New Mexico and Texas settlements. There can be no question that the Utes were being pragmatic about the Comanche peril to their expedition visitors.

The Comanches once lived beyond the Yellowstone River. They were among the first northern tribes to acquire horses (possibly via the Utes), probably by 1690. One theory is that they were driven south by Crows and Blackfeet advancing from the northeast with French-supplied muskets. "I do not believe the Comanches were driven" into the South Plains region, counters well-studied Rupert Norval Richardson. "On the contrary, it seems that they visited it, found that it was well suited to their mode of existence, and proceeded to fight for it and take it." Their record and temperament would seem to confirm Richardson's conviction.

Shoshonean-speaking, the Comanches were introduced to New Mexico by the language-kindred Utes at a Taos trade fair in 1705. Comanche eyes feasted on horses for barter there, a sight they wouldn't forget. About the Comanches Miera would comment in two different legends on two different maps (of which the following is a composite): "This nation is very warlike and cruel. . . . They say they left the region farther north breaking through various nations. . . . They obtained horses and iron weapons, and they have acquired so much skill in handling both that they excel all nations in their dexterity and hardiness. They have made themselves the lords and masters of all the buffalo country . . . to the Province of Texas . . . taking it from the Apache nation, which was formerly the most widely extended of all known in America. They have destroyed many of the Apache nations, pushing those that were left to the frontiers of our King's provinces. . . . [The Comanches and Apaches] have brought about such panic that they have left no towns, cities or ranchos of Spaniards unattacked."

Can history be better capsulized? Add another achievement to that tally of Miera's talents.

Besides their offensive capability, said a Santa Fe report, the Comanches marshaled "such solidarity that both on the marches which they continually make . . . as well as in the camps . . . they are formidable in their defense."

In the late 1740s the Utes and Comanches fell out . . . so divisively, for whatever reason, that they were after each others' scalps. The enmity had persisted.

The Comanche threat and the Sabuaganas' counsel aside, at our expedition's camp Escalante was infuriated, writing furiously about those companions who had "caused much grief" to the leaders. He singled out Felipe (the coyote) and the

Muñíz brothers who "either through fear or because they did not wish to go on, had secretly connived with the Sabuaganas ever since they learned they were opposed to our plan."

Escalante had more to complain of. The Muñíz brothers had slipped out to trade, the padres somehow had learned. No sooner had we told the Sabuaganas that God was more powerful than arms and soldiers, Escalante wrote, than they "showed themselves to be so obedient, loyal and Christian that they traded what they had kept hidden, and with great eagerness solicited arms from the heathen, telling them they were very necessary to them because they were going to pass through the lands of the Comanches." Escalante, in this instance, was a Domínguez in his sarcasm.

"Greatly to our sorrow," Fray Silvestre added, "they manifested their little or entire lack of faith and their total unfitness for such enterprises."

The friars harbored another grievance that would not be disclosed until a late-October diary entry made after the leaders again felt called upon to censure certain of the companions. While interpreting Domínguez' preaching to the Sabuaganas here, Andrés Muñíz had interposed: "The Father says that the Apaches, Navajós and Cumanches who do not become baptized cannot enter Heaven, but go to Hell, where God punishes them, and where they will burn forever like wood in the fire." The Sabuaganas "were greatly pleased at hearing themselves thus exempted from and their enemies included in the inescapable necessity either of being baptized or of being lost and suffering eternally." Though Muñíz is not herewith quoted as saying that, perhaps Escalante felt this was what he implied. The interpreter's motive, the friars concluded, was to retain "the ancient friendship" that traders maintained with the Utes.

"The interpreter was reprimanded, and seeing that his foolish infidelity had been discovered, he reformed." Escalante doesn't tell us how this infidelity had been discovered by Domínguez, who spoke no Ute. In any case Muñíz' reformation apparently was in the fidelity of his interpreting only, for Escalante's Inquisitional specification of complaints, as supplemented in that October entry, lengthened. The traders "wander two, three or four months among the heathen Yutas and Navajos with nobody to correct and restrain them. . . . some of them have given us sufficient cause in this journey to suspect that while some go to the Yutas and remain so long among them because of their greed for peltry, others go and remain with them for that of the flesh, obtaining there its brutal satisfaction."

The Father says that the Apaches, Navajós and Cumanches who do not become baptized cannot enter Heaven, but go to Hell, where God punishes them, and where they will burn forever like wood in the fire.

Again somber, the Sabuaganas descended early on the camp. Again the Comanche menace. The Laguna Silvestre returned his payment.

Silvestre had agreed voluntarily to lead them, the Hispanos argued "with the anger justified in such a situation." We know "perfectly well" that you have dissuaded him. Guide or no guide, we shall continue. No guide, and we no longer shall consider you our friends.

After an hour and a half's wrangling, the younger "chief" — he who had denied having two wives — began to harangue his brethren. We have given our word. The Laguna has promised. We "should stop talking about the matter."

As capricious as high-country thunderheads, the Sabuaganas promptly reversed themselves . . . but a new contretemps arose. The Laguna continued to refuse to guide them. It took "much urging and coaxing," apparently from both sides, for him to accept his payment anew, "although with some ill grace."

Our expedition proceeded to the ranchería, where the Sabuaganas were pulling up tipi poles. Where they were going was not stated. As a New Mexico view had it, the Utes were "like republics or itinerant nations who today dwell in one place and tomorrow in another."

Silvestre still was laggard, pretending to look for a saddle for a horse the Spaniards had given him. Nothing to do but follow the Sabuaganas' trail, "though unwillingly because we wanted to get away from them." In a quandary they sent Andrés Muñiz back to talk horse sense with the Laguna. Muñiz returned to say that the guide, "all the Yutas having left," wanted them back at the ranchería grounds. Had he lingered there because of lingering opposition from some Sabuaganas?

Our men found fellow Lagunas charging Silvestre "to conduct us with care" and "telling him how he was to proportion the days' marches." They heard that another Laguna, "still a youth," wanted to go with them. As he later would be referred to as "a boy," we may assume he was in his early teens. To avoid the delay of saddling another horse, Don Joaquín Laín took the lad riding hind-saddle. They thus named him Joaquín.

Led by Silvestre and Joaquín, they moved northwest, a direction they again would follow for days, a direction that would take them both farther from Monterey's latitude and nearer its longitude, as a caravel tacking in obverse wind.

82

Had Christianity been further discussed with the Sabuaganas? Were horses traded? Was a letter written to the Great Captain? We'll probably never know.

Just as our journeyers could have been slapping backs in camp (at the headwaters of Buzzard Creek) on the day's turn of events, "tonight it rained heavily."

September 3-5, 1776

THEY RODE THROUGH MEADOWS AND FORESTS along the east fringe of Grand Mesa, at fifty-three square miles the most expansive table mountain in what would become the United States. It was built of a lava cap up to four hundred feet high that prevented erosion of sedimentary formations beneath. Unprotected crust has worn away until the mesa stands in splendid isolation up to ten thousand five hundred feet.

This was the season nature's palette was at its most spectroscopic: blues of penstemon, yellows of marigold, purples of aster. Escalante's eyes may not have been closed to them but his diary was. Perhaps we shouldn't expect him to have entertained the soaring appreciation of the West's nature that an Audubon, an Agassiz or a Muir would feel.

Apparently along Buzzard Creek, Escalante espied a phenomenon to be seen on more than a few western streams. A flow vanishing into porous soil, then popping out like a gopher from a new hole. Carrying "as much water as two good-sized furrows would hold, . . . in places it completely disappears, yet in some places, it runs and in others it can be seen in pools like stagnant rainwater." Underground or above, the stream must be permanent, Fray Silvestre judged, because of huts along its banks "which indicates that this is a residence of the Yutas."

Camp (on Buzzard Creek) was called San Silvestre, celebrating perhaps the new guide.

Descending the plateau they came across three Ute women and a child sun-drying chokecherry, garambullo, lemita and "this year's piñon." While the garambullo hereabout was "very bitter" on the bush, they found when offered some that it was "bitter-sweet and very savory" after drying.

They could have halved the distance from their Santa Monica camp near the Uncompahgre-Gunnison junction had they not detoured to the Sabuagana ranchería. This they learned from Silvestre when they came upon a trail that ran "straight across" the Grand Mesa region. And "tonight we felt the cold very much" at camp (north of Collbran). Days were fleeing, this one detour in a grand detour having contributed to setting them up for an eventual confrontation.

Above the cirques, those alpine meadows, lay "hanging valleys," as geologists call them. They were chiseled out by glaciers tributary to the main troughs. That Escalante took no recorded notice of them is not surprising. They represented not the dramatic vistas of a Moran or Bierstadt painting but stark impediments to the expedition.

Not far along, "We . . . ascended a hill without troublesome stones but extremely steep and dangerous to climb because there were turns where the trail is less than a third of a vara wide." A vara was about thirty-three inches. "The footing is of very loose soft earth, so it is very easy for an animal to slip, and if he should lose his footing he would not be able to stop until he reached the plain below."

Ahead loomed "a chain of high mesas [Roan Cliffs], whose upper half is of white earth and the lower half evenly streaked with yellow, white, and not very dark colored red earth." After five leagues they arrived "at a river which our people call San Rafael and which the Yutas call Rio Colorado" in their language. In a manner of speaking, the Utes had hit it!

The "our people" referred possibly to explorer Rivera and certainly to Andrés Muñíz and other companions, who would have learned about the San Rafael from the Utes. That it was *the* Colorado, which our travelers had known they would have to cross, Escalante gives us no hint of their comprehending. It was not even recorded that they asked themselves this. Nor would they wonder anywhere in his diary when they would cross the Colorado. Perhaps they eventually decided it rose somewhere to their southwest.

The next year, when Miera began drawing maps of the route, he would have it figured out. His San Rafael became for a stretch the Rio de los Zaguaganas (Sabua-ganas), with the Dolores and Navajo (San Juan) as tributaries, and then the mighty Rio Colorado.

"This river carries more water than the Rio del Norte," wrote Escalante in what

84

could have been a broad clue to its identity. So high was the river, in fact, that some animals had to swim at the fording. Rivera having considered the Gunnison to be the Colorado, why not speculation that this even greater river might be it? Why not speculation that it was the long-sought Great River of the West?

The San Rafael rose, according to the Utes, "in a great lake" to the northeast; below here it "enters the Rio de los Dolores," a reiteration of that Tabehuache misinformation about its tributary. The Colorado's source is just north of Grand Lake, no great lake, in the Never Summer Mountains on the Rockies' west slope. Its Colorado state stretch, eventually to be called the Grand, would be renamed the Colorado in 1921.

Our explorers were groping with geography as our astronauts two centuries hence would grope with the moonscape. At camp (near Una Siding) Miera now made the latitude 41° 4′, a degree and half too high, his longest error of all. Themselves "fearing some defect in the observation," they decided to take another by the sun tomorrow — stopping en route so as "not to remain here where the Sabuaganas might bother us."

September 6-9, 1776

ALONG ROAN CREEK THEY HALTED for Miera to try again. Though his finding was about the same, there was no diary uneasiness over their being so far north.

"Some companions" had been sent ahead with the pack animals and the "loose herd." This is the last we hear of what presumably included the cavalcade's cattle, its quadruped commissary. The others caught up to find the companions "disgusted" because the guide had led them away from a westing (Roan Creek) trail, which "appeared according to reports [whose?] more direct," and up a canyon (Clear Creek) due north. Silvestre said his route soon turned west. "The companions who knew the Yuta language tried to convince us that the guide Silvestre was leading us by that route either to delay us by winding around so that we could not go on, or to lead us into some ambush by the Sabuaganas who might be awaiting us."

"To make us more distrustful," these companions said they had heard the Sabuaganas at their ranchería tell Silvestre to lead them not to the Lagunas but to bring them back after "he had delayed us for eight or ten days in useless wanderings."

. . . he had delayed us for eight or ten days in useless wanderings.

85

One of them had *just come
from the land of the
Cumanches Yamparicas,
whither with four others
he had gone to steal horses.*

86

"Although it was not entirely incredible" that some Sabuaganas had said this, our leaders didn't believe the guide would have agreed to such a wild-goose chase. If the Sabuaganas so counseled, these companions would have told them long since, "for at the ranchería they had not neglected to magnify greatly other difficulties, less fearsome and less likely, as well as the fact that in any catastrophe they would risk little less than we." To have elaboration on statements such as these, one wishes again that Domínguez had taken more of a hand in the diary. What other difficulties? Would not risk, presumably at Comanche hands, be shared by all alike? Or were human thoroughbreds, body and soul, worth a bit more than castas and genízaros?

Though the leaders accepted Silvestre's explanation of a "very bad hill" on the other route, all others except Laín insisted on taking it, "some because they feared the Cumanches too greatly and without foundation, and some because the route did not confirm with their own opinions." How was it known that the Comanche threat was without foundation? Were not the others, perhaps led by Miera, justly insistent against going farther north?

Whatever, a lone Sabuagana, "one of the most northern," happened by. His statement that the northerly route "went up very high" clinched it for the opposition. The party turned west, to its left. Camp (at Roan and Brush creeks) was called La Contraguía, The Mule That Pulls to the Left. Was such wit pulled by Domínguez from his vast vocabulary?

Nearby were three Sabuagana "ranchos" (used here as diminutive of rancherías) from which six men came to see ours. One of them had "just come from the land of the Cumanches Yamparicas, whither with four others he had gone to steal horses." The Comanches they sought had decamped, the Sabuagana said, probably to the east or for the Rio Napeste (the Arkansas, far to the southeast).

Should such rustling alert the Comanches, the Utes prided themselves on bravery. But loot was the objective, says anthropologist Marvin K. Opler, "not any desire . . . to win prestige by rash displays of valor." Among them "no war honors [were] institutionalized," as among the Plains Indians. Scalps were incidental. ". . . standing fights were avoided whenever possible."

Said Escalante: "Our companions were somewhat encouraged" by the Sabuagana's report. Some indeed had been in sweat. After all, most had known the Comanche as a bogey from early childhood. (These Sabuaganas, Escalante added, were the last of this band they were to see.)

Shortly they veered northwest up Carr Creek Valley, then left it for a northerly climb so "very rugged in places there was not even a trail" and with soil so loose "the animals could not put their feet down anywhere with safety."

As the men struggled up afoot, "the guide gave us irrefutable proof of his sincerity and his innocence." Was this proof for Silvestre's prior insistence that on this trail lay that very bad hill? "At the top there are some benches over very brittle shale where two pack mules lost their footing and rolled down more than twenty varas at the least. But God willed that none of those who were coming behind should be trampled upon and that the mules should not be injured."

Descending from Cuesta del Susto, Slope of the Scare, they camped in a valley (probably at the headwaters of Brush Creek). Here is one of few places along the expedition's route where no road of any kind has been punched through. When this writer approached a rancher at the mouth of Carr Creek about the prospects for driving north, he lifted his palms and shrugged. "Are you kidding?"

With a westerly drift, they topped a high ridge from which Silvestre pointed to the white cliffs of a sierra (Yampa Plateau) to the northwest. On its northern slope, he said, dwelt the Comanches Yamparicas. Shivers in some of the companions?

They stumbled down a long slope amid scrub oak and chokecherry groves that "served to prevent the horses from slipping and rolling" and camped in a glade of a canyon (of East Douglas Creek).

Past where the canyon joined a larger one (Douglas Creek) they came upon something on a cliffside that interested them. "We saw crudely painted three shields or *chimales* [Apache shields of hide] and the blade of a lance. Farther down on the north side we saw another painting which crudely represented two men fighting."

The first of these pictographs is still readily to be seen, designated by a Rio Blanco County Historical Society marker 17.4 miles south of Rangely on Colorado

. . . two pack mules lost their footing and rolled down more than twenty varas at the least. But God willed that none of those who were coming behind should be trampled upon and that the mules should not be injured.

87

State Highway 139. It was the work of the aforementioned Frémont people, who had appeared about A.D. 700 and eventually occupied much of Utah, northwestern Colorado and southwestern Wyoming. They farmed small canyon plots and built stone granaries. There is no evidence linking them to the Utes, who moved into their region in the mid-twelfth century. What may have happened to them, we don't know.

The Frémont people's pictographs were heavy with red ocher and typified by trapezoid human beings, many apparently with horned headdress, according to Gilbert R. Wenger, chief archaeologist at Mesa Verde National Park. When researching for his master's thesis in 1949, Wenger tells us, he identified the initial Escalante-cited rock art as depicting "four men, two cornstalks, a red track, several unknown figures and a white mountain sheep." This is a far cry from Escalante's description, but then this writer saw in the red-on-tan pictograph a ladder, a centipede and a plumed man smoking a stogie and walking with a cane. So much for any possibility of agreement.

Our wayfarers called this Cañon Pintado, Painted Canyon. Down this abyss they also sighted "a vein of metal" above. A companion picked up a stone that had broken away. "Don Bernardo Miera said it was one of those which the miners call *tepustete* [copper], and that it was an indication of gold ore."

(Tepustete is the first of a number of Aztec words to crop up in the diary. Readers may be able to recognize others for a flavor distinct from Spanish.)

Miera had become a geologist too. "On this matter we assert nothing," Escalante wrote, "nor will we assert anything because we are not experienced in mines, and because a more detailed examination than the one we were able to make on this occasion is always necessary." Miera, who of a certainty read the completed diary, may not, in his vanity, have appreciated these remarks. The leaders, perhaps distrusting this uncertified Miera talent, obviously didn't want to be held responsible for a rush that might produce something other than a proverbial pot of gold at the end of a rainbow that was long and tortuous, even if of chromatic though rugged terrain.

They emerged from the canyon amid tall chamiza and *jara* [osier] "of the kind they call latilla." (*Latillas* were the wattle that covered New Mexico ceiling vigas; these laths in turn were covered with dirt.) Camp was made (near Rangely) across a river they called the San Clemente. Nothing more was recorded here about the White River, a considerable stream.

THE RIVER

September 10-15, 1776

TO THE NORTHWEST, now across arroyo-cut semidesert, our explorers followed no beaten path though they came upon several trails. These were not made by Indians, but rather by buffalo, among those original mammalian trailblazers, that "come down to winter in this region." This was about the southwestern limit for the Plains buffalo, which ranged to the north and even more to the east in their thundering herds.

At their camp, El Barranco, beneath Raven Ridge, "it was necessary to watch the animals and keep them corraled all night" because of neither water nor pasturage. Were these animals at The Cliffsided Arroyo now just horses and mules?

SCALE: 50 MILES

Still in barren country, they crossed an invisible line into what in 1847 would become Mormon country, part of a projected State of Deseret of the Church of Jesus Christ of Latter-day Saints. From a *Book of Mormon* word interpreted to mean "honey bee," Deseret was envisioned to take in not only Utah but huge sections of New Mexico, Colorado, Arizona, Nevada, Idaho, Wyoming, Oregon and even California. The United States, needless to say, refused the bee access to so much potential honey.

Our wayfarers saw fresher buffalo tracks leading in today's direction. "By now we were short of supplies" not only from Ute appetites but "because we found it necessary to travel so far. . . ." Necessary? Two scouts having sighted a buffalo, other companions were sent on the "swiftest horses." After a chase of over three leagues it was killed.

Who the hunter hero was, Escalante didn't say. Nor how the buffalo was slain. In the next century, Josiah Gregg, a chronicler of the Santa Fe Trail, would admire the skill of *ciboleros*, Hispano and Pueblo buffalo hunters on the Plains. A buffalo having been singled out amid a herd, a cibolero shouldered his horse up to it and drove a lance down past its ribs into the heart, Gregg said. Aliens to these parts,

89

employing high-powered rifles that required no skill, still later would all but eliminate the multi-millions of buffalo as a species.

About sundown the hunters returned with the buffalo meat, "much more than comes from a large bull of the common variety." To the Indians, as an earlier explorer had it, buffalos were also "drinke, shooes, houses, fire [dung], vessels, and their masters' whole substance," . . . in which he could have included dress, blankets, rugs, ropes, bone tools and necessities more.

Our men named their camp (along Cliff Creek) Arroyo del Cíbolo in deference to this buffalo that would make its lonely mark in history. To prevent its meat from spoiling in the heat and to rest their animals, they laid over here for a day. There is no mention whether they jerked or dried some of the meat, an Indian and Hispano practice for packing on the march.

Beneath the Yampa Plateau, those white cliffs seen some fifty-five air miles back from the Roan Plateau, they reached their "largest river" yet. Though they didn't appreciate the significance of this moment, they named it for one of the Franciscans' noblest lights, San Buenaventura, thirteenth-century cardinal and minister-general of the Order of Friars Minor.

They of course didn't know the source of today's mighty Green River, the Wind River Mountains of southeastern Wyoming, though they learned from Silvestre that it was joined by the White River on down. *"We do not know whether this is true of the previous streams."*

As with their San Rafael (the Colorado), our explorers were unaware that this San Buenaventura was a component of Escalante's Rio Grande (de los Misterios) of the Havasupais. The San Buenaventura must be, they seemed to tell themselves, a main stream of an unrelated river system. If they were confused, so would the U.S. government be deluded a century and a half later in renaming the Grand River the Colorado when the Colorado's headwaters are those of the Green.

The San Buenaventura is the same river, wrote Escalante, that Father Posada gave as dividing the Utes from the Comanches "according to the distance which he places it from Santa Fe." Posada was the seventeenth-century priest who posited that Copala-Teguayo province and lake somewhere to the northwest. Escalante puzzles us here, for Posada had cited no such river. And the Comanches were unknown in Posada's day, as Escalante should have realized from himself having said in a letter to Provincial Murillo that tribes known at the time of the Pueblo Revolt "included the same nations which there are today except the Comanches."

"The river enters this meadow between two high cliffs [Split Mountain Canyon] which, after forming a sort of corral, come so close together that one can scarcely see the opening. . . ." Close to a chain of lead-and-yellow hills to the canyon's south they forded at the only place Silvestre said possible without swimming and set up camp (near Brush Creek) for two days, again to refresh their animals. Miera tonight observed the latitude by the North Star and came up with a reading of 41° 19′, about fifty-four minutes too high. Whatever their actual latitude, which was almost that of latter-day Eureka, California, Domínguez rightly would write that this was "the highest to which we ascended during the whole journey." They had traveled some three hundred eighty-five air miles from Santa Fe while having gained only about one hundred eighty on Monterey.

Near the campsite stood six large cottonwoods that "have grown in pairs attached to one another." On one of them Laín cleared bark for a panel and chiseled in "The Year 1776," his name and two crosses. Don Joaquín's graffiti would soon be grown over of course. The cottonwoods standing here today Bolton suggested as being arboreal mementos of the expedition but, cored later by dendrochronologists, they ringed at only sixty to seventy years.

There was no way for our travelers to know that almost within musket shot were fossils interred in rock (at Dinosaur National Monument) of land animals the size of which no human being had ever beheld. Hence they would know nothing of the enigma in why the dinosaur, after ruling our earth for some eighty million years, became extinct around the world in a geological overnight about seventy million years ago. But they would have their own dragons, fire-breathing humans and deep-clawed terrain, to contend with.

"Here we succeeded in capturing another buffalo, smaller than the first, although we could use little of the meat because the animal had been overtaken late and very far from the camp." How the "capture," by whom and to where had Diana led the chase?

"It happened also this morning [September 14] that the Laguna, Joaquín, as a prank mounted a very fiery horse. While galloping across the meadow, the horse caught his forefeet in a [prairie dog?] hole and fell, throwing the rider a long distance. We were frightened, thinking that the Laguna had been badly hurt by the

Here we succeeded in capturing another buffalo, smaller than the first, although we could use little of the meat because the animal had been overtaken late and very far from the camp.

91

fall because when he had recovered from his fright, he wept copious tears. But God was pleased that the only damage was that done to the horse which completely broke its neck," but, wondrous to behold, lived on. "The rider" should more exactly be translated "the horse-breaker," Fray Angelico Chavez informs us, Escalante's cutely equating Joaquín with a bronco-bustin' ranch hand.

The last night here Silvestre went off "without being noticed" to sleep away from camp. To escape Hispano snoring, it might jocularly be speculated. The guide's unprecedented action, perhaps noticed upon his return, would be remarked upon in tomorrow's diary.

September 16-17, 1776

AS OUR EXPLORERS LEFT CAMP Silvestre for the first time put on the woolen cloak he had been given in payment as guide. After crossing two tributaries (Brush and Ashley creeks) to the Green River, they began to pick their way up a "high and very stony ridge." Silvestre stopped for a time "as if thoughtful and confused, wishing first to go [back] along the banks of the river and then to lead us through here."

"As soon as we had reached the top we found a trail, one or two days old, of about a dozen horses and some people on foot, and on examing the vicinity, indications were found that on the highest part of the hill they had been lying in ambush or spying for some time without turning their horses loose. We suspected they might be some Sabuaganas who had followed up to steal the horse herd in this place, where it would be likely we would attribute the deed to the Cumanches. . . ."

Our leaders themselves now suspected that Silvestre, "having come to an understanding with the Sabuaganas [last night], put [the cloak] on so that he could be recognized in case they attacked us" somewhere around here.

Fortunately they gave Silvestre "no indications of our suspicion," for during the rest of the day's march "he gave us emphatic proofs of his innocence." Silvestre's behavior is not explained away. What proofs? Oh, for Domínguez' own pen. . . .

They returned to the Green, finding in their descent a meadow where "the people who made the trail had stayed a long time." From camp (beyond Horseshoe Bend) they sent two companions who "followed the trail southwest to explore the terrain hereabouts and concluded that the Indians had been Cumanches."

. . . on examining the vicinity, indications were found that on the highest part of the hill they had been lying in ambush or spying for some time without turning their horses loose.

92

Rio de San Buenaventura . . . Facing north, Escalante's "corral" gate in Split Mountain Canyon, Utah, from which
the Green River debouches, two miles northeast of where the cavalcade camped September 13–15, 1776.

They left the trail, angling westerly. Meantime, confirming the scouts' unexplained conclusion: "Silvestre told us they were Cumanches who were going in pursuit of the Yutas, whom they had perhaps learned about while hunting buffalo.

"We were convinced that this was the case, both because of the direction in which they were traveling and on account of other signs they left." Why hadn't Silvestre explained yesterday? Which Utes? What direction and what was its significance? What other signs?

From another high ridge Silvestre showed them the junction (about fifteen miles south) of the White and Green rivers that "ran south from this place." How far south would become of high import on Miera's maps.

They reached a junction of the Uinta River, their San Damián, with the Duchesne. Both flow from the Uinta Mountains to the north. The latter, which they called the Rio de San Cosme, becomes another tributary to the Green. Following the Duchesne upstream: "we saw near its banks the ruins of a very old pueblo, where there were fragments of metates [cereal grinding stones], jars, and jugs made of clay." Escalante continued un-Hispanic in his attention to prehistory and to what probably was a relic of the long-gone Frémont culture.

They camped along the Duchesne (east of Myton) where "we saw columns of smoke at the foot of the sierra, and asking the guide who he thought had sent them up, he said they might be Cumanches, or some Lagunas who were accustomed to range about here hunting." New terror for our companions? Or on the other hand, homesickness for Silvestre and the lad Joaquín at the possibility of these Indians' being of their fellow band?

Our expedition was now in the heart of the Uinta Basin and traversing what would become the Uintah and Ouray Reservation. The Uintahs, for Pine Land, are another division of Ute stock; Ouray was the chief whose name is perpetuated by a monument at Montrose.

To protect Ute ancestral rights against Anglo intruders, President Lincoln in 1861 would proclaim the Unitah reservation, to encompass almost all of the basin. Utes farther west were reluctant to move over here, but Mormon leader Brigham Young told them: "If you do not sell your land to the Government, they will take it. . . . We shall increase, and we shall occupy this [Utah Lake] valley and the

94

next and the next, and so on until we occupy the whole of them." The Utes moved.

(According to *The Book of Mormon*, Indians are Lamanites, descended from the white tribe of Joseph. This tribe was led by the prophet Lehi from Jerusalem to the Western Hemisphere in about 600 B.C. Laman, a son of Lehi, rebelled against his father. The Utes, among other tribes, were not appreciably or appreciatively susceptible to the Mormon offshoot of the religion of their Palestinian forefathers.)

The Tabehuaches, Sabuaganas and other northerly Colorado Utes in 1882 by federal decree were shunted here, hence the addition of the name Ouray. Twenty-five years later an "Indian-giver" Congress broke a treaty by opening the reservation to Anglo homesteaders. It now is a mere three hundred eighty-four thousand acres, mainly "badlands" remnants of the Uintah domain.

On this day some seven hundred miles west-southwest a presidio was completed for the new settlement at San Francisco.

... September 18-20, 1776

NO LONGER YAWING, our expedition was now, and would continue for some days to be, on almost a straight westward heading. In maintaining course, dense osiers and marshy creeks forced five crossings of the Duchesne today before camp was made near where Indian Canyon joined it.

"From the country of the Cumanches a very long high sierra descends, running from northeast to southwest as far as the country of the Lagunas. This ridge we could see for more than seventy leagues. Toward the north of Rio de San Buenaventura at this season its highest hills and peaks are covered with snow, for which reason we named it Sierra Blanca de los Lagunas, and we shall begin to ascend and cross it tomorrow where it is least elevated."

Our party's White Range, the Uintas are the only major east-west trending mountains in the United States south of Alaska and are Utah's highest, with Kings Peak reaching 13,498 feet. They were pushed by subterranean stresses into a flat-topped arch, a rather unusual geological formation. Apex ridges lie mainly on their north side while to the south, over which our expedition would travel, the arch drops off onto a sloping, though crevasse-carved, plateau.

95

✝ ✝ ✝

Again playing tag with the Duchesne, our men encountered "almost impassable terrain," with rocky precipices laming a horse and forcing a turnabout that led them through a grove of osier and tall bamboo reed. They finally left the river to their south and, climbing to the plateau, found themselves in an arroyo that "led us imperceptibly into a closed canyon, high on both sides, with no passable terrain" other than its bed. "We called [the latter] Cañon de las Golondrinas because there are many nests of swallows in it, formed with such symmetry that they looked like little pueblos."

Our explorers arrived at camp (east of Fruitland, probably on Red Creek) "very much fatigued, partly because of the difficulty of the day's journey and partly because a very cold wind blew unceasingly from the west." Should they not now have begun to worry about winter? California's Sierra Nevada, sure to be snow-inundated, still was a long way off, and snowshoes were unheard of by the Spaniards. "Leaving for dead one of our strongest horses," the veritable Rasputin from which prankster Joaquín had taken his spill, they covered a stretch troubled only by chamiza and cacti and camped at a spring (in Strawberry Valley, apparently at Soldier Springs). "Tonight it was so cold that even the water which was near the fire all night was frozen in the morning."

September 21-22, 1776

THEY NOW PASSED THROUGH "low valleys of very soft earth, the animals sinking and stumbling every instant in the many little holes which were hidden in the grass," then descended to a "fair-sized river" (the Strawberry) in which "there is an abundance of good trout, two of which the Laguna, Joaquín, killed with an arrow and caught, and each one of which would weigh somewhat more than two pounds." Lest we take this to be the Far West's first fish story, Fray Angelico affirms a Spanish-language implication that the trout were skewered by successive arrows.

They were so taken with the region's "good pastures, many creeks and pretty groves of white cottonwoods [poplars and aspens]" that they called it Valle de la Purísima. "All the advantages necessary for a good settlement" again were offered

Tonight it was so cold that even the water which was near the fire all night was frozen in the morning.

96

in this Valley of the Most Pure Virgin. But, "Silvestre told us that part of the Lagunas, who used the fish of the river as their customary food, lived in this valley at one time, and that they withdrew for fear of the Cumanches who were beginning their raids into this part of the sierra."

Crossing Strawberry River and Horse Creek, they "entered a dense grove of white cottonwoods, dwarf oak, chokecherry, and royal pine." This was the season when, though Escalante overlooked it in the writing, fall's glory begins turning aspens golden, maples scarlet, scrub oak a Joseph's coat of russets. It is as if nature had created such beauty in anticipation of man's evolution and our eventual appreciation.

"The guide, anxious to arrive as quickly as possible, went so fast that at every step he disappeared in the thicket and we were unable to follow him, for besides the great density of the wood, there was no trail, and in many places his track could not be seen, . . ." After a now-obviously homesick Silvestre had been "ordered to remain always in sight," from a ridge: "The guide pointed out to us the direction to the Lake, and, to the southeast of it, another part of the sierra in which he said there lived a great many people of the same language and character as the Lagunas."

That other part of the sierra was in fact another sierra, the Wasatch Mountains, A Low Pass Over a High Range in Ute. The Wasatch, with peaks nearing twelve thousand feet, extend from near the Idaho line to about one hundred fifty miles south. Unlike the Uintas, the Wasatch are of the more common tilted block formation; the original, sharper fault escarpment is to the west. At some time within five centuries past, underground pulsations abruptly moved them about sixty feet. Imagine your house being thrown that far at one drumfire toss. The earthquake must have been more dramatic than any recorded anywhere in historic time, geologists say. It would be interesting to know if Ute oral tradition recalls it.

Our explorers scratched their way through "almost impenetrable thickets" and an aspen grove "so dense that we thought the packs would not get through without being unloaded." Domínguez took a "hard blow" on a knee from one tree. Here Silvestre "again annoyed us by his speed so that we were forced to keep him back." Descent culminated in a well-watered and -pastured campsite (perhaps on Fifth Water Creek), which they named for San Mateo, doubtless because this was the apostle Matthew's day.

Here they themselves were now on the Wasatch Mountains. And here they now were in the watershed of the Great Basin, which no explorer would comprehend for

97

three-quarters of a century. In fact, theirs was the white man's first penetration into the Great Basin above the latitude of Father Garcés' recent pioneering through the Mojave Desert. Extending 880 miles north-south and 572 miles from California's Sierra Nevada east, it has no water outlet to the sea, no sieve anywhere.

"Tonight it was much colder than on previous nights."

Lurching down, our men faced so many "perilous defiles and slides with no other trail" that they were forced "at each step to change our direction." Atop a final ridge: "We saw in front of us and not very far away many large columns of smoke arising in the same sierra. . . . Silvestre said they must have been made by his people who were out hunting. We replied to them with other smoke signals so that if they had already seen us they would not take us to be enemies and thus flee or welcome us with arrows. They replied with larger smoke signals in the pass through which we must travel to the Lake, and this caused us to believe they had already seen us, because this is the most prompt and common signal used in any extraordinary occurrence by all the people of this part of America." Finally "a long passable slope" took them down to camp near where Little Diamond Creek and Wanrhodes Canyon join Diamond Fork.

"We warned Silvestre that tonight he must be on the *qui-vive* lest some of his people who knew of our arrival should approach the camp to see what people had come here. And about two o'clock in the morning, the hour when according to his opinion there might be one or more Indians close at hand, he made a long speech in his own language, giving them to understand that we were peaceable people, friendly and good, but we do not know whether or not anyone heard him."

. . . he made a long speech in his own language, giving them to understand that we were peaceable people, friendly and good, . . .

The Lakes

98

TO SILVESTRE AND JOAQUIN, so that they "might enter their land or settlement feeling happier and more friendly toward us," the wayfarers gave each a vara of

San Lino . . . On Diamond Fork, Utah, looking north at the mouth
of Wanrhodes Canyon near the September 22, 1776, campsite.

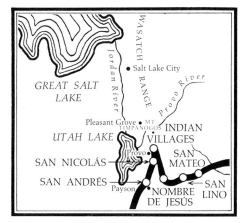

woolen cloth and of red ribbon "with which they at once set about adorning them-selves." There may be imprecision in Escalante's language here since he had not previously recorded indication of the two Lagunas' unhappiness or unfriendliness. "The guide Silvestre donned the cloak . . . wearing it like a mantle or cape, and the cloth . . . he wore like a wide band around his head, leaving two long ends hanging loose down his back. And so he paraded about on horseback. . . ."

As such he was "the living image of the [ransomed] captives whom the father redemptors bring out in their processions on the feast day of Nuestra Señora de la Merced." These Mercedarians, their order established to redeem Spanish captives from the Moors, in Spain paraded gaily garbed former prisoners on September 23, this the feast day of their patron Our Lady of Ransom.

Silvestre's being so accoutered on this fortuitous date, our friars named Our Lady of Ransom patron of the Lagunas as "a happy omen of the friendly disposi-tion of these captives" — the Lagunas generally — "whose liberty we besought of the Redeemer of the World, through the intercession of His Immaculate Mother." Captives of the devil, be it explained, and the liberty of Christianity granted through the priests' intercession.

Despite excited anticipation that led them to "set out early," Escalante paused to note "a large anthill, composed of very fine alum rock, pure and crystalline." Also he noted a succession of six hot springs that "we tasted and liked," their being "of the same sulphurous character" as one near Jémez Pueblo in New Mexico. Fray Silvestre put it thus casually as if a passing reference to the Newport and Saratoga spas of a century hence. Because three of the springs flowed into a stream they now encountered, they called it Rio de Aguas Calientes (the Spanish Fork). From these Hot Waters, "We . . . climbed a small hill and beheld the lake and wide valley of Nuestra Señora de la Merced de los Timpanogotzis [Utah Lake], as we shall call it henceforth. We also saw that all around us they were sending up smoke signals one after another, thus spreading the news of our coming. . . . Timpanogó . . . is the very special name of this lake." Actually, Timpanogo is the name, Rock River, that the Utes had attached to the American Fork, a tributary to it.

Crossing the Spanish Fork, they set up camp for which they may have saved, for this special moment, the name of Meadow of the Most Sweet Name of Jesus (southeast of Spanish Fork town). A placid Christ to the contrary, all about them meadows had been burned or were still burning. "From this we inferred that these Indians had thought us to be Cumanches or some other hostile people, and since

100

they had perhaps seen that we had horses, they had attempted to burn the pastures along the way, so that the lack of grass might force us to leave." Our party's smoke-telegrams and Silvestre's orations obviously hadn't gotten across the message that their intrusion was friendly.

No horses would be mentioned as Laguna property. Mounts had had to be provided for Silvestre and Joaquín, we recall. It is altogether likely that, so valuable were horses, few if any had fanned out this far west even from their kinsmen, the Sabuaganas. No wonder the Lagunas' profligacy with pastureland, though Escalante did add that theirs was so extensive they couldn't have burned it all off in so short a time.

Both to reassure the Lagunas and in the thrill of it all, Domínguez, again exerting his leadership, set out this same day for their ranchos with Silvestre, Joaquín and Andrés Muñíz. They "pushed their horses as hard as they could, to the point of tiring them out," over the six and a half leagues to the first of them (on the Provo River east of Orem). Approaching, they saw the Lagunas to be "very poor" of dress, their "most decent" being jackets and long leggings of buckskin. "Some men came out with weapons in their hands to defend their homes and their families, but as soon as Silvestre talked to them, the guise of war was changed into the finest and simplest expression of peace and affection." What sort of weapons? Silvestre's influence was not surprising when it developed that he was the third-ranking chief among the Lagunas . . . with a name meaning Talker. In their mien, "They have good features," most men with "heavy beards."

The Lagunas invited their visitors "very joyfully" into their "little huts of willow." (In their lack of horses they hadn't even the tipi.) No multi-roomed, multi-storied houseblocks such as our travelers must have been picturing ever since hearing of their "pueblos" from the Tabehuaches. No Cíbola, no Copala, no Teguayo. It was as when Coronado had found not sumptuous palaces but earthen houseblocks in the Zuñi realm. Yet no recorded expression of dismay . . . in fact, no reaction at all to these most unsophisticated of dwellings. Fray Francisco, where art thy pen?

Domínguez and Escalante hadn't, as we know, recorded any aspiration to discover these Eldorados, however much they may have been on the leaders' minds. For them to have recorded here that they had found none would have opened them to ridicule, they may have felt. And their finding not New Mexico–style pueblos but wikiups — there would have been mortification in emphasizing it. Mortifica-

101

tion, if such it were, Fray Francisco buried in his heart as he embraced each Laguna, making known that "we loved them as our best friends."

Guide Silvestre recounted his experiences with the expedition, told of its "purpose in coming" and dilated on "our love for him." In what terms did he explain the Spaniards' presence here?

Joaquín was "on such good terms with us that he paid no attention to his own people" but "clung to the father," Domínguez. The Hispanos themselves were surprised at "such an attitude found in an Indian boy so far from civilization that he had never before seen fathers or Spaniards." Joaquín's people talked "a long time" in wonderment at his adulation.

And Silvestre, living up to his Laguna name, talked on. "He told them with great surprise that although the Lagunas [Sabuaganas] had told us that the Cumanches would kill us or steal our horses, we had passed through the regions which they most frequent and even found their very fresh tracks, but they had not attacked us nor had we even seen them, thus verifying what the fathers had said, namely, that God would deliver us from all our enemies and from these in particular. . . ."

Lagunas flocked in from nearby ranchos. They doubtless were drawn by such curiosity as would have the whole of a village surrounding this writer in China's hinterland. The Lagunas must have pointed and gaped at Domínguez — as those remote Chinese would at this Foreign Devil wherever I came among them as a foreign correspondent. Papooses peeking from behind mothers' backs, youngsters giggling among themselves, men reaching out to touch, old ones warping their wisps in astonishment.

Domínguez gave all comers "something to smoke," again that ritual. He began to speak, a double translation through Muñíz and Silvestre, for the Lagunas "speak the Yuta language but with notable difference in the accent and in some of the words." He gave his version of "our reasons for coming."

The main one was to "seek the salvation of their souls." He stipulated "the only means whereby they could obtain it": belief in, love of and obedience to God. If they became Christians, fathers and other Spaniards would come to live with them. Patently, this doesn't square with Governor Mendinueta's acerbity on the lack of priests even to man existing missions.

The Lagunas also would be taught "to plant crops and raise cattle." If no cattle were left, did Domínguez describe them as being similar to tamed buffalo?

. . . the Lagunas [Sabuaganas] had told us that the Cumanches would kill us or steal our horses, we had passed through the regions which they most frequent and even found their very fresh tracks, but they had not attacked us . . .

Again, "then they would have food and clothing like the Spaniards." Is it not cultural imperialism — witness American tourists abroad — that "ours" is to be preferred?

If they agreed to live as the fathers taught them, "everything necessary would be sent by our Captain, who is very grand and rich and whom we call King." How does this accord with Domínguez' own knowledge of the kingdom's penury? Indeed, if the king "saw that they wished to become Christians, he would regard them as his children." Such paternalism historically had worked to isolate tribes accepting Christianity and left them unprepared to cope with wider society.

Meantime, "we must continue on our way in order to get news of the other padre, our brother," Garcés. "We needed another of their people to guide us to some other tribe known to them who might furnish us still another guide." No questions asked about a route toward Monterey or that mysterious colony?

To everything Domínguez said, the Lagunas "listened gladly and replied that they were ready to do all this."

By now they must have offered food. "It is true they have good fish," Domínguez would write, though it is to be doubted that he relished another of their staples, grass-seed gruel.

Some Lagunas eventually retired to their huts but there were others "remaining and conversing all night with our Silvestre." Home from the wars, he!

Domínguez himself stretched out, probably in one of the wikiups for privacy, with Joaquín "sleeping at his side during the brief space of time that was left in the night." Fray Francisco may have drifted into sleep ruminating on what Escalante would call the "great docility" of the Lagunas, again possibly in comparison with the stubbornness of the Hopis.

The other companions, summoned here by Muñíz, Silvestre and Joaquín, arrived a little before noon. Again, no recorded dismay at the "poor little houses."

At Domínguez' bidding, "the one who rules these people" meantime had come with two other chiefs who were here yesterday, several elders and many others. Elders too would become the king's "children."

After Fray Francisco elaborated on his talk of yesterday, the Lagunas "unanimously replied that if the fathers should come, that they would live with the Tatas (as the Yutas called the friars), who would rule and teach them." A Papa-dominated kindergarten of a commune.

"They offered the Spaniards all their land" — unconversant as they were with colonialism's land greed — "so they might build their houses wherever they pleased."

"They would scout through the country and be always on the watch for the inroads of the Cumanches, so that if they tried to enter the valley or the vicinity of the sierra, the Spaniards would be promptly warned and they all could go out together to punish them." Was there method here in the Lagunas' madness at wanting the Spaniards about? Comanche incursions "did not appear to be very frequent," Escalante did add.

"We must not delay our return for long," Escalante recorded the Lagunas' "earnest supplication."

"Give us a token," the friars asked, so that our Great Captain will be "convinced of [your] good intentions" and other Spaniards "encouraged to come more quickly."

We'll give it to you tomorrow, the Lagunas replied.

The chief was presented a hatchet, hunting knife and strings of beads, the others beads "for which they were happy . . . though we could give only a few to each because the Indians were numerous." Then they reminded the Lagunas of their promise of a guide.

We have already talked it over and decided that Joaquín should continue with you. (Was Joaquín an orphan or of parents eager to see his "education" advanced? Orphans are much pitied in Ute culture. Ute children mature young into adult ways.)

A new guide also will go. Both will travel "perhaps as far as [your] land" and return with you. None of us knows much about the country in the direction you are taking, but they can help you inquire among tribes along your route.

The Hispanos put forward a woolen cloak, hunting knife and white glass beads such as had been given Silvestre. One Laguna stepped forward to accept them. He "became, thereupon, our guide and companion, who from that time we called José María." The Hispanos simply couldn't be satisfied with Indian names.

"Finally, we told them that we now had only a few provisions and would be grateful if they would sell us a little dried fish. . . . we purchased a considerable quantity." With a dwindling supply of beads?

"All day and a part of the night they kept coming and conversing with us, and we found them all very simple, docile, peaceful, and affectionate." Fit children for the king.

✝   ✝   ✝

This morning the Lagunas assembled anew and presented the requested token. On a small piece of buckskin five men were painted with earth and red ocher. On both sides, the one with the most ocher or, "as they called it, the most blood," depicted the head chief "because in the battles with the Cumanches he had received the most wounds." Two other figures, "not so bloody," represented subordinate chiefs, including Silvestre, and another, unbloodied, was "not a war chief but a man of authority among them." A shaman? At the suggestion of one companion a cross was painted above each figure.

The Great Captain will be very much pleased to see this, the Hispanos said. The explorers would bring it back with them "so that they might see how much we esteemed their things and in order that the token itself might be a guarantee of their promises."

"We told them that if, while awaiting us, they should have any difficulty in the way of sickness or enemies they must call upon God, saying, 'Oh true God, aid us! Favor us!' But seeing that they were unable to pronounce these words clearly, we told them that they should say only 'Jesús María! Jesús María!' They began to repeat this with ease, our Silvestre very fervently leading them." Not far north of here, three-quarters of a century later, the Mormons would say "three Hosannahs" as they undertook their brand of communalization.

It was time "to continue our journey to the establishments and port of Monterey." All the Lagunas "bade us goodbye with great tenderness . . . saying they would expect us within a year." Silvestre "especially embraced us vigorously, almost weeping." He had "acquired authority among them for having brought us and being so much noticed by us."

After about three and a half leagues' travel, our wayfarers camped along the Rio de San Nicolás (Hobble Creek, northwest of Springville). All the while they had been among the Lagunas, Escalante must have been taking notes, for here was inserted a detailed section on the region that he may have drafted into the diary that night.

The valley was "surrounded by the peaks of the [Wasatch] sierra, from which

It was time *to continue our journey to the establishments and port of Monterey.*

105

flow four fair-sized rivers which water it, running through the valley to the middle of it where they enter the lake." Escalante might well have singled out 11,750-foot Mt. Timpanogos, by whatever name, that magnificently commands the Utah Lake drainage. Of the rivers, he correctly sized up today's Provo as carrying the most water. They hadn't reached the fourth, the American Fork, but had been told it was bounded by "a good deal of level land." Indeed, "with the exception of the marshes on the shores of the lake, [all] the land is of good quality, and suitable for all kinds of crops, . . . all of which can be irrigated" — and all of which the Mormons would prove so prodigiously.

The meadowland offered "abundant pastures, and in some places it produces flax and hemp [for cloth and cordage] in such quantities that it looks as though they had planted it on purpose." Also attractive thereabout were sycamores and cottonwood groves. Southerly were "two other extensive valleys" — this would have been inserted later — with plenty of water and pasturage.

In the Wasatch were "plentiful firewood and timber" and still more rangeland. Miera, in his report to the king, would cite also "very fertile . . . lands for planting all kinds of grains in their valleys." He would slip in that "veins" up there "appear at a distance to have minerals." His highness should drool at that.

Escalante, in his exuberance, estimated Utah Lake to be six leagues wide and fifteen long, about a fourth and a third too high. Miera would outdo Escalante in a prospectus on its wildlife: "This lake and the rivers that flow into it abound in many varieties of savory fish, very large white geese, many kinds of ducks, and other exquisite birds never seen before, besides beavers, otters, seals [muskrats?], and some strange animals which are or appear to be ermines [weasels?], judging by the softness and whiteness of their furs." Now a naturalist, Miera would have seen the likes of sea gulls hereabout from his ocean passage. His other "exquisite birds" might have included Treganza great blue herons, white pelicans, double-crested cormorants and Caspian terns.

To Escalante, "The climate here is good, for after having suffered greatly from the cold since we left the Rio de San Buenaventura, in all this valley we felt great heat both night and day." Had they been here in winter, he might have modified his weather report. Visiting in December, this writer couldn't see either Mt. Timpanogos or Utah Lake because of a blizzard.

The Lagunas ate some fowl — how they were taken is not stated — as well as their fish and the grass-seed porridge; hares and rabbits too. "There are also buffalo not very far to the north-northwest, but fear of the Cumanches prevents them from hunting them." Of handicrafts we learn only that the Lagunas "make nice baskets and other necessary utensils" of osier.

Curiously, no attention to dogs, ubiquitous among Indians, either among the Lagunas or anywhere along the trail. The Utes didn't use dogs to drag travois, twin poles laden with family possessions, as Plains Indians once did. They did, though, eat them, as did many another tribal people.

"In all parts of this sierra . . . live a large number of people of the same tribe, language, and docility as these Lagunas, with whom a very populous and extensive province could be formed." That the valley was lush and the Lagunas, dependent on the lake, were relatively sedentary perhaps contributed to Escalante's omitting reference to the pueblo structures the journeyers had expected to find. Perhaps these other attractions more than compensated for the missing pueblos. In any case, the Hispanos were enamored to a passion.

Escalante, envisioning a minimum of ten settlements, said that "if each pueblo should take only one league of agricultural land, the valley would provide for as many pueblos of Indians as there are in New Mexico." The then twenty-one pueblos, Hopi aside, generally had been granted four square leagues, about seventeen thousand acres.

Miera, we may remember, would recommend Utah Lake, along with Yuma and the Ánimas-San Juan junction, for one of three strategic presidio-guarded settlements of his New Empire. The "chief one" should be here, he wrote Carlos III, "for this is the most pleasing, beautiful and fertile site in all New Spain. . . . It alone is capable of maintaining a settlement with as many people as Mexico City, and of affording its inhabitants many conveniences, for it has everything necessary for the support of human life." Mexico City's population then was about one hundred thousand, more than that of New York, Boston and Philadelphia combined.

Domínguez the skeptic also would wax hyperbolic: The valley is of such "beautiful proportions, that in it alone a province like New Mexico can be established."

What these mesmerized Hispanos said about it "could be smoothly fitted into the first official American report on Utah Valley, which is Frémont's," observes Bernard DeVoto in his *Course of Empire*. Though fellow historian Dale L. Morgan has dispelled the widespread notion that Brigham Young greeted Great Salt Lake Valley with "This is the place!" for Mormon settlement, Utah Lake Valley was indeed "the place" to our wayfarers.

As for Great Salt Lake, Escalante said that to the north Utah Lake extended into a "narrow passage" that led to another, "much larger," lake. In all events, the Mormons' Jordan River flows from Utah Lake and, dropping some three hundred feet, empties into Great Salt Lake about thirty-five miles north. "The other lake with which this one communicates, according to what they told us, covers many leagues, and its waters are noxious and extremely salty, for the Timpanois assure us that a person who moistens any part of his body with the water of the lake immediately feels much itching in the part that is wet."

Fed by the Jordan and two other major rivers, Great Salt Lake is without its own outlet. Evaporation accounts for its high mineral content, about twenty-five percent, some eight times that of the ocean. Its level, governed by this and the rate of the rivers' runoff, fluctuates in seeming cycles. With gently sloping strands, a rise or fall of a few feet means hundreds of square miles' difference in its average fifty-by-seventy-five-mile dimensions.

Great Salt Lake itself is a remnant of a far greater sea that, beginning in the fourth glacial age about fifty thousand years ago, grew from a brine pond to encompass most of western Utah and bits of Nevada and Idaho. At 346 miles long and 145 wide, it was almost as big as Lake Michigan and, at 1,050 feet, far deeper. Lake Bonneville, as man would call it, drew to luxuriant vegetation along its fresh waters those mammoths and mastodons that have long since disappeared. As the climate changed, Bonneville shrank back upon itself, leaving a briny Great Salt Lake and five smaller lakes as remnants. (In our eon its salt flats are the speedway of world-record car dashes.)

"Round about [Great Salt Lake], they told us, live a numerous and peaceful nation called Puaguampe, which in our ordinary speech means 'Witch Doctors' and who speak Cumanche." The Puaguampes fed on herbs and drank from springs of good water found around the lake, the Lagunas said. Their huts were of grass covered with earth. While not enemies, they no longer were considered "as neutral as formerly" because they had approached through a mountain pass and killed a Laguna.

Besides these Indians, Miera would indicate on a map, "The people who live on the other side of their [own] lake, and [on] a high range [Lake Mountains] that they can see from their houses in the said direction, were formerly their friends, and they made the tips of their arrows, lances and war clubs of a yellow metal, in accordance with ancient traditions."

The other lake with which this one communicates, according to what they told us, covers many leagues, and its waters are noxious and extremely salty.

108

These peoples were of Shoshonean stock akin to the Paiutes, some ethnologists say. Miera, as we know, didn't realize that Indians hadn't smelted metals. Though no copper artifacts have been found hereabout, it is just possible that these Indians worked such weapons' points from raw ore.

Our wayfarers didn't consider riding the two days to the other lake, as far as the record shows, or visiting the copper-workers. Why not is the expedition's greatest mystery.

The great salt lake of the Lagunas realized a part of Baron de Lahontan's fantasy. The copper-workers might have realized another, those Mozeemleks of superior civilization. They could have tested the Copala-Teguayo tenet of Father Posada, in whom Escalante had put credence. Why didn't our padre leaders yield pell-mell to curiosity?

As if the lake and these peoples were not enough of a lure, Miera's report would say further that the Lagunas told of a river that "flows from the [salt] lake, and whose current runs toward the west. . . . They say it is very large and navigable. And if it is as they say, I conjecture that it is the Rio del Tizón discovered long ago by Don Juan de Oñate, first colonizer of New Mexico. . . . They told him that on the other side of the river there were large settlements in which lived civilized Indians."

If Miera's history were a bit confused, his recollection of the Oñate-inspired Colorado River narrative was valid . . . those Aztec-related Indians who wore gold bracelets and earrings.

"Inexplicable," says historian DeVoto of our wayfarers' lack of enterprise, for "surely their first duty was to explore any such river as a possible route to Monterey." Might not here be both the Great Sea and the Great River of the West? Could it simply be that, the Lagunas' pueblos having turned out to be what they were, the friars were disillusioned of any and all such speculation?

From what we know of Miera, he may have been a raging minority of one arguing for such enterprise. But, like Lahontan, Don Bernardo didn't need to see to believe. From Miera's conjectures about the salt lake came one of two rivers that would be the most explosive effects of the entire expedition.

A Miera map would show Utah Lake and Great Salt Lake as one — of hourglass shape, Laguna de los Timpanogos. From its northern and somewhat larger bulb swept to the west an unnamed river [presumably the Tizón] wide enough to accommodate any number of *Queen Marys* abreast. While the map's border clipped off the river, it was implicit that Don Bernardo conceived of this laguna and this river as still another drainage system . . . to the Pacific. A Great River of the West.

For Miera's settlement of Utah Lake he would propose sending artisans. "There should be . . . two skilled mechanics who know how to build barks and launches for sailing on this lake, and to transport whatever might present itself; they would serve also for fishing and for exploring its full extent, for visiting the tribes who live around it, and for learning whether or not the river mentioned is navigable . . . Thus, in a short time [the settlement] would serve to promote and supply the nearest ports of the coast of California." To Don Bernardo the river was navigable all right.

Curiously, Miera was skeptical about a southerly "Sea of the West, shown on the new maps," disbelieving theories of Fathers Garcés and Font. Don Bernardo held that the concept "apparently and without doubt is in error. I believe that all [these maps] show as the said sea is dry land, populated by various peoples who are able to live in organized societies, which is why our ancient Spaniards, from the time of Don Fernando [sic] Cortes down to the present, have longed to discover and settle the coast of California, because of many reports they had of the people who lived in those places, and the fact that the Mexican Nation emerged from them." Miera's own maps would label TIERRA IN COGNITA a blank space west of his Laguna de los Timpanogos.

The RIVER

September 26-28, 1776

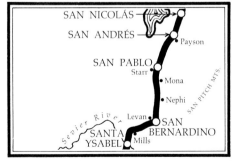

SCALE: 50 MILES

FOLLOWING THEIR NEW GUIDE JOSE MARIA, our rovers entered new territory after again fording the Spanish Fork. They camped along Spring Creek, west of Payson. "On its banks there is a species of medium-sized trees [box elders] on whose foliage live a vast number of little insects [box elder bugs] as strange to us as are the trees."

Shortly they cleared Utah Lake's south end. Miera had put their lakeside latitude at 40° 49', some three degrees above what Escalante had posited for Monterey. They had gained only about three hundred twenty air miles on their goal while advancing some four hundred fifty from Santa Fe (perhaps twice that in ground covered). It would seem logical for them to have turned westerly here and hewed to such a course.

Half a century later Jedediah Smith, a beau ideal among early Anglo explorers, would pioneer a comparable route in the opposite direction. Smith had marched up California's San Joaquin Valley in search of Miera's Great River of the West, intending to follow it east to Great Salt Lake. Failing to find it, Jedediah, with no Indian guide, surmounted the snowbound Sierra Nevada, crossed the central Nevada desert and after six tortured weeks reached the Jordan River.

Our expedition's new guide conceivably didn't know of any tribes to the southwest. José María led it instead out of Utah Lake Valley "through a southern pass" and entered "another large valley" (Juab). Because Laguna bands came hereabout for their salt it was named El Valle de las Salinas.

To camp (near Starr) the two Lagunas brought five Indians from nearby ranchos. These were given food, despite dwindling supplies, and of course something to smoke. To them were made new pledges to return to this land. They were "as docile and affable as the others," so much so that "they remained with us until nearly midnight."

Our explorers passed 11,877-foot Mt. Nebo, which marks the end of the Wasatch Range, and halted at Salt Creek, "which comes down from the eastern part of the sierra in which the salt flats are," to "get some relief from the great heat" under cottonwoods (poplars?). "From among some thick clumps of willows [osiers], eight Indians very fearfully approached us, most of them naked except for a piece of buckskin around their loins. We spoke to them and they spoke to us, but without either of us understanding the other, because the two Lagunas and the interpreter had gone ahead. By signs we gave them to understand that we were peaceful and friendly people."

Beyond Salt Creek begin the nine thousand-foot San Pitch Mountains, about thirty-five miles from north to south. The visitors perhaps were of Ute bands living

From among some thick clumps of willows [osiers], eight Indians very fearfully approached us, most of them naked except for a piece of buckskin around their loins.

111

in and about them that later were variously called San Pitch, Sampitch, Sampichya, Sanpich and San Puchi. Camp was made beneath the San Pitch at a spring (southwest of Levan).

September 29, 1776

EARLY THEY MET SIX MORE INDIANS. "We talked with them a long while and preached to them through the interpreter and the Lagunas, and they listened with great docility." After two and half leagues they left El Valle de las Salinas, "which continues on to the south," on a southwesterly bearing that, though Escalante didn't specify it, now had them on a more logical course for Monterey.

"Here we met an old Indian of venerable appearance. He was alone in a little hut and his beard was so thick and long that he looked like one of the hermits of Europe. He told us about a river nearby [the Sevier] and about some of the country which we still had to traverse." Failing to discover it until we were on its very bank," they named the river Santa Ysabel and camped here (southwest of Mills). Miera here took the latitude bearings by the North Star and found the expedition to be at 39° 4'. Four more Indians visited this evening, giving them more of the lay of the land.

> This river, according to the name which the Indians give it, appears to be the San Buenaventura, but we doubt whether this is the case, because here it carries much less water than where we crossed it in 41° 17' [near Dinosaur National Monument], although after it unites with the San Clemente [White River] it is joined by the San Cosme [Duchesne], the San Damián [Uinta], and several other small streams. Moreover, it seems likely that when we crossed it in that latitude Silvestre would have told us that this river ran near his country, as he told us other things about the sierra and of other rivers and lakes, which we found to correspond with his account . . .

While Escalante doubted the Indians' implication, Miera took it for granted. Two days later other Indians would supplement this geographical data, telling our explorers that their Santa Ysabel "entered another lake and then emerging from that lake it continued west." (Whether to California, in all probability unknown to them, seems not to have been asked.)

Here we met an old Indian of venerable appearance. He was alone in a little hut and his beard was so thick and long that he looked like one of the hermits of Europe.

112

From the Indians' combined intelligence Miera developed the second of his explosive rivers. As with Jedediah Smith, one or the other would become the most persistent and pervasive final goals in the centuries-old quest for the Northwest Passage and the Great River of the West which was to be Columbus' waterway to Cathay.

Miera and the others had not connected the Green River with the Colorado, we know, but made it central to another drainage system. Don Bernardo now would lift the Green, their San Buenaventura, over intervening mountains, a hydrologic impossibility, and connect it with Sevier Lake, the salty sink of the Sevier River. It was as if making the Mississippi jump the Appalachians to the Atlantic.

Sevier Lake, which they would not see, he humbly named Laguna de Miera. His map's border cut across his laguna's western bounds, a broad hint that it could be of greater magnitude. The map therefore does not show the San Buenaventura exiting from the Laguna de Miera but Don Bernardo's implication was clear. It flowed on to the Pacific. Another Great River of the West.

In view of the overall accuracy of Miera's maps, it is not easy to see how he could have identified the Green with the Sevier . . . but to predicate eventually is to believe. Columbus had insisted to his death that his discoveries were Cathay.

Miera couldn't know that the Sevier rises in southern Utah and flows an errant two hundred-plus miles north. Sevier Lake, its depository, is one of the larger relics of extinct Lake Bonneville. Now generally dry from the river's having been bled for irrigation along its course, Sevier Lake is a major alkaline pläya of the Great Basin.

The BEARDED

September 30-October 2, 1776

"VERY EARLY" OUR WAYFARERS WERE GREETED at camp by twenty more Indians, "wrapped in blankets made of skins of rabbits and hares." They were "as docile and affable as the preceding ones."

"These people here have much heavier beards than the Lagunas. They have holes through the cartilage of their noses and they wear as an ornament a little

SCALE: 50 MILES

polished bone of deer, fowl or some other animal thrust through the hole. In features they look more like Spaniards than like the other Indians hitherto known in America, from whom they are different in the foregoing respects." Here was another coincidental substantiation of Baron de Lahontan's imaginative tale — the Spanish-visaged Indians. And here seemingly was exploded a myth: "It is they, perhaps, who gave rise to the report of the Spaniards that . . . live on the other side of the Rio del Tizón which according to several coinciding reports is the Rio Grande [Colorado]."

That mysterious European colony. Escalante would write in 1778 that "these, no doubt, are the Yutas Barbones [Full-bearded] of whom the Reverend Father Custodian [Domínguez] and I speak in the diary of the journey which we made through those lands in the year 1776; who live in rancherías and not pueblos. They are very poor; they use no arms, other than their arrows and some lances of flint, nor have they any other breastplate, helmet or shoulder-piece than that which they brought out from the belly of their mothers." So much, one would think, for Colonel O'Conor's "flying reports" heard in Sonora and all those others, before and after, about the mysterious colony. But predications die hard, as we shall see.

These Bearded Utes spoke the same language as the Lagunas, Domínguez would write, "although with noticeable difference." Theirs was, said Fray Francisco, "a widespread and numerous nation." They called themselves Tyrangapui. Pahvants or Pah Vandüts, ethnologists call them, Water People in Ute.

Again southerly, our men traversed five easy leagues through Mills, Little and Scipio valleys and camped (south of Scipio) at a spring they called Ojo de Cisneros for their companion. So harsh was the landscape that Escalante made note of "two small trees" marking the site.

They climbed stony Scipio Pass, between the Canyon Mountains and Pavant Range, and looked upon "a vast plain" (Black Rock and Sevier deserts) that was "surrounded by sierras." Turning west, they descended the Canyon Mountains via Eightmile Creek.

They thought they saw water ahead in a marsh or lake. "We quickened our pace" only to find that they had fallen victim to a mirage, "in places salt, in others saltpeter and in others *tequesquite* [caustic soda]." They camped (north of Clear

114

Lake) "without having found any water fit to drink or pasturage for the animals, for which reason they were unable to travel any farther." Animals and men already had covered fourteen leagues, thirty-six-odd miles, the expedition's farthest day of all.

Two men who had been sent ahead now reported they thought they had seen water about a league beyond. When the moon rose, three men were sent to look for it toward the Sevier River; two others were to herd the animals there and bring back water for the rest of the explorers.

Dawn rose with none of the five men yet back. Finally one of them who had been with the animals arrived "but was unable to tell us anything about the herd, his companion or any of the rest because these two men had fallen asleep." No mention of censure, not to mention execution at sunrise.

The men in camp set out in various directions for the animals, Cisneros so hastily that he rode bareback. Don Juan Pedro himself finally caught up with them seven leagues back, half the distance along yesterday's trail and the second such accursed occurrence en route.

That afternoon the three who had gone seeking water returned with five bearded Utes, including an "attractive" chief of "mature years but not aged," whose village they had stumbled upon along the Sevier. The Utes talked "very happily" and soon "became very fond of us," and soon won the Hispanos' hearts. Not your stolid cigar-store Indian, the Utes generally seem to have been a loquacious and by no means inscrutable people.

When the chief learned that a Hispano still was missing, he ordered out his four men, most likely afoot, in four directions. "This was an action worthy of the greatest gratitude and admiration in a people so wild they had never before seen persons like us." Resonance from Father Garcés' "Who will say that this Indian is a savage?"

Even as the chief was giving his order, "he saw that the absentee was already coming and very gladly he told us the news." It is a fact that primitive peoples often see (and hear) better than the so-called civilized.

These Utes Escalante described as so long-bearded that "they looked like Capuchin or Bethlehemite fathers." Capuchins were of a reform branch of the

Franciscan order who wore long, pointed beards; Bethlehemites of an order of hospital brothers formed by a Capuchin in Guatemala.

Miera was so taken by the Bearded Utes that he would draw four on one of his maps, a Grant Wood picturization that adds much to our knowledge of their culture. Two men wear short-sleeved jerkins of almost knee length and are slung with animal-skin quivers. One of them holds a rabbit in one hand and what looks like a spear in the other. The other clings to a bow in one hand. With his other hand he holds a net with the assistance of one of two full-breasted women. One woman wears a skirt, the other appears to be nude. All wear moccasins and what seemingly are headbands.

Of such nets, Herbert S. Auerbach, a Salt Lake City merchant who was an early student of the expedition, says: They were made of the outer fibers of soapweed, sagebrush and hemp dogbane bark, twisted into cords. Fences were set up three to four feet high on willow posts "to form a crescent-shaped enclosure, into which [hares and] rabbits were driven, trapped and slaughtered."

Here Escalante joined Domínguez in sermonizing and promising to return with other Hispanos providing that these Utes "live together in a pueblo and not scattered as they do now." The chief agreed, at the friars' suggestion, to take his people to live with the Lagunas once the Spaniards had come back.

At parting, the chief setting the emotional tenor, the Bearded Utes "broke out weeping copious tears, so that even after we were a long distance away we still heard the tender laments of these miserable little lambs of Christ who had strayed only for lack of the Light." Some companions themselves "could not restrain their tears."

"This place . . . we called Llano Salado [Salty Plain], where, because of some delicate white shells which we found, it appears there had been a lake much larger than the present one." This is precious prescience, long predating the scientific postulate for Lake Bonneville. Was this Miera's conception?

Though two rivers entered the Salty Plain, the Sevier from the north and "a medium-sized one whose waters are very salty, from the east," they saw, for once, "no place whatever suitable for settlement." Mystification here. Miera's maps show a considerable river, the Salado, flowing into his laguna from the east, where none runs now. Escalante was right about one thing. Here these days there are no towns, only a few scattered ranches.

Salty marshlands deterring a southerly heading toward a pass out of the plain,

116

our wayfarers had to veer southeasterly. They camped southeast of El Cerrillo. The Small Bluff, which Miera deemed large enough to map, rises about a thousand feet above the plain as today's Pavant Butte. This butte is one of a number of extinct volcanoes that were islands in the Sevier Lake arm of Lake Bonneville.

October 3-4, 1776

NOW DETERMINED TO RID THEMSELVES of the quagmire, they slogged south-westerly to a stream that "abounds in fish and apparently disappears" on the plain. Miera would have this Rio Salado entering the quagmire, then hopping over the Cricket Mountains and into Laguna de Miera, our Sevier Lake. While Andrés Muñíz' horse fell at a "miry" ford and gave him a hard blow on the cheek, better fortune ensued in the cavalcade's floundering onto "good level land."

They camped along a creek with good pasturage and some pools "in which it was difficult for the animals to drink." Because along it was "a sort of [scum-] white, dry and narrow bank which from a distance looked like stretched canvas," they named it Arroyo del Tejedor. Their Stream of the Weaver was the Beaver River, which rises about forty-five air miles southeast in the Tushar Mountains and peters out in the Black Rock Desert.

Two days later Escalante would write that "on the preceding days a very cold wind from the south had been flowing fiercely and without ceasing. . . ." A portent.

Up and down a slight "south pass" opposite the southern end of the Cricket Moun-tains, exiting the Llano Salado they rejoined the Beaver River where it had more and better water and came upon "beautiful meadows." Both were a boon to their animals "because the salty water had done them much harm."

At camp tonight Cisneros sent for his servant Simón Lucero to join the way-farers in praying the Virgin's rosary. For whatever reason, Lucero objected. Don Juan "reprimanded him for his laziness and lack of devotion." The servant took him on and they grappled. Not surprisingly, our wayfarers were beginning to get on each other's nerves — though Fray Angelico Chavez reads into the original Spanish text an implication of some playfulness in the Cisneros-Lucero joust. Whatever, this would be the only noise of violence recorded for the entire trip.

JUST BEFORE STARTING THE MATINS, the men heard another disturbance, continuing friction between Cisneros and Lucero. After finishing the morning prayers, they hurried to them, but not in time to prevent guide José María's "getting a good scare."

"We tried to convince him that these persons were not angry, saying that although a father might chide his son, as just now had been done, he never would wish to kill him, as he thought, and that therefore he must not be afraid."

Nevertheless José María left this morning without saying goodbye. "We did not wish to say anything . . . preferring to leave him at complete liberty." He seems to have gone afoot that long way home. Andrés Muñíz now disclosed that their guide had become "somewhat disconsolate on seeing that we were going so far from his country," but Escalante thought that "doubtless the decision was hastened" by the Cisneros-Lucero squabble. The lad Joaquín's reaction was not recorded.

Though left "without anybody who knew the country ahead even from hearsay," our leaders also rued José María's decision because his salvation "he would not be able to obtain so quickly." But they would return! They attached no recorded blame either to Lucero or Cisneros, Domínguez later citing only "an unexpected contingency."

From a second camp five leagues up the Beaver River two men were sent to scout the San Francisco Mountains to their west, which would be named long later in probable deference to the Franciscan-led expedition's having passed by. The two returned after nightfall to report that they "had found no pass whatsoever by which to cross the sierra, and that it was very rough and high." (Indeed the peaks rear to almost five thousand feet above their campsite.) And between here and the sierra was "a wide plain without any pasturage or water whatsoever. Therefore we were unable to take this direction, which was the best for reaching Monterey, which was our objective." Coherence at last seemed to be taking hold.

Thwarted, though, they decided to continue south through what they called El Valle de Nuestro Señora de la Luz until they had passed the San Franciscos. In Our Lady of the Light they were coming up on the Escalante Desert, an arm of Lake Bonneville also named long later. (Utah's Escalante River and town to the southeast are some fifty miles north of any point touched by the expedition.) Though the desert is true to its designation, the Beaver afforded sufficient water and riverine pasturage. That night brought "a snowfall so heavy that not only the peaks of the sierra but likewise all the plains were covered."

Heaven found no favor with them during all the daylight hours. We visualize them now, huddled beneath their poncho-blankets, as snowbound they prayed to the Virgin Mother and chanted a litany. "God willed that at nine o'clock it should cease to snow, hail and rain."

The ground being so mushy as to be "impassable," they were forced to remain here another day, despite "the lack of firewood and the excessive cold." One is reminded of accounts of polar explorers, unable to move in a howling snowstorm, as they huddled in their tents and exhausted their pemmican. Except that our expedition in all probability hadn't even tents.

God willed that at nine o'clock it should cease to snow, hail and rain.

The DECISION

October 8-10, 1776

OUR EXPLORERS NEGOTIATED only three and a half leagues today because "many pack animals and saddle horses, and even the loose ones, either fell down or mired in the mud." And the men "suffered greatly from cold because all day a very sharp north wind never stopped blowing."

The time had come for serious meditation. Escalante totted up his diary figures to find that the expedition had moved west only one hundred thirty-six and a half leagues. (It actually had traveled about forty-five miles farther west than that, but still was about five hundred twenty air miles from Monterey.) To Miera — in a petulant tone? — "it was still a long distance to Monterey."

In any case, "partly on account of not having heard among all these last people

119

SCALE: 50 MILES

any report of the Spaniards and fathers of Monterey, partly because of the great difference in longitude between this port and the town of Santa Fe as shown on the maps," the leaders were in agreement with Miera that "there were still many more leagues to the west."

"We [friars] feared that long before we arrived the passes would be closed and we would be delayed for two or three months in some sierra, where there might be no people nor any means of obtaining necessary sustenance, for our provisions were already very low, and so we would expose ourselves to death from hunger if not from cold." Indeed, Domínguez would write, "food failed us at the critical time."

The trepidation expressed in the diary forecast the strait the Donner party would find itself in when bogged down in snow short of the Sierra Nevada to our expedition's west seventy years later. It was a strait that ensued in cannibalism and starvation. The only major disaster in Anglo migration to California, it had been brought on by dallying en route and following an ill-advised itinerary . . . just such blunders as afflicted our expedition. Of seventy-nine Donner migrants, only forty-five, aided by rescue parties from California, survived to reach the Promised Land.

Other rationale was conceived by our friars against venturing farther west. Should they indeed reach Monterey this year, they wouldn't get back to Santa Fe before June. The Utes, to whom they had promised to return soon, would decide that "we had intentionally deceived them, whereby their conversion and the extension of the dominions of His Majesty . . . would be made much more difficult."

Again, young Joaquín, "terrified and weary of so many hardships and needs, might stray away from us" in the manner of guide José María.

Finally, by turning back here they might find "a shorter and better road" from Santa Fe that would bypass the Sabuaganas en route to the Lagunas and Full Beards. This route could lead "perhaps to some other nations hitherto unknown who may always have lived on the north bank" of the Colorado. "Therefore, we decided to continue to the south, if the terrain would permit it, as far as the Rio Colorado, and from there proceed toward Cosnina, Moqui, and Zuñi."

Might not there have been both mutual- and self-recrimination here for their having made that huge detour to the north?

San Atenógenes . . . With the San Francisco Mountains to the west, the campsite along Beaver River, Utah, where the expedition was snowbound from October 5–7, 1776, and just north of where it was decided to forego continuing to Monterey.

They swung away from the Beaver River in bending southwestward to steer clear of the Black Mountains and found water for camp (southwest of Milford) in pools of rainwater on the desert floor. Here is some of the starkest terrain anywhere along their whole line of march.

At camp tonight (near 5,626-foot Blue Knoll) it was noted that the Bearded Utes "extend this far south." How this was determined, as none apparently had been seen for eight days, was not stated.

October 11, 1776

AS OUR CORTEGE rounded the Black Mountains for the southeast, Domínguez and Escalante lingered behind the others so that "we two might discuss between ourselves the means we ought to adopt to relieve the companions," especially Miera, Laín and Andrés Muñiz, "of the great dissatisfaction with which they were leaving the route to Monterey and taking this one. . . . They were very insubordinate. Everything was now very onerous to them and everything insufferably difficult. They talked of nothing but how useless so long a journey would now [have been]."

Further rationale had been advanced to them. The expedition had "already discovered so great an extent of country, and people so willing to attach themselves readily to the Vineyard of the Lord and the dominions of His Majesty (God spare him)."

The saving of Joaquín's soul was "now almost assured . . . an achievement . . . worth an even longer journey of greater difficulties and fatigues."

"Moreover, we had already made much progress toward reaching Monterey" that could be consummated later.

To all this the recalcitrants had "paid no attention," for Miera, "without any cause whatsoever, at least on our part, had conceived great hopes of honor and profit by merely reaching Monterey, and had communicated these hopes to the others, building great castles in the air."

In Miera's contending that "we were robbing them of these blessings . . . even the servants greatly tried our patience." Servants? Lucero, Felipe the coyote, genízaro Juan Domingo? Though Miera himself had argued a few days earlier that "it

122

was still a long distance to Monterey," he and the servants now "maintained that we would have arrived within a week." In a dune buggy . . . maybe.

Before leaving Santa Fe, Domínguez and Escalante had stressed that "we had no other destination than the one which God might give us." God had willed that the expedition now turn back. The friars were "disconsolate to see that instead of the interests of Heaven, those of Earth were first and principally sought." Against such materialistic opposition, they decided "to inquire anew the will of God" by putting it up to another casting of lots.

The friars overtook the others and bid them dismount. Domínguez, as leader, reiterated the now-numerous arguments for turning back and set forth "the mistakes and setbacks which we would have suffered hitherto if God had not interfered with some of their projects." If they opted for Monterey, he warned, "there would be no other director than Don Bernardo Miera, for he thought it so near at hand, and all this dissatisfaction was a result of his ideas."

A "brief exhortation" to "submit themselves entirely to God" was followed by saying part of the Rosary, reciting penitential Psalms and singing litanies. "This concluded, we cast the lot, and it was decided in favor of Cosnina [Havasupai country]. Now, thank God, we all agreeably and gladly accepted this result."

How lots were cast remains perplexing. It was accomplished by "putting in one [what?] the word 'Monterey' and in the other 'Cosnina' " is all that Escalante wrote. Scraps of paper into sombreros conceivably? Several of the companions, beyond doubt illiterate, would have had to trust the two padres' word.

Which one or more had undergone a change of mind to reduce the opposition to a minority? Were some repelled by the thought of the irascible Don Bernardo as leader? Some cynics have gone so far as to suggest that the friars tampered with the will of God. Though dice or cards were not used, their activity, straight or crooked, set an example for a Las Vegas-to-be not too many miles southwest of this point.

The friars' decision had been the only sane one, given the weather as well as the terrain and distance as we now know it. Father Garcés had turned back from his "openings" in the California mountains for fear of dying of thirst en route to them. To be fearless is not to be feckless.

Granting this, a defense of Miera is in order. As he would write the king, it was "to the great sorrow of my heart" that the expedition failed to reach Monterey. One cannot help speculating that Don Bernardo felt cheated of verifying his imaginative conclusions as to the two lakes and his two rivers.

Escalante surely was right in accusing Miera of harboring "great hopes of honor" in the fruition of their journey. But in all Christian charity, Domínguez and Escalante were young men with bright careers ahead presumably, while Miera's time to achieve immortal fame was fading. As for the "profit" whereof Escalante spoke, Don Bernardo was not among those who had smuggled along trade goods; he was of some means. Escalante's profit for Miera credibly was the honor. Glory, even more than gold, had been an incentive to the conquistadores of long ago. It is to be conjectured how "agreeably and gladly" Don Bernardo actually accepted the will of the lots.

The friars' hearts were lighter, and "quickening our pace" the wayfarers left the Escalante Desert for the southeast and descended to camp (north of Cedar City) in a "beautiful valley (Cedar) called Señor San José for our expedition's co-patron, the Patriarch Joseph."

October 12-15, 1776

ON A BEARING THAT WOULD TAKE the expedition generally south for six days, the leaders saw that some companions ahead "left the road hurriedly." They themselves hurried to come upon them talking with some Indian women "they had forcibly detained" from among about twenty gathering grass seeds and who had fled at sight of them. The seized women being so overcome that "they could not even speak," the friars, through Andrés Muñíz and Joaquín, "tried to relieve them of their fear."

These women, "Payuchis" to Escalante, were Southern Paiutes. Their ancestors were a branch of that Shoshonean wave east from the Death Valley region. These Paiutes now occupied parts of southern Utah, Nevada and California, and of northern Arizona. They spoke Ute "with some differences" but were a culture apart.

Unlike the Utes, Southern Paiute women wore basket hats and wove twined rather than coiled baskets, Anne Smith writes in her *Ethnography of the Northern Utes*. They hadn't the menstrual hut, a place of monthly seclusion, and didn't practice the sororate or levirate, under which a man would marry his wife's sisters after she died. And some Paiutes engaged in a little agriculture. All Paiutes identified themselves as such, though like the Utes they were not a centralized nation.

"When they had somewhat recovered their composure," the women told our explorers there were many of their people hereabout. While they themselves "wore only some pieces of buckskin hanging from their waists, which hardly covered what can not be looked at without peril," the women "had heard it said that toward the south there were people who wore blue clothes." They also understood that the Colorado "was not very far from here."

Escalante "knew" that the Paiutes traded only for red clothing. The Havasupais obtained blue woolen cloth from the Hopis. The women were talking of the Havasupais, he concluded. How Escalante knew about the trade in red and blue clothing, we aren't told. His citing of red garments indicates that the Paiutes "had been in some contact with Europeans, probably indirectly, before 1776," says anthropologist Robert C. Euler. To our day such Escalante observations are valued as the first word on Paiute culture.

Our men, bidding the women goodbye, asked that they tell their men "to come without fear" to tonight's campsite. Still, other Paiutes ran away as they advanced. They needed to confirm whether the Colorado was as near as the women had said and to get a Paiute guide to the Havasupais. Laín and Joaquín finally were able to catch up to a lagging male. He was brought to camp (near Kanarraville) on the rump of Don Joaquin's horse, surely the Paiute's first such experience. His reaction was doubtless not unlike the skittishness one of us might feel on first riding, say, an elephant behind a mahout. In camp, in fact, he "was very excited and so terror-stricken that he seemed to be insane. He looked in every direction, watched everybody, and was excessively frightened by every action or movement on our part." Given something to eat and draped with a ribbon, he "quieted down a little."

Seeing that the Paiute carried "a large net very well made of hemp" for catching hares and rabbits, the travelers asked where he had got it. From other Indians down the Colorado, he replied. From them the Paiutes also acquired colored shells.

"According to the distance and the direction in which he placed them, they appear to be Cocomaricopas." (It is doubtful that direct trade was carried on over such a distance, writes Euler. More likely, Mojaves, Havasupais or Hopis served as middlemen to the Cocomaricopas, who lived far southwest.)

The Paiute had "some colored woolen threads" he said he had bought this summer from two blue-clad Indians who had crossed the Colorado. The latter plausibly could have been Hopis or Havasupais.

As for the "Cosninas," the Havasupais, he gave no information either because he didn't know them, knew them by another name or "feared that we would take him by force" as guide to them.

While they themselves *wore only some pieces of buckskin hanging from their waists, which hardly covered what can not be looked at without peril*, the women *had heard it said that toward the south there were people who wore blue clothes.*

125

Pointing to the west and west-northwest, our men asked if there were fathers and Spaniards beyond.

No. Many people live that way but they are all of my tribe and language.

They showed him a kernel of corn. Have you see how it is grown?

Yes. I'll take you tomorrow to a rancho whose people have brought corn from where it is raised.

Where is this corn raised?

On a "small river" this side of the Colorado.

In the Paiute's company, the explorers came upon the rancho he had mentioned. Here were "an old Indian, a young man, several children and three women, all of them very good looking." They had "very good piñon nuts, dates, and some little sacks of maize." The dates were the fruit of the yucca, a plant of the lily family sometimes mistaken for a cactus, that is widespread in the Southwest. "Maize" is from the Spanish *maíz* for Indian corn.

Our men gave their guide a promised hunting knife and put before these Indians another knife and beads in seeking one who would lead them to those who planted corn. "The old man seized them, and impelled by his great fear, he offered to guide us, in order to get us away from there, as later became evident to us, and to give his family time to reach a place of safety by withdrawing to the nearby sierra."

With both their previous guide and the old man, they left Cedar Valley and in a few lopes parted from the Great Basin. There would be many others, Hispano and Anglo, who would top this rise before it was known there was a Great Basin.

"In the roughest part of this cut the two guides disappeared. . . . We admired their cleverness in having brought us through a place well-suited to the sure and free execution of their plan. . . ." Along the younger Paiute's "small river," Ash Creek, they camped in "a pretty cottonwood grove" (north of Pintura). Tonight Escalante noted that the Paiutes they had been among were called Huascari "in their language." There being no modern Paiute equivalent for this word, these bands probably long-since have become extinct or melded with others.

After traversing "hills of very brilliant white sand" and "stony malpaís [basaltic lava]," they descended again to Ash Creek and camped (near Toquerville). "Here the climate is very mild. . . . The cottonwoods [poplars] of the river were so green and leafy, the roses and flowers which grow here so flaming and undamaged that they showed that through here they had not yet been frozen nor frosted. We also saw mesquite trees, which do not grow in very cold lands." Mesquite, again a Southwestern fecundity, is a wild mimosa-family bush bearing pods rich in sugar.

What difference a week's travel had meant. Not for nothing do Utahans boast of this region as their Dixie. When your writer drove through here one mid-December it was like June in Santa Fe.

Along Ash Creek's west bank, the party shortly "found a well-made mat with a large supply of ears and husks of green corn which had been placed on it. Near it, . . . there were three small corn patches with their very well-made irrigation ditches."

At this apparently unattended site they "felt especially pleased" not only because it gave hope of assured food farther on but "principally because it was evidence of the application of these people to the cultivation of the soil," whereas the conversion of other Indians was "impeded by their aversion to this labor which is so necessary for living a civilized life especially in pueblos."

A bit farther downstream, they came to where Ash Creek joins La Verkin Creek, also flowing from the north, which empties into the Virgin River, gushing in from the east. An oddity here in that Verkin is a corruption and Virgin the anglicization of the Spanish *Virgen*, all three names to be bestowed decades later. To our expedition the Virgin was Rio Sulfúreo because of its "hot and sulphurous water." Escalante didn't mention the considerable hot springs close by.

A Miera map would identify this river as "Rio Sulfureo de las Piramides." Don Bernardo's "pyramids" may have been "crags of shiny black rock" cited just south of here by Escalante. Fray Silvestre wrote also of nearby "ash heaps, veins and other signs of minerals, and many stones of reddish mica."

Near here also were seen wild grape vines, "hills of chamiso (the plant which in Spain is called *brezo* ["heather"]) and red sand," *palo taray* (tamarisk) and *hediondilla* (literally "stinkweed" and here the fetid wild rue), its springs of "very medicinal qualities, according to what had been learned in New Mexico." Some latter-day organic food adherents maintain that modern man could sustain himself on such wild plants alone. In the past when game was scarce or meager crops failed many Indian tribes did.

To the cavalcade's east rose "a chain of very high mesas," the Hurricane Cliffs, some fifteen hundred feet above the plain. One of the nation's longest and most conspicuous fault planes, the Hurricane Cliffs extend from Utah's Markagunt Plateau some two hundred miles south to flank Colorado's Uinkaret tableland. In primeval upheaval, mountain blocks displaced sedimentary beds from fifteen hundred feet to as much as eight thousand feet high along their front.

Sighting "some fresh tracks of Indians," scouts led our men southwest up onto mesas (Sand Mountain) upon which "we were unable to go forward." They slid off them by "a high, rugged and very stony ridge" and camped along an arroyo (Fort Pierce Wash, southwest of Hurricane town). "Tonight our supplies were completely exhausted, leaving us only two little cakes of chocolate for tomorrow." As impassive as that.

This camp, which they called San Dónulo, was the farthest west they would touch. In air miles, they had progressed about four hundred fifty west from Santa Fe and would have had some four hundred eighty left to reach Monterey. But the Colorado, not Monterey, was now on their minds.

October 16-21, 1776

NEAR WHERE THE EXPLORERS CROSSED the present state line into the Arizona Strip, they passed hills abounding in transparent gypsum and mica. Hearing shouts from behind, they saw eight Indians on one of them. Andrés Muñíz calling out that "we had come in peace," the Indians "took courage" and descended. They held up for barter strings of *chalchihuite*, each string also carrying a varicolored shell. *Chalchihuite* was any kind of soft stone of green, a color prized by Indians of New Spain. Here in the Kingdom of New Mexico it undoubtedly was native turquoise, an object both of adornment and veneration. Modern Navajos, along with Hopis, Zuñis and some other Pueblos, work a jeweler's magic with turquoise, often in companionship with silver. "This gave us something to think about, for from below, the strings of chalchihuite looked to us like rosaries and the shells like medals of saints."

Tonight our supplies were completely exhausted, leaving us only two little cakes of chocolate for tomorrow.

These Indians spoke Ute so differently from all others they had met that neither Muñíz nor Joaquín could carry on totally intelligible conversation with them. They said they were Parussis and, partly by sign language, indicated they were the ones who planted corn on Ash Creek and that they lived downstream "for a long distance." (The Parussis also grew *calabaza* [squash], Escalante noted.) Parussi, ethnologists say, is Paiute for "white river," the Virgin, because it foams through a canyon at one point. With the Parussis was "one who spoke more of an Arabic tongue" whom they took to be a Mojave. (To the Spaniards "Arabic" meant any incomprehensible tongue as in "It's Greek to me.") Perhaps he was a go-between trader in coral and seashells.

You can reach the Colorado in two days (it was about fifty air miles), but not by going due south, the Parussis explained. The terrain that way is "very bad," there is no watering place and such a route will lead you to where the river can't be crossed because "it ran through a great canyon and was very deep and had on both sides extremely high cliffs and rocks." The Grand Canyon, of course.

The Parussis were given two hunting knives and each one got a string of glass beads. A guide will get more, the Hispanos said.

We'll put you onto a trail through a canyon (into the Hurricane Cliffs) that leads up to a mesa east of this plain, the Parussis replied. We are barefoot. From where we lead you, you can go on alone.

The friars, distrusting the Parussi disquisition, still wanted to go due south, apparently to be sure to visit the Havasupais. They theorized that the Hopis had been angered by the Havasupais' having led Father Garcés to them, a correct assumption, and had warned the Havasupais against bringing other fathers and Spaniards to their mesas. "We suspected . . . that these people having heard the news, now intended to lead us astray in order that we might not reach the Cosninas or their neighbors the Jamajabas [Mojaves].

"But at the urging of the companions, to whom it was not desirable at present to make known our suspicions" — another unexplained why — "we consented to go by the canyon."

The Parussis were offered soles of satchel leather for sandals if they would guide the expedition farther than proposed.

Two of us will put you on "a good straight road."

It was not recorded whether the Hispanos provided the leather or traded for the chalchihuites before setting out anew. On the heels of the two guides they entered

129

the canyon (Short Creek) and traversed a league and a half in which their animals were hindered by stones along frequent "dangerous stretches. . . . We arrived at a narrow pass so bad that in more than half an hour we were able to make only three saddle animals enter it. This was followed by a rocky cliff so rough that even on foot it would have been difficult to ascend it. The Indians, seeing that we would not be able to follow them, fled. . . ."

They retraced their hoofprints and camped just south of the canyon's mouth "without water for ourselves or for the animals. . . . This night we were in great need, having no kind of food, so we decided to take the life of a horse in order not to lose our own, but because there was no water we deferred the execution until we should have some."

Now moving south as the friars had wanted, they threaded an easy pass into Lower Hurricane Valley and found ample water along Hurricane and Ellen washes. They were squarely on what would become the Old Temple Road, beaten deep in the 1870s by Mormons hauling timber from Mt. Trumbull to the southeast for building their temple at St. George, Utah, to the northwest.

Though there was water now, that horse received a stay of execution, perhaps because along Ellen Wash they recognized "some of the herbs which they call *quelites* [lamb's-quarters]." Seeking to supply "our most urgent need," they gathered what few "very small" ones were at hand. Their having had nothing to eat since yesterday morning, Miera — an old soldier, to be sure, but an older man — "was now so weak that he was scarcely able to talk." They gave him some of "these ripe herbs."

At the same time the friars ordered their leather hampers "ransacked," but found only a little brown sugar loaf along with a few pieces of squash "the servants" had acquired yesterday from the Parussis and "hidden to avoid having to share them with the rest." These ingredients were boiled into "a little nourishment" for everyone.

During this stop some companions, "without telling us," climbed the Hurricane Cliffs, about a thousand feet high here. They returned to say that the ascent was "good," the land above level, many arroyos were seen "in which there could not fail to be water" and "it appeared to them that the river [Colorado] was at the end

This night we were in great need, having no kind of food, so we decided to take the life of a horse in order not to lose our own, but because there was no water we deferred the execution until we should have some.

of the plain. . . . Thereupon everybody favored changing our direction, but we knew very well how they had been deceived on other occasions and that in so short a time they could not have seen so much. . . ."

Toward the south the friars themselves saw "much good level land." Contrary to the Parussis, they had already found water. But being without food and since more water to the south "might be far away," they didn't want to be responsible for choosing a route that might prove "intolerable" to the companions. We'll take your route, they said.

In this case the companions were correct. For the expedition to have continued south would have led through rough canyon and mountain country considerably west of the Havasupai heartland.

They struggled up the Hurricane Cliffs by "a rough and very stony wash" in which Escalante had eyes to note "there is very good gypsum rock of the kind which is used for whitewashing." It was as though he were dressing up a Paiute pueblo-to-be in these parts. From a dry camp, two men set out for where they thought they had seen water.

The two having failed to return, it was thought this morning that they had gone on to seek Indian ranchos "where they could relieve their hunger as soon as possible." The friars decided to move out without waiting.

After meandering four and a half easterly leagues on the Uinkaret Plateau and across Black Canyon they espied five Indians "spying upon us from a small but high mesa." When the Indians spoke out, Domínguez and Escalante turned toward them. Four ran to hide. The friars began to climb afoot "with very great difficulty," followed by Andrés Muñíz and Joaquín. At each step, the fifth Indian "wanted to run away." The friars "gave him to understand that . . . we loved him like a son." He waited while "making a thousand gestures which showed that he was greatly afraid of us." Reaching his side, they embraced him.

"Having now recovered his composure," the lone Indian asked: Do you want to see the others?

The friars replying yes, this brave brave laid down bow and arrows, took Muñíz by the hand and together they brought out the others. Water is near, they said.

Show us where, the friars begged, holding out a swatch of woolen cloth.

131

The Indians first turned to Joaquín: How have you dared come with them?

Joaquín, "wanting to rid them of their fears in order to relieve the privation which, greatly to our sorrow, he was suffering, answered them as best he could."

"Greatly surprised at his valor," these Indians too "quieted down." Indeed, through travail and turmoil Joaquín appears to have been a quiet young spartan, a Kipling's Kim in his resourcefulness.

Three of the Indians led the expedition to an arroyo where deep holes held two large pools of good water (near Copper's Pockets). The men having sated themselves, the animals drained both pools.

At camp here the Indians, pleased at receiving the cloth, heard that the Hispanos were without provisions. Send one of your men with one of ours to our "huts," which are "somewhat distant," they suggested.

Joaquín and "one of the genízaros" were given the "wherewithal" (beads?) to buy provisions. With a pack horse, off they went. (This is Escalante's first indication of one or more genízaros other than Juan Domingo. Lucero? Aguilar?)

After midnight the train returned with "a small supply of wild sheep [meat], dried tuna [prickly pear cactus fruit] made into cakes, and grass seeds." (A Miera map shows an Indian village southwest toward 8,028-foot Mt. Trumbull, where such mountain sheep abounded.) It was reported that one of the two men sent for water last night "had been at this rancho." The other had arrived here meantime; when and where the missing man rejoined the cavalcade, we aren't told.

Our wayfarers well may have wolfed down a postmidnight meal. They now were reduced to eating such Indian food, be it observed, as Father Garcés maintained he relished. No gourmet reaction here.

Twenty of these Indians came to camp with more prickly pear tuna loaves and "several bags of the seeds of various herbs" to sell. (A botanist could have a field day speculating about what herbs.) Paying for them, the Hispanos asked for more tuna, any piñon nuts available and especially more meat.

We'll bring them by midday, the Indians said. And one, aparently prompted by the Hispanos, promised to accompany them as far as the Colorado if they waited until afternoon.

This afternoon many more showed up, among them one "said to be a Mescalero

Apache" who with two fellow tribesmen had come here two days before by crossing the Colorado. "These Apaches were their friends," the Paiutes said.

"His features were not very pleasing, and he was distinguished from the rest of the Indians by the disgust which he showed at seeing us here and by the greater display of animosity, which we noticed he was purposely showing." After all, various Apache tribes had been at war with the Hispanos for the better part of a century and a half.

Mescalero comes from mescal, a small cactus that was eaten by many Indians, the Pueblos included, over a wide semidesert region. The term Mescalero eventually would become identified with a more easterly Apache tribe; its reservation in our day is in south-central New Mexico. In our expedition's day Mescalero Apache was applied to some Western Apaches. Escalante had related, we recall, the threat of Gila and Mescalero Apaches along his return route from the Hopi mesas. A Miera map drawn earlier this year had placed Mescalero Apaches in the Hopi vicinity.

No meat had been brought, but the Hispanos bought all the Indians' tuna and about a *fanega* (from one and one-half to two and one-half bushels, according to the locality) of edible seeds.

These Indians were Yubuincariris, they now said. (Their descendants would be called Uinkarets Paiute, of the Pine Sitting Place, anthropologist Euler tells us.) They didn't grow corn, they related. Their fare included hares and rabbits.

Across the Colorado, the Yubuincariris said, lived the Ancamuchis, "who, we understood, were the Cosninas" and who planted much corn. (The Ancamuchis, suggests Euler, may actually have been Hualapais, who live to this day to the Havasupais' west.) This side of the river to the south-southwest lived the Payatammumis. (From Paiute-language analysis, Euler posits that the Payatammumis probably were Mojaves. This plateau-and-mountain region was a Tower of Babel.)

"Concerning the Spaniards of Monterey they did not give us even the least indication that they had ever heard them mentioned," but "one . . . gave us to understand that he had already heard of the journey of the Reverend Father Garcés, which together with the denial by all these that they knew the Cosninas (unless they know them by the above name of Ancamuchi), seems to verify what we have already said we suspected."

Suspected was that the Yubuincariris had been terrorized by the Hopis into thwarting Spanish passage to their mesas. This and perhaps the presence of the antagonistic Apache may have been responsible for the Paiutes' now refusing to

His features were not very pleasing, and he was distinguished from the rest of the Indians by the disgust which he showed at seeing us here . . .

133

provide a guide to the Colorado. But before they left the campsite they did point the direction to the river, though "giving confused reports of the ford," which could be reached in two or three days.

In trekking through China this writer often met similar experience. Which is the path to Meihsien? I might ask a wayside peasant at a fork. This way? A nod. That way? A nod. How far this way? A day. How far that way? A day. More often than not, I would learn, the peasant had never traveled as far from his native village as Meihsien.

Miera now became "sick at his stomach," perhaps from overeating on an empty one. This forced a layover here.

An easy seven-league day northeasterly through Antelope Valley and past Yellow-stone Mesa brought our explorers to a flowing arroyo (Bullrush Wash) with good pasturage. This region is virtually as much a wilderness these days as it was in our expedition's, a challenging locale for the new rage of "orienteering."

Continuing northeast, with many "twists and turns," they crossed what today is the southeastern edge of the Kaibab (Mountain Lying Down) Indian Reservation, home of about one hundred thirty-five Paiutes surviving from hereabout. Some six miles south of Fredonia they crossed Kanab (Willow) Creek, which apparently was dry, and ended a ten-league day by camping after nightfall and without water about four miles east of Fredonia, near Johnson Wash.

Olivares, "driven by his thirst because he had eaten too many of the seeds, piñon nuts, and tuna," went looking for water in nearby arroyos. Lorenzo failed to return, "causing us much worry."

October 22-25, 1776

THERE IS DISPUTE AMONG EXPEDITION AFICIONADOS on today's twelve-league march, Bolton swinging it back into Utah and others keeping it south of the state line. It can be debated like the Israelite itinerary through the Sinai to the Land of Milk and Honey. To your writer the terrain dictates against a Utah penetration.

Our explorers rode about two leagues north-northeast (beneath the Shinarump Cliffs) to where they found Olivares near a small pool. There was only enough water for the men to drink and to fill "a little barrel" should they fail to find more tonight.

After four eastward leagues to where White Sage Creek nears the Utah line, they came across a trail that Andrés Muñíz said the Yubuincararis had told him "was the one we ought to take" to the Colorado. After about a league to the south Muñíz became "uncertain of the signs because . . . the trail turned back."

Sending Andrés and Joaquín ahead to look for water, the leaders headed easterly across the Kaibab Mountains, which they had hoped to avoid. Predictably, rock rubble and a washboard of gulches tried their horses. Night overtook them descending "a very high ridge" from which they saw "several fires on a plain below." These had been lit by the two scouts to signal where they were, our men thought. After five leagues in this direction, twelve for the day, they came upon "three little Indian huts" where the pair had made themselves at home.

In the darkness Indians living there hadn't been able to make out how many Hispanos were coming. Despite "coaxing" by Muñíz and Joaquín, most fled the wikiups on the arrival, only three men and two women remaining. "Greatly disturbed," these beseeched Joaquín: "Little brother, you are of the same race as ourselves. Do not permit these people with whom you come to kill us." The youngster apparently had no time to respond before the Hispanos embraced and themselves succeeded in quieting them. "Trying to please us," they gave the explorers two roasted hares and some piñon nuts. Camp, called San Juan Capistrano, was made here (near Coyote Wash) amidst abundant water. The friars stretched out on their poncho-blankets to "the songs of an Indian."

Not until this morning did our leaders know there had been method in the singing. Some of the companions, including Miera, had gone, they said, to chat with the Indians in one of the huts. Don Bernardo was ill, the others told their hosts. "An old man . . . either because our men ordered it or because he wanted to, set about doctoring him with songs and ceremonies which, if not openly idolatrous (for such they might be) were at least entirely superstitious."

All the Hispanos present, again including Miera, "applauded them as harmless compliments." They should have halted the rites, Escalante wrote, "as contrary to the evangelical and divine law, which they profess." At the least, "they ought to have withdrawn."

The friars "reprimanded them" — their senior, Miera, a bad boy too — for "such harmful carelessness." This was a reason "why the heathen who deal most with the Spaniards and Christians of these regions, more stubbornly resist the evangelical truth, making their conversion more difficult every day."

One wonders if the friars' reaction was mainly the younger Escalante's. In an essay on Pueblo ceremonials, Domínguez would describe such singing as "a gabble of voices" accompanied by the "soft beating of the *tombé* [onomatopoetic, like tom-tom]" and the dancing as resembling "contradanses or minuets." Taking exception only to the scalp dance as being "tainted with the idea of vengeance," Fray Francisco said other rites "do not appear to be essentially wicked" or "to conceal further malice or superstition beneath the superficial trappings." For all his rigidity in churchly matters, he seems to have accommodated himself to the compromise of the changing times with Pueblo culture. He may have joined Escalante in censure not so much out of antipathy for the Paiute curing rite as for the Hispanos' having joined it.

Whatever, Escalante here entered in the diary those comments about the long-past conduct of some companions among the Sabuaganas — "the vile commerce in skins," the alleged interpolation into Domínguez' sermon on baptism, the "brutal satisfaction" of sex. "And so in every way they blaspheme the name of Christ and prevent, or rather oppose, the extension of His faith. Oh, with what severity ought such evils be met! May God in His infinite goodness inspire the best and most suitable means!"

One would hate to have faced juror Escalante at the Inquisition.

Our explorers stayed over a day to give time for others hereabout to become accustomed to them and to assemble at the three huts. Again Paiutes, these were of bands called Pagampachis, Cane Spring People.

Besides this, the grass seeds and other things they bought had "made us very sick . . . instead of nourishing us." And Domínguez was so troubled by a pain in his rectum (nothing like intimate detail) that he couldn't move. In almost three months' travel, Fray Francisco and Miera now had each been felled twice while the ailing Escalante recorded not a single debilitating bodily complaint for himself. The wilderness, be it recalled, would make a whole man of a sickly Teddy Roosevelt.

To sustain themselves our men finally killed that horse and had "the flesh prepared so that it could be carried." Was it then jerked?

All day Pagampachis came from nearby ranchos. They were "entertained [?] to the best of our ability." Were there contradanses, it might facetiously be asked, and minuets? Or might there have been staged an impromptu rodeo?

From these Paiutes was acquired "a clearer account of the Cosninas and Moquinos," whom they called "by these very names." They described the route to the Colorado, "which is twelve leagues from here at most," and how to recognize a ford.

And from the Pagampachis the Hispanos bought about a fanega of piñon nuts and "gave them as a present" over half a fanega of those detestable, indigestible grass seeds.

Twenty-six Pagampachis having assembled early at the camp, the friars jointly delivered the usual sermon, interpolating a reprimand for their "superstitious doctoring of the sick." Only God "has at His command health and sickness, life and death." Did Escalante deliver the censure?

Andrés Muñíz couldn't get the message across, but one of the Indians, "who doubtless had dealt extensively with the Yutas Payuchis," understood and explained to the others. (Here Escalante differentiated between the Paiutes they had met en route and those living east of the Colorado and south of the San Juan. A Miera map would situate Payuchi tipis in that region.)

If you want to become Christians, the friars said as if by rote, fathers and other Spaniards will come here to live with and teach you.

We'd like this.

"To increase their affection for us," the Hispanos handed out twenty-six half-varas of red ribbon to a grateful congregation before leaving. A Pagampachi hereupon promised to lead them to the Colorado ford. After "he had traveled with us half a league, he became so frightened that we could not persuade him to continue. The companions, inconsiderately, wanted to use force to make him keep his word, but knowing his reluctance, we let him go freely."

Still in Arizona, they threaded their way down House Rock Wash between the Kaibab Mountains to the west and Paria (Elk Water in Ute) Plateau, then swung

After he had traveled with us half a league, he became so frightened that we could not persuade him to continue.

around the latter's southwestern tip. "This afternoon we thought we saw the canyons and cliffs of the [Colorado] river which . . . look like a long row of houses, but we concluded" — on what grounds Escalante didn't say — "that it was the canyon of one of the many arroyos which are in the plain."

They camped in an "extensive valley" (House Rock) of poor land, part sandy, the rest "about four fingers" of gravel atop loose soil of different colors. Hereabout they saw deposits of gypsum, mica and apparent ore. Our diarist's frequent mention of mica plausibly was related to the padres' fervor for new colonization. What we know as isinglass was the semitransparent mica used by New Mexicans as window panes.

Our explorers rounded the Paria Plateau beneath the aptly named Vermillion Cliffs, rising some three thousand feet above the plain. They didn't try to reach the canyon they had sighted yesterday, which they later learned was the Colorado's, "because we had crossed several arroyos which had canyons as large as that one." While it is true that on this plain one may not recognize the Colorado gorge until almost upon it, why did Escalante let stand this patently false comparison with tributary canyons? The gorge is to the canyons as Arizona's Meteor Crater is to millponds.

Veering northeasterly, they followed the South Fork of Soap Creek until, hemmed in, they had to climb out of its ravine by "a very difficult slope." They camped near a good spring of good water (near Cliff Dwellers Lodge).

This afternoon Cisneros rode out to explore the valley to the north for a pass and a glimpse of the Colorado and its ford. Returning after midnight, Don Juan Pedro reported he had reached the river but didn't know whether they could cross "some mesas and high crests" on the other side. He had made his observation in Marble Canyon, to be named by Colorado River explorer John Wesley Powell in 1869 for "one great bed of marble a thousand feet in thickness." Cisneros' forbidding terrain included a crest of which Powell would say, "The echoes are so remarkable that we could call it nothing but Echo Peak."

But now they were about to enter one of the more treacheous stretches of their journey. The terrain was dangerous, their confusion compounded, and the hopes for food and shelter depended upon their finding the ford that would bring them across the Colorado.

The Crossing

FOLLOWING CISNEROS, OUR MEN FOUND the valley's northern exit to be "a bend completely surrounded by very high cliffs and crests of red earth of various formations," with plain and heights merging, Escalante wrote, in "an agreeably confused appearance."

Mountains and ridges hereabout are sedimentary deposits of ancient seas, rich in marine fossils, and of winds that blow sands to this day. Through eons the swelling beneath the earth's surface has pushed them ever upward in the elephantine wrinkling that Escalante observed. Indeed, like the Sangre de Cristo, they are rising even now.

After a stretch in which the expedition's animals broke through surface gravel and "sank to their knees, . . . we arrived at the Rio Grande de los Cosninas." Tizón, Buena Guía, Buena Esperanza, Rio Grande de los Mártires and los Misterios and appellations more. After all these days of pointing toward the Colorado . . . Escalante, the sphinx.

About twelve million years ago water began trickling south from Wyoming. Pushing sand and gravel, it hewed through plateau until it became a stream, through mountains until it became a river. Vagrant tributaries carved canyons until the river was honed into a Paul Bunyan ripsaw. In places the Colorado has cut six thousand feet deep to basement rock, a crust from some two billion years ago when our planet's molten surface finally hardened.

As its parent land rises, the Colorado is grinding ever deeper. No river on earth runs so deep so far, which is for much of its seventeen hundred miles. If let alone again, it would overrun and destroy man's ephemeral dams in the twinkling of a geological eye.

There was no Colorado mystique in our wayfarers' eyes. Like San Francisco Bay in Pórtola's, it was simply a barrier. Unlike the Monterey colonizer's obstacle, this was one that had to be crossed.

They forded what they called the Santa Teresa (Paria River) and camped on the Colorado's banks near a high, tawny tor that is as conspicuous these days as then. Because of the Paria's erosion and silting, here was a flat, deltaic approach to the Colorado. This is the site of Lees Ferry, where Mormon John D. Lee, having

SCALE: 10 MILES

139

begun ranching here in 1871, instituted a ferry the next year. A ferry would provide a vital link between Arizona and Utah until the high-arch Navajo Bridge was finished about five miles south in 1928.

With "all sides surrounded by mesas and inaccessible heights," a reconnaissance of the opposite bank was called for. "Two men who knew how to swim well entered the river naked, carrying their clothing on their heads. It was so deep and wide [about one hundred yards] that the swimmers, in spite of their prowess, were scarcely able to reach the opposite shore, and they lost their clothing in the middle of the river, never seeing it again."

These Leanders probably were Felipe the coyote and Juan Domingo the genízaro, the uninvited and unwanted pair, as Escalante later would describe them as "good swimmers." Too tired by their ordeal to have reconnoitered, they returned naked and barefoot. "So," says Bolton, "the travelers had a wardrobe shower for the unfortunates."

San Benito Salsipuedes, this camp was named — *Sal-si-puedes*, "Get Out If You Can." There is of course no such saint. This grim appellation may have derived from an expression long since forgotten, Fray Angelico Chavez speculates to us. The Spanish Inquisition forced certain of the convicted to wear a habit called a San Benito, he relates. These victims surely would have wanted out of it.

Again the scout, Cisneros rode up the Paria River bed looking for a pass by which they could cross mesas to the northeast. From those heights they could return to the Colorado in perhaps more open country where, the river being wider, their horses could cross "without the danger, encountered here, of being drowned in its waters."

While traveling all day and into the night, Don Juan Pedro descried "an acclivity very near here . . . but it appeared to him to be very difficult." Other men sent in other directions meantime had "found only insuperable obstacles" to reaching a ford "without going back a long distance." In going back the cavalcade would have entered the Grand Canyon proper.

A raft of logs was put together — presumably tied by ropes they had toted along — and Escalante and "the servants" became mariners. "But since the poles which served for propelling the craft, although they were five varas [about fourteen

140

Cuesta de las Ánimas . . . Hill of the Departed, background to the north, with a projection of the Vermillion Cliffs at middle distance, three miles south of Lees Ferry, Arizona, on the October 26, 1776, march to San Benito Salsipuedes.

feet] long, failed to touch the bottom a short distance from the shore, the waves caused by the contrary wind drove it back. So it returned three times . . . but was unable to reach even the middle of the river."

Besides the river's "being so deep and wide," its banks were so deeply mired that our explorers feared losing most or all of their animals in an attempted crossing.

The Yubuincariris and Pagampachis had told our explorers that their ford "reached only a little above their waists." From this and other landmarks they had cited, the ford had to be higher up. The Muñíz brothers were dispatched over the northern mesa, along the cliffs of which Don Juan Pedro had descried his acclivity, after having been told that, "when they arrived at the river, they should seek a good ford, or at least some place where we could cross on the raft and the animals could swim without danger." Whatever else our leaders felt about the Muñízes, they regarded them as among the expedition's foremost pathfinders. The devil has his due.

The meat of the horse, together with all the provisions bought from the Pagampachis, now had been eaten. A second horse was butchered. For three full days (October 29–31) our wayfarers waited the brothers' return. How they must have chafed at time idled away.

November 1-6, 1776

ANDRES AND LUCRECIO FINALLY REPORTED BACK shortly after noon: the only pass was the one Cisneros had seen five days earlier. A ford lay beyond.

Our men left "the unfortunate campsite" of San Benito Salsipuedes and moved up the Paria about a league to camp beneath Cisneros' acclivity. "This night . . . we suffered greatly from the cold." Their Santa Teresa was a wind tunnel.

Breaking camp, they began to ascend the Paria's east bank. "At the beginning it is very rugged and sandy and afterward has very difficult stretches and extremely perilous ledges of rock, and finally it becomes impassable." Grunting, gasping, sweating in raw wind, we picture it, they took more than three hours to negotiate about half a league. The impassable again was not the impossible — though when surveying the acclivity one may see the possibility of passability only for the likes of bighorn sheep. Our mountaineers called it Cuesta de las Ánimas, Incline of the Departed.

They descended to a campsite on an arroyo (Wahweap Creek), north of where it emptied into the Colorado. "Emptied" is used advisedly, for Wahweap today empties into Lake Powell in the Glen Canyon National Recreation Area. The lake, named for the explorer, backs up behind Glen Canyon Dam, the canyon having been named by Powell for its "many 'glens' or coves."

The dam, eight years in the building and finished in 1964, stores water to meet downstream commitments to Arizona, Nevada, California and Mexico. Turbines generate enough power for a city of a million. The lake, extending one hundred eighty-six miles northeast at high water, lures the city-sated with swimming, fishing, boating and water skiing. Wahweap Marina, in Arizona, is about on the expedition's November second camp.

Despite the dam's benefits, there is much controversy over its environmental impact on plants and wildlife, its submerging many of Powell's "glens" and other natural wonders. Of the latter Escalante himself cited "a multitude of narrow valleys, little mesas and peaks of red earth which at first sight look like the ruins of a fortress." From here on for several days much of the expedition's route nowadays is under Lake Powell.

Striking east-southeast, the cavalcade returned to the Colorado . . . at a brink about five hundred feet above. The "descent to the river is very long, high, rough and rocky, and has such bad ledges of rock that two pack animals which went down to the first one were unable to climb up it in return, even without the pack saddles."

We don't know if these beasts were left stranded in midair, so to speak, but we do learn that the Muñízes had failed the expedition. Not only had they "not told us of this precipice" but "we now learned that they had neither found the ford, nor in so many days even made the necessary reconnaissance of such a short stretch of country, because they spent the time seeking some of the Indians who live hereabouts. . . ." If the brothers had found those Indians, Escalante surely would have so stated.

. . . a multitude of narrow valleys, little mesas and peaks of red earth which at first sight look like the ruins of a fortress.

143

The padres resisted insistence by "the companions" that, despite the perils of descent, an attempt be made at once to cross the Colorado here. To the other side they saw no way to go forward except by the "deep and narrow canyon" of Navajo Creek. If this then-unnamed "little river" were a cul-de-sac, they might be forced to climb back up the cliff here, which would be "extremely difficult."

They sent Juan Domingo down on foot to swim the river and see if Navajo Creek were not impassably hemmed in. Thereafter, Lucrecio Muñíz, credibly in contrition for the brothers' failures, asked permission to follow the genízaro on horseback. Carrying "equipment for making a fire," he "would send up smoke signals" if he found an exit. Perhaps because he feared being dragged under by the current, Lucrecio wore no trousers, "no more shelter than a shirt."

From the brink the others watched as Lucrecio's horse "swam for a long stretch and when it faltered the water reached almost to its shoulders." They judged the river here, while deep, to be shallower than at Salsipuedes. That there were no quagmires at either side was of further comfort.

Juan Domingo and Lucrecio having failed to return by nightfall, the cavalcade camped on the brim, "not being able to water the animals although the river was so close by."

Their second horse having been devoured, "we broke our fast with toasted leaves of small cactus plants and a sauce made of a berry they brought from the banks of the river." Others apparently had scrambled down and up. "This berry is by itself very pleasant to taste, but crushed and boiled in water as we ate it today it is very insipid." Whose recipe for what kind of berry?

As the day latened without the appearance of the "two emissaries," the friars themselves became tired of tarrying. Any moving, wherever it might lead, apparently was better than sitting. Any of us with military experience knows that, such becomes the tension of waiting, it can be less nerve-rending to move out for the attack at once. So be it, the explorers after all would descend today. If Navajo Creek Canyon were indeed impassable, they could, they hoped, continue upstream along the Colorado's west bank in search of that Indian ford. "With great difficulty they got the animals down, some of them being injured because, losing their footing on the rocks, they rolled down long distances."

We broke our fast with toasted leaves of small cactus plants and a sauce made of a berry they brought from the banks of the river.

But men and animals . . . all made it. Camp was set up on the strands. Juan Domingo swam back across to report that he hadn't found an exit but that Lucrecio had left his horse in the middle of the arroyo canyon to follow fresh Indian tracks. A third horse was slaughtered.

With Lucrecio still missing, they left Andrés here under orders to await his brother only until afternoon and to try to overtake them before morning. Along the bank, moving north-northwest, they coped with many ridges, gullies and, returning to Utah, "a very deep canyon" (Warm Creek) in which there was much copperas (green vitriol).

Finding a "little-used trail" here, they turned north-northeast and made camp beneath "a high mesa," calling the site Santa Francisca Romana. (Through efforts of Professors C. Gregory Crampton and David E. Miller of the University of Utah, expedition devotees, U.S. Geological Survey maps today carry this as Romana Mesa, the only one of the expedition's sainted campsites to be so preserved.)

"Tonight it rained heavily here and in some places it snowed."

It was raining when Andrés arrived alone at about six in the morning. That his brother had not reappeared "caused us great anxiety" because he had been gone three days so scantily attired and without provisions. A deserted Lucrecio — a lone castaway Hispano in an ocean of uncharted currents and unfathomed depths, amid peoples as bestial as Jonah's whale. He had to be rescued.

"And so the genízaro decided to go to look for him," to track Lucrecio's trail from where he had last seen him. For all of Juan Domingo's fortitude, Escalante didn't condescend here to give him a name — though the genízaro was given a supply of horsemeat. "The meek," as the Gospel (Matthew 5:1) says, "shall inherit the earth."

The rain ceasing, our main party traveled northeast until "we were stopped for a long time by a heavy storm and a torrent of rain and large hail, with horrible thunder and lightning."

Their having "chanted the Litany of the Virgin . . . God was pleased that the

We were stopped for a long time by a heavy storm and a torrent of rain and large hail, with horrible thunder and lightning.

145

storm might would cease." They rounded Gunsight Butte to its southeast. A short while later God withdrew His pleasure. Renewed rain and a barrier of boulders helped them decide to make camp close to another brink of the Colorado.

Cisneros, off to scout for the Paiutes' ford, returned to observe that from above the river looked "very wide, and judging from the current it did not appear to him to be deep, but that we would be able to reach it only through a nearby canyon." Through Don Juan Pedro's canyon flowed Padre Creek, named long later for our leaders, until inundated by Lake Powell.

Two others, unnamed, were sent to survey the canyon and ford the river. They returned saying "it was very difficult." The padres "did not give much credence to their report and decided to examine everything ourselves next day" with Cisneros. After their experience with the Muñíz brothers' reconnaissance our leaders had turned obversely wary.

"Before nightfall the genízaro arrived with Lucrecio." No word of commendation. No word of thanksgiving. And no word of what had kept Muñíz these three days.

November 7, 1776

"WE" — PRESUMABLY DOMINGUEZ, ESCALANTE AND CISNEROS — "went forth very early to inspect the canyon and ford, taking along the genízaros Felipe and Juan Domingo, so that they might ford the river on foot since they were good swimmers." Felipe was no longer a coyote but a genízaro, which shows that by this period such terms of admixture were interchangeable.

To lead their horses into Padre Canyon "it was necessary to cut steps in a rock with axes for the distance of three varas or a little less." The horses made it on their own, though without packs or riders, the rest of the way down.

About a mile down Padre Creek Canyon the five men reached its mouth and the Colorado. They followed the river downstream "about two musket shots [in distance], sometimes in the water, sometimes on the bank, until we reached the widest part of its current where the ford appeared to be. One of the men [Felipe or Juan Domingo] waded in and found it good, not having to swim at any place. We followed him on horseback a little lower down, and when halfway across, two horses which went ahead lost their footing and swam a short distance. We waited, although in some peril, until the first wader returned from the other side to guide us and then we crossed with ease, the horses on which we crossed not having to swim at all."

Thirteen days after the expedition's coming upon the Colorado at Salsipuedes, its canyonlands had been crossed by white men for the first recorded time at what would become known in perpetuity as El Vado de los Padres.

The Crossing of the Fathers, alas, is no longer. When your writer was boated over it he asked a National Park Service navigator for the fathometer reading. "About four hundred fifty feet." A moment later the question was repeated. "About fifty feet." This still was a thrill.

Escalante put the ford at "a mile wide, or a little more." As the river was only about a hundred yards across here, Fray Silvestre probably was taking into account the downstream trek and a diagonal crossing to the southeast.

The vanguard "notified" — by what means? — the others to lower the pack saddles and other effects with lassos and ropes from "a not very high cliff to the bend of the ford," then to lead the rest of the animals down their Padre Creek Canyon path.

"They did so and about five o'clock in the afternoon they finished crossing the river, praising God our Lord and firing off a few muskets as a sign of the great joy which we all felt at having overcome so great a difficulty and which had cost us so much labor and delay . . ."

Muskets or musket shots? More likely the latter. In any case, this was the only recorded "noise of arms" to have reverberated throughout the entire journey.

On the east bank, amid good pasturage and all the water that could be desired, they camped at what was resoundingly called The Most Pure Conception of the Most Holy Virgin.

For many years the crossing site would be in dispute and in fact mapped as at the mouth of Kane Creek, about a mile to the north. In the 1930s Dr. Russell G. Frazier made five trips, by motorboat and overland, in search of the exact location. On his second foray Frazier, chief mine surgeon for the Utah Copper Company, penetrated what he was convinced from Escalante's description had been the expedition's side canyon. He found therein two series of steps, one of twelve, the other of twenty-five. A jigsaw puzzle, these pieces didn't fit with the diarist's statements that the axed-out steps were only about three yards' distance.

Indians had crossed hereabout from time immemorial, to be followed by post–1776 Spanish traders, Mormons and other pioneers. The traders had added to the

. . . about five o'clock in the afternoon they finished crossing the river, praising God our Lord and firing off a few muskets as a sign of the great joy which we all felt at having overcome so great a difficulty . . .

147

steps, Frazier conjectured. Indeed, Antonio Armijo, of whose published diary the surgeon appears to have been unaware, would write of his 1829–39 trading trek to California: "We stopped the train and repaired the upgrade of the canyon, the same one which has been worked by the padres."

On his fourth trip Frazier and companions implaced a copper plaque at the canyon's entrance. It was he who named its stream Padre Creek.

Then, on the final trip in 1937, Frazier's son and a brother "pointed excitedly to a sloping wall . . . in which were cut six ancient steps 'three yards long or a little less' " that, though "very badly weathered and not easily seen unless the light is just right, . . . still show traces of having been cut by some steel instrument." (Trader Armijo's upgrading had perhaps been of Indian-carved steps.)

"To stand in the footsteps of the padres" was to Frazier, who would join the third Byrd Antarctic expedition, "the greatest thrill of my life." The plaque, rescued before the Crossing of the Fathers was drowned, is treasured by the Utah State Historical Society.

Our wayfarers doubtless would have been beguiled at this fervor over what to them had been a struggle for survival. In all events, Escalante now inserted a retrospective entry on how the struggle could have been eased of "much bad terrain" and "much hunger and thirst" had they but had a guide.

After surmounting the Hurricane Cliffs, they should have headed northeast, thus avoiding their southern loop through the Arizona Strip. They should have kept on to the Paria River north of their campsite San Juan Capistrano, thus avoiding the southern loop around the Paria Plateau. From the river they should have struck east-southeast to the Colorado via Wahweap Creek.

"But doubtless God disposed that we should not obtain a guide, perhaps as a benign punishment for our sins, or perhaps in order that we might acquire some knowledge of the people who live in these parts."

These, "a large number," are "all of pleasing appearance, very friendly, and extremely timid." For the latter trait, our wayfarers called them Yutas Cobardes, an unflattering Timid Utes. Blessed are the meek . . . ?

All the country hereabout "has very high cliffs and peaks. Eight or ten leagues to the northeast [actually east] of the ford there is a high, rounded peak which the Payuchis, whose country begins here, call Tucané, which means Black Peak, and it is the only one hereabouts which can be seen close at hand. . . ."

One Miera map would designate Tucané as Cerro Prieto, Black Peak, and another as Cerro Azul . . . that legendary Blue Peak of silver. Today it is Navajo Mountain, a 10,416-foot laccolith surmounting Rainbow Plateau. It dominates the northern realm of the Navajo Reservation, which chews big bites out of Utah, Arizona, and New Mexico. Sacred to the Navajos, it is to be avoided as home of their thunder god.

THE OBDURATE

November 8-15, 1776

AFTER EDGING THEIR WAY UP from the Colorado by a long, sloping ridge, our explorers turned southerly over a "well-beaten trail" atop Rainbow Plateau. Though picking up many human tracks, they met no Indians. They also found spoor of wild sheep as thick as those "of great flocks of domestic sheep." Apparently they espied too some sheep on the hoof, for these were described as larger and "much swifter" than the domestic variety.

Swinging east beyond a cliff (Tse Tonte), they camped beneath it. A fourth horse was killed. "Tonight we felt much colder than on the other bank." Elevated and now farther from the Vermillion and other more northerly cliffs, here they were more exposed to the region's sometimes gale-stiff west winds.

Losing the trail, they were thwarted by rocks and ridges from continuing south toward Navajo Creek Canyon. They turned easterly but like obstacles soon prevented their "being able to take a step forward." They camped. Nearby they sighted ranchos of Yutas Payuchis, "neighbors and friends of the Cosninas." Visiting the Havasupais had been a stated purpose for taking this route. Through Joaquín and other companions they sought a parley. "But either because they suspected that we were friends of the Moquinos, toward whom they are very hostile, or because they had never seen Spaniards and greatly feared us, we were unable to induce them to come."

Though these Paiutes might never have seen Spaniards, their fear could have

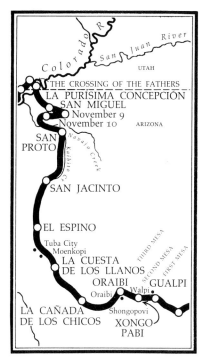

SCALE: 50 MILES

149

been rooted in reports of raids by such mounted strangers from Navajos, Apaches and Hopis. Being of small, unfederated bands like their kinsmen "Timid Utes" west of the Colorado, they would be no match for these white men or, for that matter, any manner of disciplined intruder. Survival was in keeping to hidden hinterland.

The friars set out for the Paiute ranchos with Andrés Muñíz and Joaquín. The latter two went among them while Domínguez and Escalante remained on a height alone so that the Indians might be reassured. After Muñíz had coaxed them for over two hours, five approached. When close, "they turned and fled, and we were unable to stop them."

Andrés learned, though, that the Paiutes had no spare provisions to sell. Some Havasupais lived nearby, he was told, but they were off gathering piñon nuts. Not far from here the expedition would find two roads, one leading to Havasupai country, the other to the Hopi pueblo of Oraibi. However, to proceed now they must return to the base of the cliff and indeed go down to Navajo Creek, the canyon bed that Juan Domingo and Lucrecio Muñíz had explored from its mouth at the Colorado.

A route over the rocks and ridges apparently was plotted for Andrés Muñíz, for our men now retraced their way and camped half a league beyond their site of the night before last at the head of the descent into the canyon.

The lost trail having been found, they inched down a canyon wall "made up entirely of cliffs. The Indians have repaired it with loose rocks and logs and in the last place they have a stairway of the same materials, more than three varas long and two wide."

They came to Navajo Creek where it is joined by Kaibito (Willow Springs in Navajo) Creek. Climbing back out of the canyon along a craggy ridge between the two streams, they traversed "some perilous benches of rock which could be made passable only by the use of crowbars."

Again they were literally carving their way. Getting free of the Colorado was proving almost as rugged, if not as time-consuming, as getting across it.

La Purísima Concepción de la Virgen Santísima . . . From near Padre Butte and the campsite at the Crossing of the Fathers, Utah, facing south toward Rainbow Plateau, Arizona, over the route for November 8, 1776.

They camped amid "plentiful firewood to withstand the severity of the cold." The firewood likely was piñon. To present-day Southwesterners its burning, in the semicircular corner fireplaces native to the region from first Spanish days, is something to come home to. Resinous, piñon smell aburning — not quite as tangy as sandalwood — much like the Greek wine retsina tastes. Its fragrance would have been sharpened by the wintry tang of the air that November eleventh evening.

Still on the trail, they came upon a site that, "judging from its vestiges," was a camp frequented by Havasupais when en route to visit the Paiutes. (What manner of litter identified it as such?) Ice was broken in a spring and men and animals drank their fill.

While the others went ahead, the padres stopped to build a fire and "massage Don Bernardo Miera, who was now about to freeze on our hands, for we feared he could not withstand such extreme cold."

Farther on, our men left the road for Oraibi, "according to the instructions of the Payuchis," to follow another headed for Havasupai territory. Along this way they passed several uninhabited "little houses" about which many cattle and horses had been pastured. No Havasupais in the flesh.

At camp (on the Kaibito Plateau) the leaders were put out over the companions who had gone ahead. These, carrying "vessels" for water, had failed to fill them at the spring, "for which inadvertance we suffered," besides the cold, "great thirst tonight."

Thirst of men and animals was slaked three and a half leagues along at a pool amid rocks. They then continued across a sandy plain.

To more closely approximate the expediiton's trail, your writer turned off Arizona 98 south of Page and drove southwesterly on Navajo 21. "Sandy" is an understatement. So soft and deep is the sand that there was nothing to do approaching scores of dips but to gun my sedan and hope to plow through. The only reassurance was the far-between presence of hogans, round branch-and-earth-covered Navajo dwellings, that gave promise of assistance from Navajo herders. Though such was not required, I felt as wrung-out upon reaching The Gap and U.S. 89 as though having ridden with our wayfarers. Their horses must have had four-wheel drive.

Momentarily our explorers expected to come upon Havasupais . . . and food. Their having eaten nothing but "a piece of toasted hide" since last night, a porcupine proved to be so "very appetizing" that camp (south of Preston Mesa) was named El Espino in its honor. Eating of the spiny creature was tabu, we recall, even among the Sabuaganas. Its serving "only to stimulate the appetite," a fifth horse was carved up. As with some Indian tribes, horses were becoming "much to the taste" — that Domínguez phrase for the Utes' regard for fine horses.

Early our men came upon a small farm, "very beautiful and well-arranged," irrigated from six springs. Harvested abundantly had been corn, beans, squash, watermelon and canteloupe planted amid peach trees. Besides wikiups there was a "little house very well made of stone and mud" in which were found baskets, jars and other houseware. The interlopers judged from tracks that the rancho's presumed Havasupai occupants had been away for several days perhaps picking piñon nuts in the high sierra (Coconino Rim?) to the south-southwest.

From here roads led in different directions. "Now we could not go farther afield to see the Cosninas, both because of lack of provisions as well as on account of our severe suffering from the winter weather." So, after five weeks' seeking them, the expedition wouldn't see Havasupais after all. No conversion of Havasupai souls. No plotting of their sites for Hispano settlement. No inspection of their silver-laden Blue Mountain. God's elements dictated against fulfillment of God's will.

The wayfarers now would go instead directly to the Hopi mesas. Out of the web of the rancho's roads, one pointing southeast they deemed most likely to get them there. After crossing a stream carrying "as much water as a fair-sized [irrigation] ditch," Moenkopi (Hopi for Running Water) Wash near Tuba City, they began seeing Hopi cattle "in large herds." They camped on Moenkopi Plateau about fifteen miles northeast of the Little Colorado, Don Juan de Oñate's Colorado of a century and three-quarters earlier.

Now we could not go farther afield to see the Cosninas, both because of lack of provisions as well as on account of our severe suffering from the winter weather.

153

After an arid nine-league day to the southeast, they stumbled upon water in a valley flush with *chico* (a kind of sagebrush), camping south of Howell Mesa, probably at Hochi Spring. With Hopi cattle herds milling about, the companions begged permission to kill a cow or calf. Had horsemeat palled? Though assured that these were "strays or common stock," the padres ordered that none go near them. "Considering . . . that this might stir up some trouble with the Moquinos and defeat our purpose, which was to use again the means of the evangelical light and meekness to combat their willful blindness and inveterate obstinancy, we ordered another horse killed. . . ." Patently, Escalante speaking of the Hopis from sad experience. This horse would be the sixth and last to fall victim to our expedition's appetites. Be it pointed out that these appetites never were reduced, as had been those of the first Portolá expedition to Monterey, to subsisting on "scaly" mules, our men "smelling frightfully" of them.

. . . we ordered another horse killed. . . .

November 16-19, 1776

MOVING EAST-NORTHEAST across what would become the border of the U.S.-endowed Hopi Reservation, the expedition came finally to the foot of the Hopis' Third Mesa and its pueblo of Oraibi. Our leaders, ordering the others to remain below until summoned, began the 400-foot-high climb with Cisneros at their side.

One ponders their thoughts at approaching this most obdurate of all the obdurate Hopi pueblos. Was Escalante recalling his callous treatment? Was Domínguez reflecting on the threats to Father Garcés? Was Cisneros seized with trepidation? The diary was becoming attenuated. We don't even know if the three men rode or walked.

At the first houses "we were surrounded by a great number of Indians, large and small. . . . We asked them for the cacique and the chiefs, and when we wished to go to the house of the cacique, they restrained us, one of them saying in the Navajó tongue that we must not enter the pueblo."

Are you "not our friends?" Cisneros asked "spiritedly" in Navajo.

The Oraibis quieted. An old man led them to his house, "made us welcome" and provided a room and "the viands which they eat." The rest of the Hispanos presumably were sent for and given food and lodging by reluctant hosts.

Tonight the cacique and two old men visited the friars, gave them "to understand that they were our friends" and assured them they would sell needed provisions. At least the visitors had not been forced to remain on the street and denied sustenance, as had been Garcés' fate here. What would tomorrow bring?

"Very early in the morning" — the Oraibis eager to be rid of their uninvited guests? — the travelers were brought flour, beef tallow, a traditional almost paper-thin cornbread "and other kinds of food." These were bought "promptly . . . because of the most necessary things they brought us the least." Most likely the Oraibis, their larders low, simply had no more to part with.

For lack of an interpreter they were unable to take up the matter of submission to Spanish rule — what a cross to bear! — but were able to explain "some things to them. . . . They listened attentively but said nothing except that they wanted to maintain friendship with the Spaniards."

I have sent word to the other pueblos to offer you hospitality, the cacique volunteered, and to sell such provisions as you may need to reach Zuñi.

This afternoon, the expedition rode on to Second Mesa and Xongopabi (Shongopovi) Pueblo, where "they welcomed us courteously, promptly giving us lodging."

The leaders of this pueblo and nearby Xipaolabi (Shipolovi) and Mossonganabi (Mishongnovi) having gathered, the padres tried to preach in Navajo, via Cisneros, and by sign language.

We don't understand, they made understood. At Walpi you will find persons versed in Castilian who will tell you "what everybody wished to know."

You have understood us. You yourselves should reply.

Oraibi's leaders have told us we must lodge and sell you supplies. We must cultivate your friendship "without treating of or admitting any other subject" since we don't want to become Christians. No slave church . . . and that's it.

At this point the Hopi who had housed them was given a woolen cloak for his wife, who "gladly accepted" it. A brother of hers promptly took it and "threw it toward us with a deep frown."

Thinking that "his hostility . . . arose from a suspicion of some evil purpose," the friars explained the cloak as "innocent recompense."

155

The brother, "wishing to make amends for the affront he had shown us," now "put us in a predicament even worse than the first, many of us finding ourselves unable to understand a thing."

The other Hopis dispersing, the brother pointed to Escalante and Cisneros and said "he had heard what had taken place" in Oraibi last summer. He had been present at Walpi when the Havasupai had told Escalante "about the road from Moqui to the Cosninas, and that now we had come by this same road." If the cloak were accepted, "relatives and neighbors would be angry. He said this to satisfy us, but we were unable to understand clearly the other thing regarding which he wished to tell us, although it is not very difficult to infer it from the foregoing events."

What to make of this curious bit of reportage? Contrary to Escalante, it *is* "very difficult to infer" what he himself was trying to say. If it were that the expedition's having arrived from the west had angered the Hopis, that they suspected the Havasupais of having connived in plotting its route, why didn't Fray Silvestre say so? This, at any rate, appears to be the logical deduction.

Whatever, this afternoon they went on to First Mesa, to be "welcomed very joyfully" by the Tanos (Pueblo refugees) and Walpis and lodged by the Tanos' cacique at Hano Pueblo.

The friars were visited by "an apostate" named Pedro from Galisteo Pueblo (about twenty miles south of Santa Fe and no longer extant), "who was now old and had great authority in this pueblo of the Tanos." The Hopis, Pedro said, "were now at fierce war with the Navajó Apaches, who had killed and captured many of their people." They had been "hoping that some fathers or Spaniards would come to these pueblos in order through them to beg from the Señor Governor some aid or defense against these enemies. So they had been especially delighted when they learned that we were coming . . . because they hoped we would aid and console them."

The stir aroused by Navajos — their ambush plot, their smoke signals — we recall from Escalante's previous visit to Walpi. Navajo Apaches? Separate and distinct in historic times from other Apaches, the Navajos like them are of Athabascan lineage. Both peoples are believed by anthropologists to have come out of northwestern Canada as the last wave of Asian migrants to the Southwest. The Navajos, who call themselves *T'áá Diné*, "The People," had appeared on the northern fringe of the Pueblos in the sixteenth century but were not so named until the 1620s. For

Gualpi . . . Walpi Pueblo, on the Hopi First Mesa, Arizona, where the party spent November 18–19, 1776.
(This painting is adapted from 1897 photographs by A. C. Vroman.)

a long time the Spaniards saw no reason to distinguish between them and other Apaches.

When first encountered, the Navajos were centered in the upper Chama Valley and adjacent regions. In the late seventeenth century Pueblo rebels took refuge among them, transmitting the use of the upright loom that in time would make the weaving of wool a Navajo art that persists to this day.

The Navajos gradually moved — and were pushed by the Southern Utes — out of north-central New Mexico and south-central Colorado through the Gobernador and Largo canyons south of the San Juan River toward their present heartland in and far about northeastern Arizona's Chuska Mountains. Meantime, besides raising staple crops on seemingly barren earth, they became pre-eminent herders, particularly of sheep.

The Navajos began to seize much of their livestock in raids on the pueblos and Hispano settlements. They took captives as well . . . in swelling numbers. After the Comanches, the Navajos, notable horsemen too, periodically arose as a pre-eminent scourge of New Mexican domain. In time the Spaniards and Indian allies would retaliate with equal ferocity. Church records show more baptisms of Navajo captives — genízaros they would become — than of any other non-Pueblo Indians.

Small wonder that the sedentary Hopis were fearful of Navajo aggression on this November 18, 1776.

To Domínguez and Escalante this alarm fortuitously provided "one of the finest of opportunities" to induce the Hopis to return to the faith and to colonial subjugation. Summon the chiefs of the other pueblos, they told Pedro, so that tomorrow we may discuss "this matter at length and seriously."

I shall go with you to Santa Fe, Pedro now suggested, to speak to the Señor Governor for the Hopis and Tanos about an "alliance" and the aid we need.

We shall take you gladly and "use our good offices" with the governor, the friars replied, but all the Hopi pueblos should be represented in a deputation, each one by a person of authority.

From the other mesas the chiefs of only one other pueblo, Mossonganabi, arrived to join the leaders of the First Mesa pueblos in the Tanos' kiva. The friars were invited to meet with them in this sacred chamber. Another interpreter would be

Antonio el Cuate, a Spanish-speaking apostate from Santa Clara Pueblo, translating into Tewa while Pedro did the same into Hopi. (Of Antonio the Twin, Escalante had spoken in one of his letters to Provincial Murillo in Mexico City. "Not long ago" some fellow Santa Clarans had gone to the Hopi mesas to bring him home. The Hopis, "judging that they meant to take him by force attacked and would have killed them if the very unhappy apostate himself had not restrained them." Fray Silvestre, presumably during his earlier visit here, had "exhorted as much as I could to convert him to the fold of the Church" but without success. It is unclear whether Antonio the Twin had wanted to return to Santa Clara or still was forcibly held by the Hopis.)

We are agreed that Pedro should go with you to Santa Fe, the leaders said. Please do "everything possible" on our behalf.

We shall do so because we love you "like children" and commiserate in your troubles. But you won't be able "to free yourself from suffering these troubles" until you cease to offend God. Beyond this ("taking advantage for greater clarity and force, of the afflictions of which they had just told us"), you will suffer "eternal punishments."

If they would submit, "they would have constant and sure help from the Spanish arms against all the heathen who might attempt to attack them, as did the Christian pueblos of New Mexico."

This was the utmost of dissembling. Spanish arms couldn't defend many outlying Spanish settlements not to mention the pueblos on and near the Rio Grande.

Be that as it may, "This caused them to see at the same time the uselessness and inconstancy of the friendships and alliances which they had celebrated many times before with the Yutas and Navajós."

Whether or not you accept Christianity, the friars said, we will take your ambassadors to Santa Fe and speak on their behalf.

"They replied that they knew the governors were sending the fathers to persuade them to submit to their authority but that they had not and still did not wish to." Again, "they gave us to understand that, since there were many more heathen nations than Christian, they wanted to follow the more numerous party. . . ." Finally, "they lived in a country which was very inconvenient for the service which, once converted, they would have to render the Spaniards."

Harsh country . . . no surplus for missionaries and officials. And no surplus of time to minister to Hispano wants and dictates.

They gave us to understand that, since there were many more heathen nations than Christian, they wanted to follow the more numerous party. . . .

159

. . . we withdrew very sadly to our lodging, realizing that the obstinancy of these unhappy Indians was invincible.

"When we had overcome the apparent force of each one of these arguments, finding now nothing to contradict, the men of the assembly talked a long time, each in turn, beginning with those of the greatest authority and continuing in the order of their importance. And although each one spoke individually, he expressed himself in the form of a dialogue, and concluded his discourse by asking various questions of the others, who replied by assenting or denying respectively according to the nature of the questions."

These two centuries later Frank Waters and this writer sat in on a similar contemplation in the adobe office of Taos Pueblo's governor. Waters, an acknowledged friend of the Taoseños, had written an article commemorating the thirtieth anniversary of his novel *The Man Who Killed the Deer* and celebrating the reacquisition from the U.S. government of their Blue Lake and some fifty thousand surrounding mountain acres. We were seeking permission from the governor and his council to send a photographer to this sacred lake to illustrate the article. Having made our request through an interpreter, we listened silently as the elders, their heads shrouded in white blankets, spoke one after another in Tiwa. Minutes sometimes elapsed between one monologue and another. After about an hour, the interpreter turned to Waters and me: "The answer is no."

In the discourses in the Tanos' kiva, "they related the traditions of their ancestors and exhorted that they be observed, concluding that it was better to suffer their present troubles and calamities than to violate these traditions [and] become Christians, because the old men had told them and counseled them never to subject themselves to the Spaniards." The answer was no.

In "taking advantage . . . of the afflictions," the friars had overplayed their hand. The chiefs, having talked themselves into renewed resolve, decided that no pueblo emissaries would be sent to Santa Fe. Better to face the Navajos alone, they were saying, than to have anything at all to do with Spanish clerics and officialdom. Just as, though it would never have occurred to our friars, Christians had faced lions and gladiators rather than submit to Roman gods and dictates.

Not only this obstinancy but Pedro himself broke new news. "Now they do not wish that I should go to see the Governor because, since I am a Christian, they say that he will not let me return to Moqui."

Pedro, whom Escalante had characterized as an apostate, actually "feared this much more than the others." Home is where heart and hearth are. Though an apparent Christian, he wanted above all to remain among the apostate Hopis, "and so we were unable to get him to carry out his first intention. . . . we withdrew very sadly to our lodging, realizing that the obstinacy of these unhappy Indians was invincible." Once there Escalante doubtless harangued Domínguez and the others anew on the righteousness of his conviction: reduce and relocate the Hopis. Not for nothing would anthropologist Edward H. Spicer look back upon the Hopis as "probably the most famous 'apostates' in the history of Spanish Christianity."

Our disappointed travelers would leave for Zuñi Pueblo next day while they still could "because it was now snowing constantly."

Sometimes it still snows constantly hereabout. In the winter of 1968–69, for one, snow fell so long and heavily that the Air Force deployed helicopters to rescue isolated Navajos and cargo planes to drop fodder to their snowbound livestock.

The hOMEWARDING

November 20-23, 1776

ESCALANTE'S LOG now resumed the brevity of the expedition's first days, the route well-known and Fray Silvestre having described it in reports on his 1775 trip there. They apparently camped in the vicinity of Keams Canyon on November twentieth and not far west of Steamboat Wash on the twenty-first.

On November twenty-second, at a camp presumably just west of Klagetoh, Domínguez, Escalante and three unnamed others left the rest, the animals "now worn out," and pushed ahead. That day the five men covered eleven leagues before their horses became so exhausted

161

"we had to halt." From a site seemingly on Black Creek a bit southeast of Pine Springs, next day they "travelled on the gallop" for twelve leagues despite "troublesome flurries." Tonight they "suffered greatly from the cold."

November 24-December 12, 1776

IN THEIR PATENT EAGERNESS to reach comparative civilization, the five set out "as soon as it was daylight." They crossed I-40 a little east of Houck. Just before reaching the present New Mexico state line, they felt forced to halt and build a fire because "we feared we would freeze in this valley." They couldn't have hunkered down long, though, to make the time they would. Farther along they halted again, to change horses — the first such occurrence cited in the entire diary. Having ridden twelve leagues this day, they arrived "after nightfall and greatly fatigued" at the pueblo and mission of Nuestra Señora de Guadalupe de Zuñi.

"Not having sufficient strength to continue immediately," the friars next day wrote almost identical letters, epitomizing the diary, to Governor Mendinueta and Provincial Murillo, the former signed jointly, the latter by Domínguez. A number of Domínguez' comments in our preceding account of the expedition have been drawn from the letter to Murillo. Both letters assumedly were sped by courier to Santa Fe.

The following day, November 26, the eight other companions arrived. Though left unrecorded, it can be taken for granted that the friars as well as the others enjoyed the creature comforts of the mission convento, Escalante's headquarters, and perhaps of magistrate Cisneros' residence. Though man cannot live by bread alone, he relishes it as well. One wonders if the youth Joaquín saw this Indian metropolis as skyscraper adobe, if as a child of the wilderness he might even have felt confined within adobe walls.

"On account of various incidents" our travelers laid over at Zuñi for seventeen days. One such incident certainly was to edit Escalante's diary into a suitable journal. Another was Domínguez' official visitation of the Zuñi mission. It may be, as in a question we raised earlier, that the inspector had held off this visitation and that of the two succeeding missions in anticipation of initiating the expedition and of visiting these pueblos en route back to Santa Fe. In all events, that's the way it worked out.

Domínguez was noncommittal about the Zuñi church structure, but cited a new altar screen "as seemly as this poor land has to offer, which was paid for by Father Vélez [de Escalante] and the Indians of the pueblo." Most such adornments were "King's gifts" — that is, supplied from his royal stipend. While only in referring to the San Felipe bulto did Domínguez show up Miera by name, he had to know that the Zuñi creations were Don Bernardo's. "That this citizen [Miera] sold them seemed intolerable" to Fray Francisco, E. Boyd concludes in her monumental *Popular Arts of Spanish New Mexico*. Here Domínguez limited what Miss Boyd calls his "derogatory paper-chase" of Miera and his art to a further observation that an altar painting of Our Lady of Guadalupe was set in "an old frame, newly half gilded. . . ."

Domínguez' taking exception to Miera's selling his art to the missions seems rather sanctimonious even for that penurious era. Don Bernardo was making a living, utilizing his talents as best he knew how. Though his carvings and paintings may not have been the equal of those Fray Francisco had admired in Mexico City, they were, Miss Boyd reiterates, of the best quality then produced in New Mexico. There were no Medici here to underwrite a New Mexican Michelangelo.

Of the Zuñis Domínguez noted perceptibly that theirs "is an entirely different language from all those known and observed in the kingdom." No comment on Zuñi élan.

Our clerical leaders must have timed their departure to take in an annual fiesta honoring Our Lady of Guadalupe, patroness not only of this mission but of all the Americas. On December twelfth there would have been masses, Indian dancing, not a little feasting.

December 13-16, 1776

ABOUT FIVE MILES ALONG, our homewarding wayfarers passed to the north of Corn Mountain. Were any of them aware of the role this had played until the early eighteenth century in Zuñi hide-and-seek with Coronado and his successors?

Escalante didn't break down a four-day, thirty-league trek to Acoma into campsites, but it is altogether likely that the cavalcade spent a night at El Morro, The Bluff, as Miera would depict it on an expedition map. From prehistoric times a natural pool at the base of this 250-foot sandstone outcropping had attracted passers-by along a well-beaten east-west trail.

Now a national monument sometimes called Inscription Rock, El Morro is graffiti at its acme of acceptability. Charles F. Lummis, whose *The Land of Poco Tiempo* and other works celebrated the primitive West, in 1926 wrote in the monument's register: "No other cliff on earth records a tithe as much of romance, adventure, heroism."

Petroglyphs had been incised here as early as A.D. 1200. It is likely that members of the Coronado expedition drank from the pool. The earliest deciphered Spanish inscription: "Passed by here the Adelantado [Forerunner] Don Juan de Oñate from discovery of the Sea of the South on the 16th of April, 1605."

In another era soldiers, camel-drivers, migrants to California — these and others carved history into sandstone here. But among hundreds of inscriptions none has been found of Domínguez, Escalante or members of their party, not even of Miera. They doubtless were too eager to be on their way to have paused for this sort of immortality.

About halfway along they dropped south of the 8,400-foot Zuñi Mountains and recrossed, after 133 days, the Continental Divide at about eight thousand feet.

Probably on their third day they struck El Malpaís, detritus of three distinct basaltic tidal waves, the latest less than a millennium ago. The Badlands is an understatement, their one hundred twenty thousand acres more tortured than any terrain our astronauts met on the moon.

Wending about six miles across El Malpaís, our travelers were fortunate to have a prehistoric trail both to find their way and to save their animals' hooves. The trail is nicely engineered of small chunks of lava, with yawning fissures spanned by bridges of larger ones.

To be seen hereabout, though Escalante mentions El Malpaís not at all, are cave-like lava tubes, some over fifty feet in diameter and one almost eleven miles long. Here also are inverted cinder cones, one of them half a mile across, a thousand feet deep and of almost perfect proportions; ice caves with delicate ceilings of crystal, formed and maintained by nature's critically adjusted temperatures, and crystal-clear stalagmites rising from rinklike floors; splatter cones, formations ten feet or so high, and sinkhole ponds of lava, from several feet to over an acre across, with a variety of distinct ecological communities representing various stages of biological parade — some cozying an algae that radiates a translucent glow, others nourishing bullrushes, cattails, even fish.

Bizarre shapes, created during lava's hardening, confronted our journeyers everywhere — dwarfs and dragons and whatever else they may have conjured up;

and everywhere junipers stunted and twisted, contorted into writhing crones and clowns. If they had been aware of it, semicircular lava walls and fire rings at the mouths of those horizontal tunnels — these betokened campsites of Indians on the move.

On their fourth day our men climbed the 357-foot height to Acoma, popularly known today as the Sky City, by a trail that, as Domínguez recorded in his visitation report, "makes a number of boxed-in turns, so difficult that in some places they have made wide steps so that the pack animals may ascend with comparative ease." These days we may drive to the top.

"Immediately," wrote Escalante, "there fell a heavy snow which prevented us from continuing as soon as we desired." This would be his last diary observation, other than of distances, directions and stopping places, until the expedition's arrival in Santa Fe.

December 17-19, 1776

ACOMA WAS ONE OF NEW MEXICO'S seven Keres-speaking pueblos (all extant today) that Domínguez formally visited. The People of the White Rock, as their name translates, probably have inhabited it continuously longer than any other settlement in the United States except the Oraibis on their mesa. The White Rock is topped by seventy crusty acres, these split by a narrow but deep cleft.

The first to see it through Spanish eyes, Coronado's Captain Alvarado called Acoma "the strongest position ever seen in the world." Stronger, that would make it, than a Granada or a Gibraltar. Because of such, the Acomas were more intractable at the outset of Spanish colonization than even the Zuñis and Hopis.

In Oñate's 1598 year of arrival he sent a detachment this way. Its commander and eighteen men ascended to get some cornmeal the Acomas had promised. Without warning, the Indians attacked, killing him and twelve others. The survivors escaped back to San Juan Pueblo and Oñate.

The conquistador then sent seventy men under the slain commander's brother, who thirsted for revenge. They mounted an assault. On the third day, while most of the soldiers preoccupied the Acomas on well-used trails to the top, thirteen men slunk up an isolated one. With a celebrated leap the squad leader cleared that deep chasm and threw logs across. He and his companions, having taken the Acomas by surprise, joined the main force in hacking a way into the pueblo.

Immediately there fell a heavy snow which prevented us from continuing as soon as we desired.

165

There are such horrible precipices that it is not possible to look over them for fear of the steep drop.

While killing some six hundred Acomas, the Spaniards burned the town and took another six hundred prisoner. Of these, seventy warriors were assassinated, one by one, their bodies thrown over the cliff. The five hundred-odd remaining captives were marched to Santo Domingo Pueblo to the northeast. In a "trial" Oñate sentenced all males over twenty-five to loss of a foot, the rest of both sexes to lifelong servitude. Though there was no Geneva Convention in those days, we know about this crime because Oñate was tried for it in Mexico City.

The Acomas were at the forefront of the Pueblo Revolt and the rebellion during the Vargas Reconquest. Finally, far closer to the pivot of Spanish power than the Hopis, they felt forced to accommodate to Spanish rule.

Meantime, they had accommodated to Christianity. Sometime between 1629 and 1641 a church was built, almost all of its materials packed over an improved cliffside trail (perhaps the one climbed by our expedition) called to this day El Camino del Padre for the missionary of that day. Vigas were dragged from the Cebolleta Mountains thirty miles away. Rocks and earth were hauled up in animal-skin bags. . . . The Israelites erecting Pharoah's temple.

Though this church was damaged during the revolts, it "probably incorporates," say Adams and Chavez, "more of the original structure than any of the surviving seventeenth-century churches in New Mexico." Certainly more than San Miguel, Santa Fe's "oldest church" in the nation.

A wonderstruck Domínguez, in another of his rare complimentary superlatives, wrote: "This makes what the Indians have built here of adobes with perfection, strength, and grandeur, at the expense of their own backs, worthy of admiration."

Here, though, Domínguez took another swipe at an unnamed Miera. "There is an ordinary painted wooden niche to hold a completely carved St. Stephen of rather medium size. The Indians bought this statue, or image, along with the niche." One wonders if Don Bernardo rose to contention with the inspector on such occasions as the late Thomas Hart Benton would excoriate avant-garde critics of his paintings for being "victims . . . of God-awful self-cultivation."

While awed by the church, Domínguez was further impressed by the site and its people. "There are such horrible precipices that it is not possible to look over them for fear of the steep drop."

For water, across that deep cleft was a natural cistern forty yards around and about as deep. Here rain collected and snow was swept. ". . . there is a guard to prevent pollution." For the mission, twelve women brought twelve small jarsful daily.

Acoma . . . The Sky City pueblo, New Mexico, the party's stopping place December 16–20, 1776, with *Katzimo* (Enchanted Mesa) in the background.

Crops were grown and livestock corralled in the far below. Dependent on rain, the fields had suffered "great drought" for three years now. Five to six leagues north-northeast corn and "each kind of green vegetable" were irrigated at Cubero by today's San José River. But tending these fields exposed the Acomas to assault. "Apaches [are] so insolent that if this pueblo were not by nature defensible, perhaps nothing would remain of it."

As it was, Acoma's population had dwindled from 1,114 to 530 in only eight years. Domínguez blamed not only the Apaches but epidemics and the fact, as told him by the missionary here, that "still others are wandering about [or] have fled to Moqui for fear of the famines and wars." Russian-born refugees in Europe after World War II, Bengalis from Bangladesh, Black Africans in search of a mouthful — it's a story far older even than the Diaspora.

December 20-21, 1776

FOUR LEAGUES TOOK OUR HOMEBOUND TRAVELERS to Laguna Pueblo, which had been Escalante's first New Mexico parish and was Domínguez' final mission visitation. It stood "on the flat top of a little hill, which . . . consists on the whole south slope of small whitish stones, very soft and sandy." Nowadays its church alone is kept whitewashed as when, says Fray Francisco, the whole pueblo could "be seen from afar on any road."

Laguna, named for a small lake nearby, was (and is) the youngest of all the New Mexico pueblos. Of how it came into being there are various versions. One is that a Father Miranda "went throughout the land, even to the most rugged sierras, collecting the wandering sheep of numerous nations." Another is that the pueblo's nucleus came from Keres who had fled to Hopi country. Dissidents of Cieneguilla (southwest of Santa Fe), Cochiti and Santo Domingo pueblos coalesced here, goes another. Finally, Keres rebels who had taken refuge at Acoma moved to this site. Perhaps two or more of these factors contributed to Laguna's founding. In any case, Laguna signified formal submission to New Mexico's governor on July 4, 1699.

By 1706 a church was under construction, the one inspected by Domínguez. Perhaps in his own haste to be on the way, Fray Francisco had little to say of the church though he did note it was of mud-cemented stone, not adobe. Nothing here of Miera's to criticize. Illustrative of the missions generally is his staff roster: a chief fiscal (a general assistant to the father who saw to it that the Indians performed their religious duties) and three subordinates; two sacristans (boy assistants who received intensive religious instruction) and eight subordinates; eight cooks, four bakers, two little girls to carry water and "caretakers for the horse, for the pigs, if there are any, and for the little hencoop, and nothing more." Some of the above worked on one-week shifts, biweekly or monthly. Collected from parishioners by the fiscal of the week were a sheep, native beans, broad beans, eggs, lard, salt, flour, tallow and milk.

Of the 699 Lagunas, "I say that they are humble, timid, and obedient" — as the foregoing testifies.

December 22-27, 1776

AFTER SIX LEAGUES THE CAVALCADE HALTED "at a place called El Alamo." Escalante's directions, east-northeast, put the campsite tonight in or near Cañada de los Apaches — now on the tiny, separatist Cañoncito (Little Canyon)) Navajo Reservation — northeast of Mesa Gigante. Miera didn't position El Alamo on any of his maps; your writer hasn't found it on any modern ones. It is hard to see why the travelers wouldn't have gone south of the mesa, a veritable giant at eleven hundred feet above surrounding terrain.

To the south-southeast the men crossed the Puerco (Muddy) River and after nine leagues came to Isleta Pueblo "on so small an elevation that it might pass for a plain" that was "about a musket shot and a half" from the Rio del Norte. After almost five months, back at the Rio Grande. When the river was in flood, "it cuts off the settled part as if it were an island, which is doubtless the reason why it was named Isleta."

Isleta is one of four Tiwa-speaking pueblos along with Taos and Picurís in the northern Rio Arriba and Sandia in Rio Abajo. It was the southernmost pueblo "mouth, or entrance, to this kingdom," wrote Domínguez.

Isleta's church dates from about 1613. Say Adams and Chavez: "With, of course, extensive repairs and rebuilding, [it] has one of the best claims to be the oldest church in New Mexico" — hence the oldest in the entire United States.

With the Pueblo Revolt, about one thousand Hispano settlers from Rio Abajo

169

gathered at Isleta before retreating south. Though the two thousand Isletans had not formally joined the rebellion, the governor and his some one thousand fleeing Rio Arriba survivors reached here to find their pueblo deserted and its church "burned and ruined . . . and a cowpen inside."

The governor returned the next year, 1681, in an abortive attempt at pueblo-wide reconquest. He met resistance at Isleta. It was short-lived. The Isletans said they thought the Spaniards were Apaches. When the Spaniards remarked upon the church's condition, the Isletans maintained that rebels from other pueblos had been responsible. The governor burned the pueblo en toto and took back to El Paso del Norte its 385 men, women and children (others having run away).

Reconqueror Vargas found the pueblo in ruins "except for the nave of the church, the walls of which are in good condition." Thereafter, some former Isletans were gathered up from around El Paso and amongst other pueblos, the Apaches and eventually the Hopis. Another melting pot. Pueblo and mission were re-established.

Domínguez, soft-spoken about this church too, earlier had, however, dismissed its father for keeping mission provisions "in a private house" — which made him, say Adams and Chavez, "a 'proprietor,' a most grave fault in the Franciscan Order, because he kept and sold merchandise for his own use and profit."

The pueblo was of "three beautiful blocks," wrote Domínguez. "Everything is of adobe, very prettily designed and much in the Spanish manner." Rio del Norte-fed irrigation yielded "copious crops," including "vinestocks, and they usually make a little wine." As for the Isletans, "They are well inclined to Spanish customs, for many use mattresses on their beds, and there are many bedsteads."

Cause for comment, since many Hispano New Mexicans themselves slept on floors.

Though Fray Francisco didn't mention it, a phenomenon had occurred here the previous year that caused much stir among the Isletans and nearby Hispanos. The well-preserved corpse of a priest rose from burial to the surface of the church's mud floor. Repeatedly reburied, this apparition would repeat itself roughly every twenty years into modern times.

The priest had been stabbed to death in 1756, an Isleta tradition being that he was victim of a drunken Hispano rancher who believed the priest was preying on his wife. Through the years at least four, maybe six, clerical investigations were conducted, according to Fray Angelico Chavez, who unearthed the story. As to the body's frequent surfacing, a theory is that, in the church's proximity to the Rio

They are well inclined to Spanish customs, for many use mattresses on their beds, and there are many bedsteads.

Grande, shifting sands were responsible. An exhumation as recent as 1948 found the corpse still well-preserved. Why this should be, while bodies buried nearby quickly decomposed, is a mystery yet to be unraveled.

Christmas Day came and went while the expedition was at Isleta. Nothing likely was made of it other than celebration of a Christmas Eve mass. The closest New Mexican approximation to modern Christmas occurred on Epiphany, a feast on January 6 commemorating the coming of the Magi from the east to Christ's cribside. Santa Claus and turkey would wait three-quarters of a century for conquerors from the east . . . as would *farolitos*, a modern New Mexican trademark, for brown paper bags within which manufactured candles are placed to light the Christ Child's way.

December 28-29, 1776

PERHAPS FORDING THE RIO GRANDE two leagues north at the Hispano settlement of Pajarito, Little Bird, our men reached the Villa de San Felipe de Albuquerque and its 763 souls after another two leagues.

The Albuquerque region had been settled by farmer-ranchers in early colonial days, its inhabitants having been among those Rio Abajo refugees during the Pueblo Revolt. The community itself was founded in 1706 with residents drawn from Bernalillo, sixteen miles north, and nearby districts. Named for the viceroy the Duque de Alburquerque, which spelling Domínguez used, it would lose through time its first *r*. It was New Mexico's third villa, or town of importance, after Santa Fe and Santa Cruz. These days it is Old Town, an arts and crafts center, of New Mexico's most populous community, often called the Duke City after its namesake.

Albuquerque old-timers grumble these days about the urban clog. That's nothing new. Thirty-three years after its founding some Albuquerqueans, in petitioning for a new settlement site to the south of Isleta, complained that their "present condition" was "very limited, with scarcity of wood, pasture for our stock, . . . and many footpaths encroaching upon us [and] scarcity of water."

Our wayfarers' host church, which Domínguez described as facing east, would collapse within twenty years despite its "very thick walls." The present church, built on the same site in the 1790s, faces south.

The villa consisted of twenty-four houses (a metropolitan sprawl?) near the mission, Fray Francisco noted, and upstream ranchos with well-irrigated fields of

171

watermelon, vineyards and orchards (apricot, peach, apple and pear) as well as the usual field and garden crops.

Just across the river lay Atlixco "on a beautiful sandy plain which comes down from hills like those on the east bank." *Atlixco*, the present Atrisco, is Aztec for Upon the Water and probably had been named for New Spain's beautiful Valley of Atlixco. North of it was Lower Corrales, Corrals for its presumably numerous livestock.

December 30, 1776

BEYOND THE HISPANO RIVERINE SETTLEMENT of Alameda, Poplar or Cottonwood Grove, another four-league day took them to a community beneath "a sierra called Sandia because there is a pueblo and mission of this name here." *Sandia* means "watermelon." Tradition gives it various derivations: that watermelons grew abundantly from Spanish-imported seeds in the mountains' canyons and hereabout; that striped ridges to its 9,605-foot peak and their pinkish reflection at sunset looks like the ripe fruit; that it recalled the shape of a mountain of the same name in Spain with a heart resembling a melon's pulpy center.

Sandia Pueblo stood (and stands) just east of the Rio del Norte "on the same site of the old mission which was destroyed in the general uprising of this kingdom." A first church had been built here in the later 1620s, but the Sandians had deserted the site during and after the 1680 Pueblo Revolt. The pueblo had been reconstituted in the late 1740s, mainly with Tiwa refugees and a few Christian Hopis led away from the mesas. "The church . . . is unusable, being in such a deplorable state that it truly saddens the soul to see the marks of the barbarities they say have been perpetrated here. . . . it has no roof, and only the walls remain to indicate what the temple was like."

The missionary at the time of Sandia's reconstitution had tried to restore the church but soon realized "it was useless and that everything was going to fall flat together." Despite successor padres, "So it has remained."

Perhaps the Sandíans had been too preoccupied with fending off Comanches and other nomads. The previous year Domínguez had heard in El Paso del Norte that Sandia had been "completely devastated." In his writ of visitation, however, he said that, while "about thirty sons of the pueblo died at the hands" of the Comanche nation in 1775, the encounter had occurred outside the pueblo.

172

Meantime, the old baptistery, still roofed inside the ruins, was used for church services. To accommodate Sandia's remaining 275 souls, it was only thirty-six feet long, fifteen wide and ten and a half high and "looks like a coach house."

As for the convento, "The thing that bears this name here resembles nothing more than the old half-fallen houses that are usually found in Indian pueblos near Mexico City." Since there was no sacristy, church valuables were kept in a convento cell "under the missionary's eye" in chests "made like the counters of cheap shops." Here is Fray Francisco, however acerbic, with an eye for such details as are missing from Escalante's running account of the expedition.

December 31, 1776 - January 1, 1777

ABOUT TWO LEAGUES UPSTREAM the cavalcade passed through Bernalillo, a diminutive for a settler family named Bernal. Its eighty-one "citizens are considered Spaniards. . . ." This was the homeplace, we recall, of our Andrés Muñíz and Juan de Aguilar. Whether there was a halt for family reunions, we don't know.

After five more leagues, Santo Domingo, a final pueblo stop. Here were two churches: one, say the records, "demolished" during the revolt yet "rebuilt for a fortress and living quarters by the apostates," and the other, alongside it, erected sometime in the 1740s to 1760s.

In the newer church's choir loft were kept two guitars, three violins, two bugles and two military snare drums — more musical instruments than Domínguez inventoried for any other pueblo. Bugles and snare drums were military features at vespers and masses on settlements' major feast days, Adams and Chavez tell us, along with the firing of muskets and cannon. At some pueblos a snare drum, not the Indian drum, was (and is) beaten on patron saints' days. At Santo Domingo "the snare drum is still accompanied," they note, "by a battered, screeching bugle."

Here Fray Francisco again took exception to Miera's art, an oil painting of Our Lady of the Conception, bought by a former missionary, and a bulto of patron Santo Domingo, bought by the Indians. The oil "was painted by an incompetent craftsman, but it serves for devotional purposes. . . . And my statement about the said painting will indicate that [the bulto] is not very fine."

Santo Domingo had "a very fine view in all directions, made pleasant by the river and its woods and poplar groves." Though Domínguez didn't note that the fine view could be a defensive one, he added that the whole pueblo was "surrounded

173

by a rather high adobe wall with two gates . . . for resistance against the enemy, for day by day they show more daring against the natives of this kingdom."

The 528 Santo Domingos were Keres-speaking, Domínguez, with a musical ear, observing that they were called Chachiscos because their dialect commonly employed the syllables *cha, chis* and *cos*. "Truly it is the prettiest and easiest of all the languages in these regions."

Don't look for the two churches Fray Francisco described. They and part of the pueblo were swept away by a churning Rio Grande in 1886. Today's church was built in the early 1890s. And a new plaza is the scene of perhaps the most impressive of all New Mexico's pueblo ceremonial dancing, chanting and drumbeating.

One wonders if there were mass and pueblo ritual for our wayfarers on New Year's Day.

January 2, 1777

THEY CUT EAST-NORTHEAST, leaving the Rio Grande, and probably ascended the five hundred-foot-high La Bajada (The Descent) Mesa. In their time this was known as La Majada, which means a natural overnight shelter for sheep. A one-letter change in spelling after 1800 was influenced by a local euphemism, Fray Angelico tells us. "Since 'majada' sounded very much like a common Spanish word for excrement, it was used — to give one example — for the load with which a child soiled his pants or diaper. Then it was extended to mean a *faux pas*, but it still sounded vulgar, as when we say in English that a person makes a boo-boo. This, no doubt, hastened the metamorphosis. . . ."

A four-lane highway today climbs the escarpment about four miles east of our expedition's presumed route. To New Mexicans it is known as La Bajada Hill.

". . . we arrived at the Villa de Santa Fe."

January 3, 1777

TO GOVERNOR MENDINUETA, "We presented this diary, the token of the Lagunas of which mention is made, and the Laguna Indian [Joaquín]. And because everything stated in this diary is true and faithful to what happened and was observed in our journey, we signed it in this mission [St. Francis]. . . ."

Fray Francisco Atanasio Domínguez
Fray Silvestre Vélez de Escalante

. . . we arrived at the Villa de Santa Fe.

174

THE REVELATION

A MAGNIFICENT FAILURE?

In groping with the "mysterious regions" the Dominguez-Escalante expedition had pierced a route "through country as difficult as any" in the future United States, as the widely traveled Bernard DeVoto saw it — some of which "may fairly be called the most difficult." Despite mountain, canyon and fierce river, no shattering of limb, no loss of life; despite dispute and sullen disagreement, no breakdown in unity and command. New Indians aplenty but, "without noise of arms," none of the carnage that would bloody the thrust of Manifest Destiny. What had our expedition contributed to Spain's desperate effort to solidify territory — their last-gasp Winning of the West?

No road was opened from Santa Fe to Monterey.

The firmest of commitments flouted, no fathers and Hispanos were sent to the Utes and Paiutes.

The Hopis continued as obdurate as ever.

The Havasupais and more westerly tribes were not even visited.

Of stated objectives, aside from mingling with previously unvisited Indians, only the mysterious colony was reached. Or was it?

Of unstated objectives, undiscovered was magnificent Copala-Teguayo, unseen the Great Sea of the West, unprospected the Sierra Azul.

Ah, but this exception: the Great River — nay, Great Rivers — of the West!

Nor would little Spanish effort come of the struggles and wonderment experienced by our twelve men and the Laguna lad Joaquín. It was as though Columbus had made his first momentous voyage, then failed to sail back those three times more; as though Spain, once having heard of the admiral's tropical islands and strange peoples, had lost all curiosity and interest.

Symptomatic of Spanish lethargy toward the expedition, its diary took its time getting on the way to higher authority. Don Bernardo de Miera y Pacheco, in his report to Carlos III, spoke of "the map drawn by me and enclosed with the diary that we are sending to Your Majesty" by order of New Mexico Governor Mendinueta. Miera's report, written in Chihuahua, was dated October 26, 1777. Perhaps Don Bernardo himself had carried the diary and map that far while riding there on personal business. Their receipt was officially noted at Chihuahua on July 30. In further time they were transmitted through Mexico City, where Viceroy Bucareli presumably had a copy transcribed of each, and sent on to Madrid.

Why, given the weight that Bucareli had attached to the "mysterious regions," were the Spaniards so numb to the expedition's new lands?

Spain, in her spun-out antagonism toward Protestant Britain, was being drawn into the American Revolutionary War, thereby draining imperial resources. New Spain, in her defense of the borderlands, was ever more occupied by the Comanches, Apaches and other nomads, further draining the colony's resources. There was no money for new official expeditions, none for new missions, presidios and settlements to the farther north. In those jingoistic mercantilist days the truism held as true as in later world capitalist days: You can't make money without investing money.

From the outset of the American Revolution Spain opened her continental and Caribbean ports to patriot privateers and provided the colonists with credit for arms. Spanish munitions moved from the Spanish Main to New Orleans, then up the Mississippi and on to revolutionists on the Ohio River. The Spaniards incited Southern Indian allies against Tory settlements and offered sanctuary to American rangers who entertained the same military objectives.

By 1776 frontier crises had become so critical that Carlos III removed the borderlands from viceregal control and set up a Comandancia General de las Provincias Internas. It was a reform pushed by Visitor-general José de Gálvez, now minister of the Indies. Named commanding general, viceroy in all but title, was the French-born El Caballero Teodoro de Croix, a Spanish soldier-politician.

Croix next year reached Chihuahua, temporary capital of the Deepest Provinces. By then Juan Bautista de Anza, not only back from San Francisco but fresh from new victories in Sonora, had been appointed governor of New Mexico to succeed Mendinueta. Anza thus came under Croix's command.

In the geopolitical shuffle New Mexico lost its proud title of kingdom to become a mere province and Anza had to make do without the title captain-general for an eventual full colonelcy. But Santa Fe remained a capital and Anza, by whatever nomenclature, would prove to be the greatest Indian fighter and ablest peacemaker in all New

Mexico's history down to and through the days of U.S. generalship.

Of solemn promises to the Utes and Paiutes, not a further word is recorded in known official papers. Domínguez' conscience being what it was, the only answer can be that such communication has been lost or not yet discovered. We can be sure he was driven to lamentation. Did the Utes conclude, as the friars had warned they might, "that we had intentionally deceived them"?

With only twenty-nine priests in the custody, Governor Mendinueta had been sustained in that question that had so perturbed Domínguez: "How can there be any for those [Indians] that may be newly conquered?" There patently were none to release for new missions. True, Anza in 1778 would shepherd eighteen new friars to the New Mexico custody when he took over as governor. With solace required at beleaguered existing missions, none of these padres could be expended, from all evidence, for the farther north.

Meantime, Domínguez had been elevated to custodian of New Mexico's Franciscans and returned from Santa Fe to El Paso del Norte. He had chosen trusted Escalante as vice-custodian with headquarters at San Ildefonso Pueblo. Mindful of Provincial Murillo's admonition to "avoid all noisy judicial proceedings," Domínguez now lamented to his superior in Mexico City: "Jupiter rains calamities upon me, but with the favor of Heaven I keep insisting that there is a remedy for everything and that it can be applied without making a din."

A din he had been making, nevertheless. His visitations had stirred some priests, angered by his high standards and decisive reforms, to forment trouble for him. They presented "even risk to my own life"; one priest "took the liberty of drawing his knife from his pouch and speaking his mind." Charges against Domínguez, their nature unknown, were forwarded to Mexico City. Malicious rumors, details also unknown, reached El Caballero de Croix in Chihuahua.

Yet Domínguez' conscience demanded rectification of wrongs. "And what nature will be necessary for this? That of a Nero or Caligula, not my own tender and compassionate one that truly loves my brethren."

In due course Domínguez' visitation papers had reached his provincial headquarters in Mexico City. His title page bears these remarks in an unidentified hand and probably of a later date:

> Report that is intended in part to be a description of New Mexico, but its phraseology is obscure, it lacks proportion, and offers little to the discriminating taste.

This superior and acid tone — so much for what historians today regard as the most informative single document on eighteenth-century New Mexico. It was filed away and forgotten. Perhaps miracle is not inappropriate to describe its survival through turbulent, anticlerical generations to be stashed among bundles of unsorted papers at the National Library of Mexico. Here in 1928 it was discovered, thick with dust, by Dr. France V. Scholes. This distinguished historian at once recognized its significance. It is to be hoped that the diligence of future Dr. Scholeses will be rewarded with documents that may answer some of the many questions raised by our expedition's diary and ensuing related events . . . parchments, if you will, such

as those of another era dug out of Palestinian caves not long ago. Evidence is ample that there are more than a few Spanish "Dead Sea Scrolls" yet to be sifted through.

One of Escalante's first acts as vice-custodian was to issue, on Domínguez' orders, a *patente*, or "official letter," on their joint "scheme of government" in New Mexico. This found Fray Silvestre, now about twenty-seven, pronouncing strictures on missionaries who for the most part were much his senior in an obedient effort to get many to mend their ways. Among them:

With Franciscans committed to "sublime poverty," any kind of trade — in boys, girls, pelts, whatever — "is an intolerable abuse and clear violation of it."

Indian labor beyond that required for food and other services "to eke out our existence" should not be forced and Indians should not be punished for resistance to it, for it would be "natural for them in their rusticity not only to abhor the minister but even to conceive no little repugnance for Christianity."

Finally, since as priests "we do not cease to be fragile men," no women should be permitted in a rectory or visited at home who are "suspect either because of their youth or beauty, or, finally, because of their customs and ill fame."

In the winter of 1777–78 Escalante visited Domínguez in El Paso, probably to confer over their continuing concern with such laxity as Fray Silvestre had proscribed in his patente. Whatever the consequences, they were determined to drive the clerical moneychangers out of the temple that was New Mexico.

Beyond direct clerical concerns, Escalante had been contributing more to posterity's knowledge by making

179

notes from Santa Fe archives on New Mexico's history and geography. This was done at the bidding of Fray Juan Agustín Morfi, an early day war correspondent, who in turn was recording his own observations while traveling with Commanding General Croix along the northern frontier. Father Morfi wrote prolificly. Fray Silvestre's research for him, published in part in the nineteenth century, has been a useful historical tool.

Of his vice-custodian's effort, Domínguez wrote Provincial Murillo that Escalante "served the king by spending some time in searching the government archive, and although Lord Mendinueta wanted to certify to this, the father did not permit it because of the rumors that many of the religious [missionaries] were already spreading about him." What these rumors were Fray Francisco didn't state but Escalante's association with him obviously was tarring Fray Silvestre with the same brush of reprisal.

Domínguez also wrote Murillo asking approval to name Escalante vicar and ecclesiastical judge, a position vacant "because of the irregular refusal of my predecessor" to fill it. For want of the judicial authority vested in the office, "souls have suffered the evils" of clerical misconduct. Nothing came of this request, perhaps because Murillo himself shortly was replaced.

Domínguez begged Provincial Murillo "once, twice and thrice" to allow him to resign. He quoted St. Francis, "I do not wish to be my brothers' executioner." He was losing "the serenity and peace of mind which I so greatly need." And "my eyesight is nearly gone, especially in my left eye which I think is going to lose it."

Fray Francisco was still in El Paso in October, 1778, by which time another custodian had indeed arrived. A letter

of that month is our last direct word from him for over seventeen years. "I have been deeply disturbed," he wrote the new provincial, "by the realization that my faithful conduct [is considered] superfluity. . . ."

For Miera, no glory, not to mention gold. Abasement even, all those unkind things said about him by the two friars. Thick-skinned, Don Bernardo seems, in having trumpeted the expedition diary to his monarch.

Yet no map drawn previous to the expedition's "prodigious exploratory *tour de force*," writes Carl I. Wheat in his *Mapping the Transmississippi West*, "offered even a fraction of the broad and remarkably accurate coverage that Miera was able to include on his map in respect to a vast, newly-discovered — though only partially understood — area of the American West."

Actually, there are seven recognized manuscript versions of the Miera expedition map. Of these, six were known when Wheat wrote his treatise in 1957. He broke these down, from their ornamentation, into the undeco-

---

The map on the opposite page is one of seven known versions of the Domínguez-Escalante Expedition route inspired by expedition member Don Bernardo de Miera y Pacheco. From the Archivo General in Mexico City, it is of the Bearded Indian type, as can be seen from the drawing at left-center, and the original may be a Miera original. This reproduction appeared with Dr. Herbert E. Bolton's Pageant in the Wilderness, *published in 1950, and is reprinted here with copyright permission of the Utah State Historical Society. Bolton apparently had the map hand-copied rather than photographed, according to Carl I. Wheat in his* Mapping the Transmississippi West. *In so doing the University of California professor sought to improve on it by correcting a misspelled* LAUNA *in the legend* LAGUNA DE LOS TIMPANOGOS *and* LACUNA *in* LAGUNA DE MIERA. *Also Bolton's reproduction has more color painted onto some of the lakes, around the frame of the title cartouche and on what is the Pope's lion-drawn chariot. Miera's legends are translated in part in the text of this volume.*

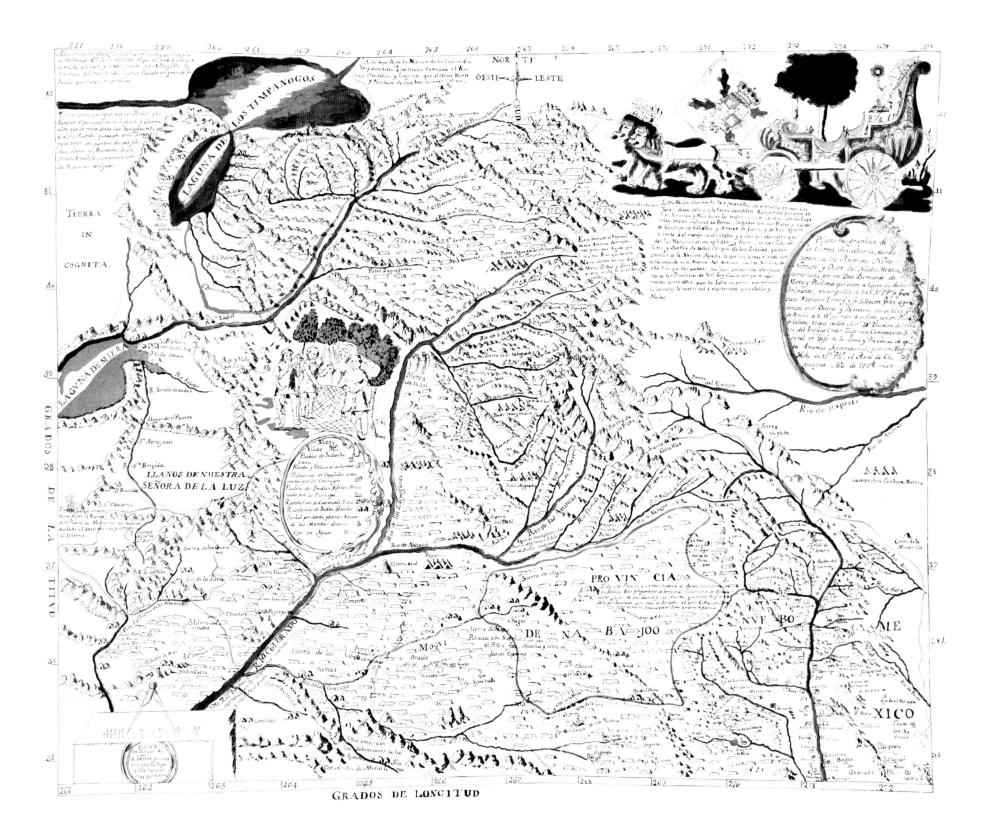

rated (one version), tree and serpent (one version) and Bearded Indian (four versions). Aside from decoration, all differ to a minor extent in inscriptions and geographical minutiae — and in that the undecorated version is dedicated to Viceroy Bucareli while all the others are to Commanding General Croix. The seventh manuscript map, an undecorated version, was acquired by Yale University from a private collection.

None of the maps is signed. Copyists did much of the cartography in those days from earlier versions of a map or sketches furnished by the original cartographers. Of his six, Wheat believes that the undecorated version and one of the Bearded Indian types, the latter specifically declaring the region to have been "surveyed by me," are possible, perhaps probable, Miera originals.

Both are held by the British Museum, doubtless having been obtained, says Wheat, because "for centuries British diplomats and naval officers assiduously collected such documents, wherever they appeared." Espionage has a long history. Other manuscript copies are with the Ministry of War in Madrid, the Archivo General in Mexico City and the Library of Congress (two).

For more than a century no version of Miera's expedition map was published, though other cartographers studied one or another version with, as has been intimated, dynamic consequences. Only in our times have his maps been recognized for the masterpieces they are.

In Miera's letter to the king, we recall, he had recommended presidios at the Ánimas–San Juan junction, Utah Lake and the Gila's confluence with the Colorado. The latter presidio would serve as a way station from Sonora to California, "protect and aid the converted tribes in its vicinity," facilitate communications among it, Utah Lake and New Mexico and, of utmost urgency, "check the ravages" of the Apaches to the east.

Further, Don Bernardo recommended driving the Western Apaches toward the Buffalo Plains where they and the Comanches, "the two most obnoxious tribes," would "soon destroy each other." To this end he urged auxiliary military outposts eastward in Arizona on the Gila, on the Mimbres River near present Santa Rita, New Mexico, and on the Rio Grande north of El Paso. For himself he volunteered command of the Mimbres outpost: "I do promise (God giving me life and health) that in the term of three years . . . to give quiet and peace . . . and to have three settlements established and at least one mine of gold, silver, and copper discovered and in operation." In our day Santa Rita has become the scene of huge open-pit copper-mining operations.

Don Bernardo concluded by telling the king he was taking the liberty of presenting to El Caballero Teodoro de Croix "a copy of this plan for his use." The fact seems to be — his dedication of manuscript maps to the commanding general is broad evidence — that he was in Chihuahua job-hunting.

As has been evidenced throughout this book, Miera was not one to hide his talents under his sombrero. "But we shouldn't judge him too harshly for that," counsels Miera-aficionado Michael F. Weber of the Museum of New Mexico. "Up here in the beyond, one had to speak up to be heard by faraway officials."

Speak up though he might, Miera seems to have been rejected by close-at-hand Croix. Possibly he was deemed too old for the front lines. Old soldiers even then just faded away.

Miera sent another letter to the king, undated and undatelined. Using the third person, he wrote of having "passed the best part of his youth in the service of Your Majesty without ever receiving any recompense. . . ." He appears now to have been hurting financially as he "supplicates" for "one of the captancies to be created " (by Croix?), for command of the New Mexico militia "with a salary for his maintenance" or for "any other capacity Your Majesty may consider suited to him." At the same time, for a son Don Anacleto who had soldiered for sixteen years, he begged "promotion to an official rank."

Neither request seems to have been honored or even acknowledged.

From the Miera-cited Gila-Colorado junction Anza in 1776 had escorted the Yumas' ever-helpful Salvador Palma to Mexico City, where the chief was lionized and was baptized in the great cathedral on the Zócalo. At Palma's continued urging, Spanish presence was established on orders from Croix three years later in a mission and settlement at Yuma and another eight miles downstream. No Miera-posited presidio was built at either site but cabins for about ten soldiers were thrown up at each. Father Garcés betook himself to the Yuma mission-settlement. Still no apparent premonition.

All the while colonists, some three hundred en toto, were moving up the Anza Trail through Yuma. While they buttressed Spanish control of California, settlements there belied a prediction of our old acquaintance José de Gálvez: not only did they not produce royal revenue but they ran a deficit on the empire's exchequer. It was not a proposition which could be supported for long.

As for that other decade-ago prediction by the present minister of the Indies, an amiable count would make "Russian aggression" felt by sailing into San Francisco Bay in 1806 and getting himself involved in a tragic romance with a señorita. Six years later a Russian trading post was set up eighty-five miles north. Though such trade was offi-

cially banned, local Hispano officials winked at and welcomed it. It was *tovarish* and *compadre*.

The last we hear directly from Miera is a celebrated map of New Mexico he drew on Anza's orders in 1779. Apparently a solicitous Anza had given him a fulltime job, for Don Bernardo bylined himself as an Exempt Soldier of the Royal Presidio of Santa Fe. An "exempt soldier" was one of the noble or upper classes who had lacked the funds to pass through military college but enjoyed such officer privileges as wearing a sword and being exempt from garrison chores.

After doing what he could to shore up New Mexico pueblo and settlement defenses, Anza made his first order of business to break the Comanches. To do this he must first break Cuerno Verde — Green Horn for his headdress. He would attack this most formidable of Comanches even as the chief was coming down from southern Colorado to attack New Mexico. And rather than campaign head-on, northeastward beyond the Taos Mountains as was historic wont, he would surprise Cuerno Verde by striking, Indian style, at the Comanches' rear flank with great hopes of success.

With some six hundred troops, militia and Indian allies, Anza in August, 1779, moved up the Rio Grande's west bank and on to the Arkansas River, the first recorded Hispano use of this route. The campaigners climbed the Rockies' Front Range just south of Pike's Peak. Espying Comanche quarry from the heights, they overwhelmed a ranchería of about one hundred twenty lodges in the foothills. Cuerno Verde indeed had left recently to raid New Mexico, Comanche prisoners said.

Three days south near modern Pueblo, Colorado, the New Mexicans caught up with the fully accoutered Cuero Verde, "his horse curvetting spiritedly," and a bodyguard of fifty warriors. Trapped in a forested ravine, the Comanches dropped behind their horses and made "a defense as brave as it was glorious," said Anza. Green Horn was slain. The commander had administered to the Comanches their most telling defeat ever.

En route home the campaigners shortly crossed the Arroyo de la Sangre de Cristo, the first recorded use hereabout of what would become the designation for the Sierra Madre.

In this same 1779, a year after ally France's declaration, Spain went to war in part "to drive the English from the Gulf of Mexico and neighborhood of that province [Louisiana Territory]," said Minister of the Indies Gálvez, "liberating ourselves by this means of the damage to our commerce and national security in which their ambitious designs keep us." Aside from resources mandatory to contain the nomads on the borderlands, Gálvez decreed that all of New Spain's available funds, talent and vessels be channeled into this war effort. A war fund drive was begun throughout New Spain, impoverished New Mexico itself contributing a substantial 3,677 pesos.

Unlike France, Spain did not enter the war as a formal ally of the East Coast colonists. She was beginning to be stung by malcontents in her own colonies. To rally to the cry for independence, Heaven forbid! The war would exhaust these other Americans or their federation would dissolve in bickering. If not, they surely could be picked off

later. Above all, this half-nation must not be permitted itself to expand to Spain's American heartland.

By this time, incidentally, Spain had been filched of those long-sought mid-Pacific havens Rich in Gold and Rich in Silver. Far-sailing Captain James Cook discovered them for Britain in 1778, though their native Hawaiians did him in on a return voyage the next year.

Anza, upon return from his Comanche triumph, learned that the Hopis were in dire straits from drouth, disease and Ute and Navajo depredations. They were taking to the hills, even uniting with their enemies, including Apaches, to stay alive. Attuned to Domínguez and Escalante, the colonel saw succor as a means to attain their reconversion and resubjugation.

Through a priest Anza offered the Hopis supplies and an alternate settlement site along the Rio Grande near Socorro. To Commanding General Croix he cited Escalante as the most recent person to have inspected "carefully and efficiently" the Hopi province and sent copies of those Escalante reduce-and-relocate recommendations with which we are familiar. From Fray Silvestre's "piety, energy of mind, and zeal" and from other reliable reports, the colonel agreed with proposals the friar "advances to oblige [the Hopis] by force to return to the old dominion of both kings," Heavenly and temporal. Meantime, in fact, Hopi refugees had begun to arrive amid New Mexico's pueblos.

Go to the Hopis, Croix ordered Anza. Take Escalante "if he is in the province." But temper your proposals to Hopi mood. We don't want to see them forming an alliance — against which former Governor Mendinueta had warned — with the Utes, Navajos and Apaches. What we want is their friendship and agreement to our siting a presidio among them. Attainment of these ends, Croix said, would help surround the Apaches, open communications with Sonora and California, allay the Havasupais and offer a good example to the Utes and Navajos.

In December, 1778, Escalante had baptized, in Santa Fe, a two-year-old Apache girl taken in battle. Records also show that in February, 1779, he performed a marriage in the capital. By then he probably had lost his title of vice-custodian along with Domínguez' resignation. And in 1779 he was relegated again to Zuñi, with an assistant.

For "A prophet is not without honor, save in his own country" substitute "religious jurisdiction" for the latter phrase. Fray Silvestre had been esteemed, if not always agreed with, by Mendinueta, Bucareli, Anza and Croix. His research had provided much of the contents of observer Father Morfi's *Descripción Geográfica del Nuevo México*, completed in 1782. In this work Morfi praised Escalante for his contribution and made a couple of singular allusions to him. In an arroyo near Santa Cruz "a ball of silver the form and size of an egg was found. Having been mixed with quicksilver, this was separated from the silver in the presence of the [former] Señor Governor, Don Pedro Fermín de Mendinueta, of Fray Silvestre Vélez Escalante and various others to the surprise of all, since no one had used quicksilver in all the kingdom."

Again, "In the mission of Zuñi which I administered, the principal altar having been made, that is to say, *el Covate*, the Indians furnished to my companion who was Fray Silvestre Vélez de Escalante as much Prussian blue as he needed without more cost or labor than gathering it up from a mineral river which they had discovered."

Despite the title of Father Morfi's work, there is no other record that he ever visited New Mexico. Apparently he had indeed gone at least to Zuñi, perhaps purposely to visit his correspondent Escalante. Morfi's meaning and syntax are not always of the clearest. By "administered" he may have meant that he took over for a few days during an Escalante illness — too short a time for his name to have appeared on Zuñi's baptismal, marriage or burial registers. As for *el Covate*, there is no such word in the New Spain or New Mexico lexicons. "Probably it was an altar cloth of blue," says historian Alfred Barnaby Thomas, "used on certain feast days."

In this *Geographical Description* Father Morfi would say the final word on Escalante: "Despite his youth, among the most meritorious of the Custody because of his talent, his erudition, his hard labors, and above all because of his virtues, which led him to sacrifice his hopes, health, and life for the conversion of those souls, for, going back to the Province [Mexico City] to recover his health, he died at Parral [a town on the Camino Real] in April, 1780." Escalante's end had come at about thirty years of age.

As even more Hopi refugees came to the pueblos, Anza set forth in September, 1780, with 126 men — Escalante lamentably unavailable — and provisions for Hopis still on their mesas. At Oraibi the cacique "had resolved to die here," he told the colonel, though he said all Hopis who wanted to leave with the Hispanos were free to do so.

Anza learned that the Hopis ironically blamed their sad state on their "ill-treatment [of] and haughty attitude" toward Father Garcés in 1776. The padre had predicted their present calamities as a consequence of their obduracy, they said. "Because of this they eulogized him." Of his old friend, Anza added: "I consider that this zealous religious has always merited it." This was, as we shall see, a fortuitous personal eulogy.

Compared with Escalante's 7 pueblos and 7,494 population, Anza counted 5 towns and only 738 Hopis remaining these 5 years later. Many left with the colonel, others remained . . . their descendants live here to this day.

No presidio was emplaced among the Hopis, probably because of the priority of military appropriations to that war far to the east. There the Spaniards fended off a British stab at seizing St. Louis and penetrating the Louisiana Territory in a strategy to encircle the colonies from the west. Spain in turn sought encirclement of the infant federation by raiding up the Illinois River, moving to the east bank of the Mississippi and capturing West Florida.

After all that talk about a road from New Mexico to Sonora, Anza finally traced one in late 1780. Avoiding the route proposed by Miera through Escalante because drouth plagued Zuñi country too, the colonel led 117 men down the Rio Grande to about present Caballo. The party swung southwest across the Mimbres Mountains and River, over the Hatchet Mountains in today's New Mexico Panhandle and on to Arispe, Sonora, to which Croix had moved his headquarters. The trip, which Anza estimated at 221 leagues, took 39 days. Anza thought that the Miera-Escalante route would cut the distance to 150 leagues. Not until 1795 would this road be tracked.

At Yuma soldiers and settlers abused the Indians and seized their lands over protests of Father Garcés and three other priests. The Hispanos proffering few expected gifts such as Anza had presented Chief Salvador Palma and his people, the padres could offer only the consolation of the church. None might recall Father Serra's prediction that the gentle Indians hereabout could "turn on us like tigers," though the padre who had urged "a large force of arms" here was back as a Garcés colleague.

When in July, 1781, cattle of a passing settlers' convoy trampled their mesquite beans, turn tiger the Yumas did. Chief Palma, torn between his people's anger and his own disposition, ordered that Garcés be spared. An apostate Christian stirred up the people against the priests: "If these remain alive, all is lost, for these are the worst!" They were clubbed to death, some forty soldiers and settlers slain, all women and children taken prisoner. Palma lifted Garcés body in his arms and wept. An appropriate epitaph for both: "Who will say that this Indian is a savage?"

While other Spaniards were able to ransom the captives the next year, they couldn't muster the power to punish the Yumas. Overland passage would be cut for about forty years. The California settlements once again had to rely on undependable sea communications.

The Yuma debacle having occurred within the Croix zone of command, the general, not the most sterling of characters, had to have scapegoats. Anza and even the dead, defenseless Garcés were responsible. Hadn't both led everyone to believe that Chief Palma and his Yumas were firm friends of the Spaniards? Overlooked by Croix were repeated warnings by the colonel that the Yumas, while friendly — yes, would remain so only if treated with friendship. Though whiffs of Croix's calumny reached Anza, he continued doing his duty in New Mexico.

Spain's attempted encirclement east of the Mississippi snapped when the 1783 peace treaty gave the American patriots all British territory west to the Mississippi and south of Canada. The Spaniards did flank the victors to the south by acquiring all of Florida.

Miera died in Santa Fe in 1785 without a hint of what his cartographic extravaganza would do to the Far West . . . unless by chance he had heard that in 1782 a certain Manuel Agustín Mascaro in Mexico City drew a map of Spanish North America incorporating his findings almost en toto.

Mascaro accepted the course of the San Buenaventura, though he robbed Miera of immediate posthumous fame by expunging his name from Sevier Lake. To the lake's west he depicted a river that Father Garcés had heard about from Indians in the San Joaquin Valley. This river, eventually the San Joaquin, became in effect a link between the lake and Father Crespí's San Francisco River. The Great River of the West.

Mascaro accepted Miera's opinion that streams rising north of the Colorado on the Rockies' west slope flowed to the Pacific. This concept would persist throughout the Spanish and Mexican periods and well into the United States era, molding Western exploration to its matrix.

In 1783 Croix, promoted to viceroy of Peru, was replaced by the governor of Alta California as frontier commandant. This successor persisted in Croix's back-stabbing. It was customary for officers to list their accomplishments in an annual service report. Anza was forbidden by the successor to cite his opening a trail to California; the honor was for the Baja California Indian who had accompanied his first expedition as a somewhat impotent guide. Again, Anza was told he could not list his victory over Cuerno Verde; this honor was for a subordinate soldier.

Anza was not alone a victim of such debasement, for Spain and her colonies were peculiarly hard on their pioneering heroes. Cortés had been denied the viceroyalty and demeaned by both Madrid and fellow conquistadores; Don Diego de Vargas, after reconquering New Mexico, had been dismissed and jailed. Spite, greed, envy . . . even churchmen were targets of malice in the Spanish Americas.

Up in Santa Fe, Anza pursed his lips, clenched his teeth and carried on — even after he was ousted as governor in the mid-1780s and forced, humiliatingly, to wait long for a replacement. Indeed, this was perhaps the finest hour of his career.

Now fighting the Apaches and Navajos, the colonel meantime was working a pacific will on the Comanches. "With kindness and rare political sagacity," epitomizes Thomas in his *Forgotten Frontiers*, the colonel "won their affection, reconciled them with their bitterest enemy, the Utes, and then bound both to Spanish power by a defensive and offensive alliance against the Apaches" in 1785–86. He forced the Navajos into this compact and to declare war on their Apache allies.

The colonel's peace with the Comanches would endure into United States times when Yankee savagery and blindness provoked them again to ride a bloody warpath against the white man.

Anza's gubernatorial relief finally arrived in late 1787. A final comedown, the colonel was reassigned to command his old, original presidio at Tubac. He may never have reached there, for the next year he dropped dead, at fifty-three, just as he rode into the frontier headquarters town of Arispe. He died with his boots on.

Anza's name all but faded from memory until historians began poring through archives over a century later. Gradually, his pre-eminent place was recognized in the frontier hall of fame. Proud and another Domínguez in his blunt suffering of lesser men, he surely was — but more than any frontiersman before and after he was acute, honest, rugged, persevering, visionary. Juan Bautista was a man.

While little fanfare would be made of the Domínguez-Escalante drama until modern times, their diary was not wholly overlooked.

The viceroy of 1791, seeking to pin down Spanish Pacific Coast claims as far north as the Vancouver Island region, saw a need for "discoveries overland from the port of San Francisco and from the presidio of Santa Fe." While awaiting royal approval, he said, he intended studying the Domínguez-Escalante papers. Did he find them as intriguing as we do?

The viceroy's expeditions were never more than a notion. After the French Revolution in 1789, Spain fell again into France's claws. A new alliance, a new declaration of war against Britain. With the rise of Napoleon, Spain became ever more a French pawn. All this was to the neglect of her colonial empire. In due course Napoleon forced her to cede most of the Louisiana Territory back to France. Hungry for martial sustenance, Napoleon sold the territory to the United States behind Spain's back in 1803.

Shortly the Domínguez-Escalante diary was cited again and often in *Pichardo's Treatise on the Limits of Louisiana*

and New Mexico. Therein a Father Pichardo sought "to disprove the claim of the United States that Texas was included in the Louisiana Purchase." With the extent of the Mississippi's watershed at diplomatic dispute, the priest included as appendices a copy of the diary and of a Miera map.

The map had been drawn in Chihuahua in 1778 and copied by a Father Vega in Mexico City, this priest-polemist wrote. "But, unfortunately, the said map . . . was very badly done." Whether Pichardo was referring to the original or to Vega's copy is unclear. ". . . a comparison of this map with the itinerary of Fathers Domínguez and Vélez . . . will show that they agree in very few points." Miera's directions and campsites are remarkably true to the diary. Whatever, Pichardo included the map "because it is the only one so complete."

Baron Alexander von Humboldt, perhaps the greatest scientific mind of his day, was privy to the diary while in New Spain from 1799–1804. Humboldt, a Prussian, cited it as reliable in his *Political Essay on the Kingdom of New Mexico*, published in 1811.

Domínguez had been correct in surmising that his faithful service was considered a "superfluity" in Mexico City. It merited him permanent exile on the frontier and permanent deprivation of advancement in his order. Records from provincial headquarters indicate that he was sent as chaplain to the Royal Presidio of Carrizal, in Chihuahua Province, soon after his resignation as custodian. Other provincial records show him assigned to Zia, Jémez and Santa Ana pueblos in 1788 and Isleta in 1791 though his name, for unexplained reasons, doesn't appear in registers of these missions. After that provincial archives place him at Janos presidio, again in Chihuahua. From there comes our last word from him.

To the provincial of 1795 Domínguez wrote of his twenty years as a missionary in New Mexico and chaplain at frontier presidios. "I now seek shelter under the beneficent shadow of your Very Reverend Paternity's wing and beg . . . that the status and exemptions of definitor may be granted and obtained for me, since I deserve it for the said period." A definitor was a member of a provincial's four-man council or an old-time custodian. There is no recorded reply to Fray Francisco's pathetic appeal.

The last time his name appears as chaplain at Janos is in 1800. The little further evidence available implies that he died before the spring of 1805 without ever having been permitted to return to the "delightful and alluring cradle" of his birth. He was about sixty-five.

While no priests or colonists were sent to the Utes, trading parties, licit or otherwise, continued to go among them.

In 1805 one Manuel Mestas of Abiquiu, a seventy-year-old genízaro interpreter of Ute, drew favorable comment from New Mexico's governor. Mestas recently had made three treks into Ute territory and recovered stolen horses and mules.

That same year the Lewis and Clark expedition came upon horses with Spanish brands, along with bridle bits and other trade goods, among Shoshones in central Idaho. A sergeant-diarist recorded that "it is only by their acct 8 day travel to the South to the Spanish country." Eight days' hard riding could have meant the Bear River, a major tributary to Great Salt Lake.

In 1813 seven Abiquiu traders traveled as far as Utah Lake. The governor, hearing of this, ordered them to tell the magistrate at Santa Cruz what had taken place. None gave any particulars on the route, an indication it was well-known by now. Testimony had it that the Lagunas would trade nothing but slaves "as they had on other occasions." The New Mexicans informing them that the present governor had banned such purchases, the Lagunas, no longer "docile," petulantly killed eight of the traders' horses. Farther along, those Bearded Indians, so affable of a generation ago, now stood with "their arms in their hands, saying their trade would be arrows." When the Hispanos overheard plotting to kill them (an indication they were familiar with the language), they spirited themselves away in dead of night. It appears that both Lagunas and Bearded Utes had been alienated, to use Domínguez' words, because "our people ordinarily play infamous tricks on them." There could have been mistreatment. En route home the Abiquiu traders lost a mule and horse to drowning in the Colorado, at what crossing they didn't say.

In 1803, even before President Jefferson had effected the Louisiana Purchase from Napoleon, he sent Captains Meriwether Lewis and William Clark to the Far Northwest, Spanish territory. They were especially to trace the Columbia River, recently discovered by sea, which Jefferson identified with the Great River of the West. They also were to be on the lookout for the Great Sea of the West.

In Mexico City meantime, Humboldt had seen, as well as the Domínguez-Escalante diary, cartographer Mascaro's map that had appropriated Miera's geography. To a map of his own the baron adapted much second-hand Miera detail, including the mountain-hopping San Buenaventura, Sevier Lake identified as Salt Lake with "western limits unknown" and Utah and Great Salt lakes combined as the

Timpanogos with an effluent he called the Yamparicas River.

En route home in 1804, Humboldt stopped off in Washington and presented a copy of his map to Jefferson. A diligent armchair explorer, the President doubtless was delighted. He gave Zebulon Montgomery Pike access to the Humboldt map before the lieutenant's exploration of the Southwest.

Like the Lewis and Clark mission, Pike's was to probe Spanish territory in further manifestation of Manifest Destiny. He sighted, though didn't climb or name, Pike's Peak in 1806. South of there he was picked up by a New Mexican detachment. Treated with courteous suspicion as the spy he was, Pike was marched to Santa Fe and on to Chihuahua, where he was released to make his way to the Gulf of Mexico and the United States East Coast. There in 1810 he published *A Map of the Internal Provinces of New Spain* that was almost identical with the Humboldt map, published the next year, and achieved comparable worldwide note.

Five years after their expedition's return, Clark in 1811 finished and published a map based on his and Lewis' observations and ideas of others. Clark preserved various Miera-Mascaro-Humboldt-Pike aberrations south of their trails. He further reflected Domínguez-Escalante-Miera geographical concepts in showing a "Rio de San Clementi" — too close to their San Clemente (White River) to be coincidental — flowing into an unnamed river, assumedly the San Buenaventura. This river in turn flowed into the "Multnomah" that today empties into the Columbia as the Willamette. Across this region is inscribed "Indians Yamparicas" near where Miera had indited "Cumanchis Yamparicas."

With the prestigious Humboldt, Pike and Lewis and Clark as exemplars, other cartographers were quick to copy and elaborate. One or another map would have four rivers, two from Lake Timpanogos (Utah-Great Salt) and two from Salado, Buenaventura or, yes, even Teguayo (Sevier Lake), debouching into San Francisco Bay, the Columbia River and numerous Pacific points.

The notion of other rivers died in time, "but that of the Buenaventura River became, finally, the most stubborn of the myths," as historian Morgan has it in his *The Great Salt Lake*. "It lasted longest, died hardest and left the most enduring impress on history. . . ."

So, though the expedition diary and Miera's maps would sit in the archives to wait long for the publishing, their contents were becoming widely known and winning over the famous.

Other myths also died stubbornly.

Teguayo . . . In 1834 what was left of this lake-kingdom was identified as Lake Teguayo of Salt in the vicinity of Sevier Lake by the responsible French cartographer Brué. A German cartographer's adopting Brué's designation was, however, the last Teguayo is heard of.

Sierra Azul . . . In 1780 Commanding General Croix had been urged by a civil assessor "to verify the discovery of mines of virgin quicksilver" within his command. While at Zuñi Escalante had "confirmed this information, vowing that he had even held some of the evidence in his hands," the assessor said. Fray Silvestre had "offered to avail himself of the information the Indians had given him and with them to look for it, provided the necessary troops be supplied him for the purpose. . . ." The assessor's statement probably was made without awareness that Fray Silvestre had died three months earlier.

In a two-century lifetime Sierra Azul would be situated

not only in the Zuñi-Hopi region but, among other sites, in New Mexico's west-central Datil Mountains, at Arizona's Sunset Crater and amid central Arizona ranges. In the latter Anglo sourdoughs would find those rich mines that Hispano generations had dreamed of.

The Mysterious Colony . . . Though our expedition would seem to have dispelled this myth in its encounter with the Bearded Indians, in 1811 a Santa Fe merchant named Don José Rafael Sarracino set out, according to a contemporary account, "to locate a Spanish settlement which the Yutas have always asserted lay beyond their territory, supposedly completely surrounded by wild Indians."

"After having traveled for three months, [Sarracino] was finally stopped by a large river. Among the Indians living there he found many articles manufactured by Spaniards such as knives, razors, and awls . . . [he was told] that the manufacturers of those articles lived across the river (somewhere between the north and west). Since they could not tell him exactly where he could cross the river, he decided to return home." This river could have been the Snake. Though no known Hispanos traded north of this Idaho-Oregon-Washington watercourse, British and Anglo-American fur companies did.

By the 1820s Mountain Men — Spanish, Anglo, French-Canadian — were trapping beaver and betimes exploring into Domínguez-Escalante country and far beyond to the west and north. The Miera-postulated rivers out of the Great Basin to the Pacific eluded them, but such other great rivers as the Bear and the Snake did come within their compass.

Antonio Armijo, as we have seen, opened a road from Abiquiu to the Four Corners and the Crossing of the Fathers in 1829–30. From the Virgin River, near our expedition's ford, the New Mexican trader and his companions blazed a southwesterly route through latter-day St. George and Las Vegas, then south of Death Valley. Near future Barstow they picked up the Garcés-pioneered route to San Gabriel mission and Los Angeles. After bartering wool blankets for horses and mules, they returned to New Mexico.

Domínguez-Escalante territory was penetrated in 1831 by a twenty-one-man trading party led from Taos by trader-trapper William Wolfskill. Slicing south of the padres' route, Wolfskill and company were the first to traverse what became known as the Old Spanish Trail to Los Angeles.

With many variants, this trail would follow our expedition's route to the Dolores, then verge northwest to cross the Colorado near Moab and the Green near Green River. At Castle Dale, the Old Spanish Trail veered southwest usually to follow the north-flowing Sevier River en route to Parowan. Thence it turned west to Newcastle and southwest to Las Vegas, where it picked up the Armijo trail.

The first emigrants from the United States to California set out from Kansas Territory expecting to find — incredibly, as late as 1841 — a salt lake "with two outlets, both running into the Pacific, either apparently larger than the Mississippi River." The Oñate-Miera Tizón in duplicate.

Headed by one John Bartleson, the party made its way with wagons over Wyoming's South Pass and on to Great Salt Lake. No navigable outlets. Thirty-two men, a wife and her baby set out over a route the Domínguez-Escalante expedition could have pursued. The terrain worsening, they deserted their wagons in Nevada desert and riding on, stumbled upon the Humboldt River, traced part of the California Trail-to-be, crossed the Sierra Nevada and made a terminus east of the San Joaquin-Sacramento junction and San Francisco.

Captain John C. Frémont — another spy in the sense of Lewis and Clark and Zebulon Montgomery Pike — intruded into much Spanish territory without invitation or permission. Of his second Far Western exploration (of four expeditions) he wrote about an 1843 visit to Great Salt Lake: "It was generally supposed that it had no visible outlet; but among the trappers, including those in my own camp, were many who believed that somewhere on its surface was a terrible whirlpool, through which its waters found their way to the ocean by some subterranean communication." This was a tale to beat even Miera's.

For his derring-do Frémont came to be called The Pathfinder. Some historical revisionists would make that The Pathmarker, for many of his trails had been or were found by those trappers he cited — the likes of Kit Carson, Jim Bridger and Tom (Broken Hand) Fitzpatrick.

Miera's concept still was utmost in the captain's mind when he wrote that in proceeding west from Great Salt Lake "I felt no other anxiety than to pass safely across the intervening [Nevada] desert to the banks of the Buenaventura."

But by the next year Frémont, camped beside Utah Lake near where the Domínguez-Escalante expedition had treated with the Lagunas sixty-eight years before, changed his mind. A map he would draw carried an inscription that this entire region was "surrounded by lofty mountains; contents almost unknown, but believed to be filled with rivers and lakes which have no connection with the sea." The Great Basin, he so named it.

Miera's day was finally done.

The Domínguez-Escalante diary, as extrapolated by Humboldt, was cited by a Lieutenant Gouverneur K. Warren in a report embodied in a voluminous official study of possible railroad routes to the Pacific published in 1859. While crediting the expedition with the first Spanish penetration of Utah, Warren caught such perpetuated Miera errors as Humboldt's accepting that Lake Salado (Sevier) "receives the waters of the Rio de San Buenaventura [the Green], its western limits being unknown." Nevertheless, while "the explorations of our government" have produced "more accurate results," the Humboldt account should not be neglected "as it has formed the basis of many classifications of the great mountain system." Miera's extrasensory perception of the Rockies.

The next year a summary of the diary was written for inclusion in a report by Captain James H. Simpson on his 1859 explorations in Utah. The abstracter was one Philip Harry of the Bureau of Topographical Engineers, who drew on a manuscript copy held by Peter Force, a Washington editor, historian and archivist. In a commentary Harry noted that at a bend of the Dolores were "some extensive and interesting ruins of an ancient Indian pueblo, which are pointedly adverted to both by Escalante and Captain Macomb." Here "the routes of Escalante and Captain Macomb diverge," the latter having gone on more directly west in 1859 to explore the Colorado.

"By many it has been supposed that Escalante called [the Santa Ysabel-Seviere] the San Buenaventura, and, moreover, that he asserted it to flow into the Pacific," Harry himself wrote pointedly. "So far from his saying that the Santa Isabel debouches into the Pacific, he merely states, on hearsay, that it enters a salt lake and emerges from it to run westwardly."

How a diary copy fell into the hands of Peter Force would be an intriguing trail for bibliophiles to track. Force's probably is the one now in the Library of Congress. Other manuscript copies are held by museums and libraries in Guadalajara, Madrid (two), Seville, London, Paris, Chicago and Berkeley, California.

Of what became of other members of our expedition, we know only that Laín died in 1799.

What of Joaquín? Our final word on the Laguna lad comes in Domínguez' letter to Provincial Murillo sent from Zuñi en route back to Santa Fe. That Joaquín had accompanied the party this far, said Fray Francisco, "has sweetened the inevitable bitter things that so long a journey offers, because we have now assured the safety of his soul."

Santa Fe baptismal records were searched long beyond 1777 by Dr. Myra Ellen Jenkins, New Mexico's state historian, at this writer's request. We found many Ute baptisms. Many Joaquíns. But none of the origin and age of our Joaquín. Perhaps he was baptized in another New Mexico community . . . to become yet another genízaro. Or conceivably he found his way back to Timpanogos either alone, given his self-reliance, or with one or another of those Hispano trading parties. His parting with his compadres of the road, especially with Fray Francisco, must have been wrenching.

And what of that buckskin token — the one depicting the ocher-bloodied chief and guide Silvestre — that the padres were to take back to the Lagunas? Was it in time thrown casually away? Or is it now in some old wooden chest? Is it, its saga unknown, even in some museum?

Some of our expedition's mysteries may be solved through discovery of more documents. Maybe the question of the buckskin token will be answered by a reader of this book.

A magnificent failure?

On the long trail of history the expedition made hardly a whit of difference. Miera's maps aside, on the shorter path of New Spain's being it made little more difference. Her own liberty bell pealing, New Spain would mutate into the United States of Mexico in 1821. Republican hopes then dissipated before turmoil and new dictatorships. In our Southwest the year 1846 and conquest by another United States was coming up fast.

Eight years before that one Frederick Wislizenus, a keen-eyed, sharp-minded traveler of the Southwest, had written: "A transformation of this remarkable country seems then at hand. . . . It is perhaps only a few years until the plow upturns the virgin soil, which is now only touched by the lightfooted Indian or the hoof of wild animals. Every decade will change the character of the country materially, and in a hundred years perhaps the present narratives of mountain life may sound like fairy tales."

Had the German-American Wislizenus been on hand in his "remarkable country" only until 1876 he would have seen what a transformation could be wrought. At our nation's 1976 bicentennial Wislizenus' perception has been vindicated far beyond Jefferson's, the President having reckoned the populating and developing of the West in terms of centuries.

The Hispanos of our expedition's day never could have done it. They lacked a sufficiency of what these days we call manpower, capital and know-how in a litany of cliches. Even as of today, compare conditions in Sonora and Chihuahua with those in New Mexico, Arizona and California to their north.

This is not to denigrate Mexico. Compare Anza's Comanche policy with his Anglo successors' treatment of Wislizenus' "lightfooted Indian." His "hoof of wild animals" — recall the decimation of our buffalo. Look upon our denuded mountains and sometime dust bowls where his "plow upturns the virgin soil." Witness our unneeded dams, bulldozed minerals, exer-extruding highways.

Wislizenus' "fairy tales" is in part as fit an appellation as any for sagas such as our expedition's. Today there are no exotic Indians to be approached for the first time, no golden cities and mysterious colonies, no great river and great sea. Do our moon landings, so mechanical, and penetrations of outer space, so robotistic, stir us as do the tales of old?

With no new earthly frontiers for us to explore we indeed turn back to those tales as romantic sustenance beyond the bread alone of assembly lines and "in" and "out" baskets. Thus the eternal pull of Homer's epics, of the chronicles about a Cortés and a Coronado, of the annals of a Kino, a Serra, a Garcés, of the journals of a Frémont in our West, a Stanley in Africa, a Lawrence in Araby . . . of the narratives of a Domínguez, Escalante, Miera and the vecinos, castas and genizaros on a road they couldn't have realized would one day be regarded as high adventure.

Not a failure, then, but a magnificent heritage, our 1776 expedition . . . its saga a fitting bicentennial gift from our earlier-day Americans of the West.

194

LA BIBLIOGRAFÍA

TWO SOURCES were essential to *Without Noise of Arms*, Dr. Herbert E. Bolton's *Pageant in the Wilderness, The Story of the Escalante Expedition to the Interior Basin, 1776*, and Eleanor B. Adams' and Fray Angelico Chavez' *Missions of New Mexico, 1776, A Description by Fray Francisco Atanasio Domínguez*.

Pageant in the Wilderness, translated, annotated and with an itinerary by Dr. Bolton, was published by the Utah State Historical Society, Salt Lake City, in 1950. The famed historian's last major work, it is, while vital, below the standard of such other Bolton volumes as are cited in the bibliography below. Fortunately, the diary has been retranslated by Fray Angelico Chavez for the Domínguez-Escalante State-Federal Bicentennial Committee and will be published by the Utah State Historical Society with an original Spanish version.

The diary is attenuated, simply because the route was so well known, for the early and latter days of the expedition. Domínguez, who wrote of visitations to all New Mexico missions, provided background on that part of the route the diary covered only scantly. Moreover, Fray Francisco wrote lengthily, as we have seen, on the peoples, cultures, geography and economy of New Mexico in historic 1776.

Missions of New Mexico, 1776, which includes other priceless contemporary documents, was long out of print after its publication by the University of New Mexico Press in 1956, and was available only through rare-book dealers at more than three times its original price. To meet a latent and growing demand, the New Mexico State Cultural Properties Review Committee has sponsored a new edition.

In the following bibliography, some material for *Without Noise of Arms* was gleaned from every book or article cited. Those marked with an asterisk (*) were particularly useful in coping with the diary's many unanswered questions. It is to be hoped that another bibliography some day may be compiled to include new documents that will have been discovered in Santa Fe, Mexico City, Madrid and other archives around the world.

*ADAMS, ELEANOR B., "Fray Silvestre and the Obstinate Hopi," *New Mexico Historical Review*, XXXVIII-2, Albuquerque, 1963.

———, "Letter to the Missionaries of New Mexico," *New Mexico Historical Review*, XL-4, Albuquerque, 1965.

———, "Writings of Silvestre Vélez de Escalante," *New Mexico Historical Review*, XL-4, Albuquerque, 1965.

*———, and CHAVEZ, FRAY ANGELICO, eds., *The Missions of New Mexico, 1776, A Description by Fray Francisco Atanasio Domínguez*, University of New Mexico Press, Albuquerque, 1956, reprinted 1975 for the New Mexico Cultural Properties Review Committee in cooperation with the State Planning Office.

ALTER, CECIL J., "Father Escalante and the Utah Indians," *Utah Historical Quarterly*, I-II, Salt Lake City, 1928–29.

———, "Father Escalante's Map," *Utah Historical Quarterly*, IX, Salt Lake City, 1941.

Arizona, A State Guide, Hastings House, New York, 1949.

AUERBACH, HERBERT S., "Father Escalante's Itinerary," *Utah Historical Quarterly,* IX, Salt Lake City, 1941.

————, "Father Escalante's Journal With Related Documents and Maps," *Utah Historical Quarterly,* XI, Salt Lake City, 1943.

————, "Father Escalante's Route," *Utah Historical Quarterly,* IX, Salt Lake City, 1941.

————, "Old Trails, Old Forts, Old Trappers and Traders," *Utah Historical Quarterly,* IX, Salt Lake City, 1941.

BAHTI, TOM, *Southwestern Indian Tribes,* KC Publications, Las Vegas, 1971.

BAILEY, JESSIE BROMILOW, *Diego de Vargas and the Reconquest of New Mexico,* University of New Mexico Press, Albuquerque, 1940.

BANCROFT, HUBERT HOWE, *History of Utah,* The History Co., San Francisco, 1889.

BANNON, JOHN FRANCIS, ed., *Bolton and the Spanish Borderlands,* University of Oklahoma Press, Norman, 1964.

BARNES, WILL C., *Arizona Place Names,* University of Arizona Press, Tucson, 1935.

BEAN, WALTON, *California, An Interpretive History,* Mc-Graw-Hill, New York, 1968.

BOBB, BERNARD E., *The Viceregency of Antonio María Bucareli in New Spain, 1771–1779,* University of Texas Press, Austin, 1962.

*BOLTON, HERBERT E., *Anza's California Expeditions,* 5 vols., University of California Press, Berkeley, 1930.

*————, *Coronado, Knight of Pueblo and Plains,* University of New Mexico Press, Albuquerque, 1964.

*————, "Escalante in Dixie and the Arizona Strip," *New Mexico Historical Review,* III-1, Albuquerque, 1928.

*————, *Pageant in the Wilderness,* Utah State Historical Society, Salt Lake City, 1950.

*————, *Rim of Christendom, A Biography of Eusebio Francisco Kino, Pacific Coast Pioneer,* Russell and Russell, New York, 1960.

————, *The Spanish Borderlands, A Chronicle of Old Florida and the Southwest,* Yale University Press, New Haven, 1921.

————, *Spanish Exploration in the Southwest, 1542–1706,* Scribner's, New York, 1916.

BOWMAN, J. N., and HEIZER, ROBERT F., *Anza and the Northwest Frontier of New Spain,* Southwest Museum, Highland Park, Calif., 1967.

*BOYD, E., *Popular Arts of Spanish New Mexico,* Museum of New Mexico Press, Santa Fe, 1974.

CARROLL, H. BAILEY, and HAGGARD, J. VILLASANA, eds., *Three New Mexico Chronicles,* Arno Press, New York, 1967.

CARTER, HARVEY LEWIS, *'Dear Old Kit,' The Historical Christopher Carson,* University of Oklahoma Press, Norman, 1968.

*CHAPMAN, CHARLES E., *History of California; the Spanish Period,* Macmillan, New York, 1921.

*CHAVEZ, FRAY ANGELICO, "The Kingdom of New Mexico" in *This Is New Mexico,* George Fitzpatrick, ed., Horn and Wallace, Albuquerque, 1962.

*————, *My Penitente Land,* University of New Mexico Press, Albuquerque, 1974.

*————, *Origins of New Mexico Families,* University of Albuquerque and Calvin Horn, Albuquerque, 1973.

*————, "Valle de Cochiti," *New Mexico Magazine,* LI-1/2, Santa Fe, 1973.

CHRISTIANSEN, PAIGE W., and KOTTLOWSKI, FRANK E., eds., *Mosaic of New Mexico's Scenery, Rocks, and History,* State Bureau of Mines and Mineral Resources, Socorro, N.M., 1967.

*Cline, Gloria Griffen, *Exploring the Great Basin*, University of Oklahoma Press, Norman, 1963.

Colorado, A Guide to the Highest State, Hastings House, New York, 1970.

*Cook, Warren L., *Flood Tide of Empire, Spain and the Pacific Northwest, 1543–1819*, Yale University Press, New Haven, 1973.

Cordova, Gilberto Benito, *Abiquiú and Don Cacahuate: Folk History of a New Mexican Village*, San Marcos Press, Los Cerrillos, N.M., 1973.

Corle, Edwin, *Listen, Bright Angel*, Duell, Sloan and Pierce, New York, 1946.

Crampton, C. Gregory, *Standing Up Country, The Canyon Lands of Utah and Arizona*, Knopf, New York, 1964.

*———, and Griffen, Gloria C., "The San Buenaventura, Mythical River of the West," *Pacific Historical Review*, XXV-2, University of California Press, Berkeley and Los Angeles, 1956.

Curtin, L. S. M., *Healing Herbs of the Upper Rio Grande*, Southwest Museum, Los Angeles, 1965.

Cushing, Frank H., *My Adventures in Zuñi*, Felter Press, Palmer Lake, Colo., 1967.

*———, *The Nation of the Willows*, Northland Press, Flagstaff, Ariz., 1965.

Dawson, J. Frank, *Place Names in Colorado*, Dawson Publishing Co., Denver, 1954.

*DeVoto, Bernard, *The Course of Empire*, Houghton Mifflin, Boston, 1960.

Dodge, Natt N., *Flowers of the Southwest Deserts*, Southwest Parks and Monuments Association, Globe, Ariz., 1973.

The Encyclopedia Americana, Americana Corp., New York, 1953.

Engelhardt, Zephyrin, *The Missions and Missionaries of California*, 4 vols., James H. Barry Co., San Francisco, 1908.

*Espinosa, Jose Manuel, "The Legend of Sierra Azul," *New Mexico Historical Review*, IX, Albuquerque, 1934.

*Euler, Robert C., *Southern Paiute Ethnohistory*, University of Utah Press, Salt Lake City, 1973.

Fewkes, J. Walter, *Prehistoric Villages, Castles, and Towers of Southwestern Colorado*, Smithsonian Institution, Washington, 1919.

Folmer, Harry, *Franco-Spanish Rivalry in North America, 1524–1763*, Arthur H. Clarke Co., Glendale, Calif., 1953.

*Forbes, Jack D., *Apache, Navaho and Spaniard*, University of Oklahoma Press, Norman, 1971.

*Frazier, Russell G., "El Vado de los Padres," *Desert Magazine*, III, El Centro, Calif., 1940.

*Garces, Fray Francisco, *A Record of Travels in Arizona and New Mexico, 1775–1776*, John Galvin, ed., John Howell–Books, San Francisco, 1967.

Gerhard, Peter, *A Guide to the Historical Geography of New Spain*, Cambridge University Press, London, 1972.

Gillmor, Frances, and Wetherill, Louisa Wade, *Traders to the Navajos, The Story of the Wetherills of Kayenta*, University of New Mexico Press, Albuquerque, 1965.

*Goetzmann, William H., *Exploration of Empire*, Vintage Books, New York, 1972.

The Grand Colorado, The Story of a River and Its Canyons, T. H. Watkins, ed., American West, Palo Alto, Calif., 1969.

Gregg, Andy, *Drums of Yesterday: The Forts of New Mexico*, Press of the Territorian, Santa Fe, New Mexico, 1968.

GUNNERSON, DOLORES A., *The Jicarilla Apaches*, Northern Illinois University Press, DeKalb, 1974.

*HACKETT, CHARLES WILSON, ed., *Pichardo's Treatise on the Limits of Louisiana and Texas*, University of Texas Press, Austin, 1934.

*HAFEN, LeROY R., and HAFEN, ANN, *Old Spanish Trail, Santa Fé to Los Angeles*, Arthur H. Clarke Co., Glendale, Calif., 1954.

HAFEN, LeROY R.; HOLLON, W. EUGENE, and RISTER, CARL COKE, *Western America, The Exploration, Settlement and Development of the Region Beyond the Mississippi*, Prentice-Hall, Englewood Cliffs, N.J., 1970.

HAMMOND, GEORGE P., and REY, AGAPITO, *Don Juan de Oñate, Colonizer of New Mexico, 1595–1628*, University of New Mexico Press, Albuquerque, 1953.

HARRINGTON, H. D. *Edible Native Plants of the Rocky Mountains*, University of New Mexico Press, Albuquerque, 1967.

*HARRY, PHILIP, "The Journeyings of Father Escalante . . ." in Simpson, Capt. J. H., *Report on Explorations Across the Great Basin of the Territory of Utah in 1859*, Govt. Printing Office, Washington, 1876.

*HILL, JOSEPH J., "Spanish and Mexican Exploration and Trade Northwest from New Mexico Into the Great Basin, 1765–1863," *Utah Historical Quarterly*, III-1, Salt Lake City, 1930.

HODGE, FREDERICK WEBB, *Handbook of American Indians North of Mexico*, 2 vols., Bureau of American Ethnology, Washington, 1907–10.

JUDD, NEIL M., *Men Met Along the Trail, Adventures in Archaeology*, University of Oklahoma Press, Norman, 1968.

KENNER, CHARLES L., *A History of New Mexican–Plains Indian Relations*, University of Oklahoma Press, Norman, 1969.

KIDDER, ALFRED VINCENT, *An Introduction to the Study of Southwestern Archaeology*, With an Introduction on Southwestern Archaeology by Irving Rouse, Yale University Press, New Haven, 1966.

KUBLER, GEORGE, *The Religious Architecture of New Mexico*, University of New Mexico Press, Albuquerque, 1972.

LAMB, SAMUEL H., *Woody Plants of New Mexico*, New Mexico Game and Fish Department, Santa Fe, 1971.

LAS CASAS, BARTOLOME DE, *History of the Indies*, Andrée Collard, ed., Harper and Row, New York, 1971.

LEIGH, RUFUS WOOD, *Five Hundred Utah Place Names, Their Origin and Significance*, Deseret News Press, Salt Lake City, 1961.

LLOYD, ALAN, *The Spanish Centuries*, Doubleday, Garden City, N.Y., 1968.

LUMMIS, CHARLES F., *The Land of Poco Tiempo*, University of New Mexico Press, Albuquerque, 1969.

*MACOMB, CAPT. JOHN N., *Report of the Exploring Expedition From Santa Fé, New Mexico, to the Junction of the Green and Grand Rivers of the Great Colorado of the West in 1859*, U.S. Engineer Department, Washington, 1876.

MADARIAGA, SALVADOR DE, *Hernán Cortés, Conqueror of of Mexico*, University of Miami Press, Coral Gables, Fla., 1942.

The Magnificent West, Crest of a Continent, American West, Palo Alto, Calif., 1973.

McHUGH, TOM, *The Time of the Buffalo*, Knopf, New York, 1973.

McNITT, FRANK, *Navajo Wars, Military Campaigns, Slave Raids and Reprisals*, University of New Mexico Press, Albuquerque, 1972.

*MORGAN, DALE L., *The Great Salt Lake*, University of New Mexico Press, Albuquerque, 1973.

*Morison, Samuel Eliot, *The Oxford History of the American People*, Oxford University Press, New York, 1965.

New Catholic Encyclopedia, McGraw-Hill, New York, 1967.

New Mexico, A Guide to the Colorful State, Hastings House, New York, 1962.

O'Neil, Floyd A., ed., *The Southern Utes, A Tribal History*, Southern Ute Tribe, Ignacio, Colo., 1972.

Ormes, Robert, *Guide to the Colorado Mountains*, Swallow Press, Chicago, 1972.

*Ortiz, Alfonso, *The Tewa World — Space, Time, Being and Becoming in a Pueblo Society*, University of Chicago Press, 1969.

Palmer, William R., "Paiute Indian Government and Laws," *Utah Historical Quarterly*, II, Salt Lake City, 1929.

———, "Utah Indians Past and Present," *Utah Historical Quarterly*, I, Salt Lake City, 1928.

Pearce, T. M., ed., *New Mexico Place Names, A Geographical Dictionary*, University of New Mexico Press, Albuquerque, 1965.

Perrigo, Lynn I., *The American Southwest, Its Peoples and Cultures*, Holt, Rinehart and Winston, New York, 1971.

*Pourade, Richard F., *Anza Conquers the Desert*, Copley Books, San Diego, 1971.

Powell, John Wesley, *The Exploration of the Colorado River*, University of Chicago Press, 1973.

*Priestley, Herbert I., *José de Gálvez, Visitor-General of New Spain, 1765–1771*, University of California Press, Berkeley, 1916.

Richardson, Rupert Norval, *The Comanche Barrier to South Plains Settlement*, Arthur H. Clarke Co., Glendale, Calif., 1933.

Rickett, Harold William, *Wild Flowers of the United States, The Southwestern States*, McGraw-Hill, New York, 1973.

Roca, Paul M., *Paths of the Padres Through Sonora*, Arizona Pioneers' Historical Society, Tucson, 1967.

*Santamaria, Francisco J., *Diccionario de Mejicanismos*, Editorial Porrua, Mexico City, 1959.

Scholes, France V., "Notes on Sandia and Puaray," *El Palacio*, XLII, Museum of New Mexico Press, Santa Fe, 1937.

*Schroeder, Albert H., "A Brief History of the Southern Utes," *Southwestern Lore*, XXX-4, Denver, 1965.

———, "Shifting for Survival," *New Mexico Historical Review*, XLIII-4, Albuquerque, 1968.

Simmons, Marc, *Witchcraft in the Southwest*, Northland Press, Flagstaff, Ariz., 1974.

*Sinclair, John L., "The Mustangs of Lucero Mesa," *New Mexico Magazine*, L-1/2, Santa Fe, 1971.

*Smith, Anne M., *Ethnography of the Northern Utes*, Museum of New Mexico Press, Santa Fe, 1974.

Southwest Indian Country, Arizona, New Mexico, Southern Utah and Colorado, Lane Books, Menlo Park, Calif., 1973.

*Spicer, Edward H., *Cycles of Conquest: The Impact of Spain, Mexico, and the United States on the Indians of the Southwest*, University of Arizona Press, Tucson, 1962.

Swadesh, Frances Leon, *Los Primeros Pobladores*, University of Notre Dame Press, Notre Dame, Ind., 1974.

*Thomas, Alfred Barnaby, *Forgotten Frontiers*, University of Oklahoma Press, Norman, 1969.

———, "Governor Mendinueta's Proposals for the Defense of New Mexico, 1772–1778," *New Mexico Historical Review*, VI-1, Albuquerque, 1931.

———, *The Plains Indians and New Mexico, 1751–1778*,

University of New Mexico Press, Albuquerque, 1940.

THOMPSON, GREGORY COYNE, *Southern Ute Lands, 1848–1899; The Creation of a Reservation*, Ft. Lewis College, Durango, Colo., 1972.

THOMPSON, LAURA, *Culture in Crisis, A Study of the Hopi Indians*, Russell and Russell, New York, 1973.

TILDEN, FREEMAN, *The National Parks*, Knopf, New York, 1970.

*TYLER, S. LYMAN, and TAYLOR, H. DARREL, "The Report of Fray Alonso de Posada in Relation to Quivira and Teguayo," *New Mexico Historical Review*, XXXII-4, Albuquerque, 1958.

Utah, A Guide to the State, Hastings House, New York, 1943.

*WALLACE, ERNEST, and HOEBEL, E. ADAMSON, *The Comanches, Lords of the South Plains*, University of Oklahoma Press, Norman, 1952.

*WARREN, GOUVERNEUR K., "Memoir to Accompany the Map of the Territory of the United States From the Mississippi River to the Pacific Ocean . . ." in *Reports of Explorations and Surveys to Ascertain the Most Practicable and Economical Route for a Railroad from the Mississippi River to the Pacific Ocean*, XI, B. Tucker, Washington, 1859.

*WATERS, FRANK, *The Book of the Hopi*, Viking, New York, 1963.

———, *The Colorado*, Rinehart, New York, 1946.

WEBER, DAVID J., *The Taos Trappers: The Fur Trade in the Southwest, 1540–1846*, University of Oklahoma Press, Norman, 1971.

WEBER, WILLIAM A., *Rocky Mountain Flora*, Colorado Associated University Press, Boulder, 1972.

*WHEAT, CARL I., *Mapping the Transmississippi West, 1540–1861*; Vol. 1, *The Spanish Entrada to the Louisiana Purchase, 1540–1804*, Institute of Historical Cartography, San Francisco, 1957.

¡GRACIAS!

Without Noise of Arms could not have been written without the friendship and inspiration of Fray Angelico Chavez of Santa Fe, the pre-eminent living authority on our Southwest's Spanish era. Fray Angelico read every line of the manuscript, caught the writer in lapses and suggested piquant interpolations.

My manuscript was similarly scrutinized and assiduously picked apart by Albert H. Schroeder, interpretive officer for the National Park Service's Southwest Regional Office, Santa Fe, and David H. Snow, curator of archaeology for the Museum of New Mexico, Santa Fe.

History is a fragile, controversial, and highly personal thing. Even primary sources — read by me in translation — lend themselves to discordant interpretation. I take sole responsibility for final formulation of opinions, sometimes at odds with those of my "board of advisers," in a book that is replete with whys and why nots.

Among others who helped, I thank Dr. Myra Ellen Jenkins, New Mexico's state historian, Santa Fe, whose brain is an infinity of facts; Dr. Bertha P. Dutton, director of the Museum of Navaho Ceremonial Art, Santa Fe, an authority on Indians prehistoric to present; Dr. Michael F. Weber, curator of history, Museum of New Mexico, Santa Fe, on expedition member Miera y Pacheco; Gilbert Wenger, archaeologist at Mesa Verde National Park, Colorado, on expedition-cited rock art; Polly Schaafsma, Arroyo Hondo, New Mexico, also on rock art.

And Natt N. Dodge, Santa Fe, on wildlife along the trail; Douglas B. Evans, National Park Service naturalist, Santa Fe, similarly; Drs. C. Gregory Crampton and David E. Miller, University of Utah, Salt Lake City, on the Utah route generally and the Crossing of the Fathers specifically; W. L. (Bud) Rusho, Bureau of Reclamation, Salt Lake City, similarly.

And John L. Sinclair, Bernalillo, New Mexico, on the expedition's horses; Dr. Don Rickey, Jr., Bureau of Land Management historian, Denver, on the Escalante Ruin; Monsignor Jerome Stoffel, Logan, Utah, on the expedition in Utah; John Crenshaw, editor of *New Mexico Wildlife,* Santa Fe, on this specialty; John V. Young, free lance writer, Los Alamos, New Mexico, on many facets of the expedition; and Dr. Marc Simmons, Cerrillos, New Mexico, on the evanescent Father Morfi.

My gratitude goes to Dr. Melvin T. Smith, director of Utah's Division of State History, Salt Lake City, and chairman of the Domínguez-Escalante State-Federal Bicentennial Committee, for copyright permission to include portions of Dr. Herbert E. Bolton's *Pageant in the Wilderness,* published by the Utah State Historical Society in 1950.

To track down source material, Virginia Jennings of the New Mexico State Library and Stephanie Eger of the Museum of New Mexico History Library, both in Santa Fe, expended time and energy far beyond that demanded of their positions.

Encouragement was given by Chris Krahling, director of the New Mexico American Revolution Bicentennial Commission, and Janie Chavez, formerly of the New Mexico Parks and Recreation Department.

Paul Weaver and James K. Howard of Northland Press offered invaluable advice and tough-minded criticism. Robert O. Jacobson of Northland Press puzzled through a bewildering assortment of maps to produce the refined expedition maps herein.

Albuquerqueans Wilson Hurley, our notable illustrator, and his lovely wife Rosalyn, were of constant good cheer. Their opinions helped mold and reinforce mine on the contentious but altogether gifted Miera y Pacheco, a leading character in our drama.

INDEX

France: 6, 7, 184, 188; arming of Indians, 76, 80; French and Indian War, 7; participation in American Revolution, 184
Franciscan Order: 116, 170, 178, 179
Francisco (Laguna chief): 77; *see also* Oso Colorado *and* Captain
Frazier, Dr. Russel G.: 147, 148
Fredonia, Arizona: 134
Frémont, John C.: 72, 107, 191, 192, 194
Frémont culture: 72, 94
Frémont people: 88
French and Indian War: 7
French Revolution: 188
Fruitland, town of: 96
Fuente de San Bernabé: 66
Full Beards: *see* Ute Indians
Full of Flowers River: *see* Rio Florido
Fur trade: 8, 16, 63, 191

Galisteo, New Mexico: 31
Galisteo Pueblo: 156
Gap, The: 153
Garcés, Father Francisco: 10–13, 15, 18, 22, 23, 25–28, 30, 32–35, 61, 69, 79, 98, 103, 110, 115, 123, 129, 132, 133, 154, 155, 183, 185–87, 191, 194
Geneva Convention: 166
Gila Apache Indians: *see* Apache Indians
Gila Bend, Arizona: 13
Gila River: 10–12, 22, 25, 182
Gileños: 12
Glen Canyon Dam: 143
Glen Canyon National Recreation Area: 143
Gobernador Canyon: 158
Gold: 4–6, 12, 56, 88, 124, 182
Golden Age of Spain: 4, 5, 8
Golden Cities of Quivira: 4, 31

Golden Gate: 26
Golden Hinde: 4
Gómez, Fray Fernando Antonio: 14, 21–23, 29, 75
Grand Canyon: 4, 20, 32, 59, 129, 140
Grand Lake: 85
Grand Mesa: 73, 83, 84
Grand River: 85, 90
Great American Desert: 71
Great Basin: 3, 40, 71, 97, 98, 113, 126, 191, 192
Great Plains: 4
Great River of Good Hope: 5
Great River of San Francisco: 11, 12
Great River of the West: 7, 12, 53, 85, 109–11, 113, 177, 187, 189
Great Salt Lake: 54, 108, 109, 111, 189–92
Great Salt Lake, The: 190
Great Salt Lake Valley: 107
Great Sea of the West: 12, 53, 72, 109, 177, 189
Great Slave Lake: 13
Green Horn: *see* Cuerno Verde
Green River: 90, 92, 94, 113, 191, 192; *see also* Rio de San Buenaventura
Gregg, Josiah: 89
Guadalajara: 21, 192
Gualpi: *see* Walpi
Guatemala: 116; Guatemalan apes, 9
Guide's Fountain camp: *see* La Fuente de la Guía
Gulf of California: 4, 8, 67
Gulf of Mexico: 8, 42, 67, 184, 190
Gunnison River: 30, 72–74, 84, 85; North Fork of, 74, 75; *see also* Rio de San Javier
Gunsight Butte: 146

Hancock, John: 32
Hannibal: 32

Hano Pueblo: 17, 19, 156
Hapsburgs: 4, 8
Harry, Philip: 192
Hatchet Mountains: 186
Havasu Canyon: 20, 28
Havasupai Indians: 18, 20–22, 25, 27, 32–35, 69, 79, 90, 125, 129, 133, 137, 149, 150, 152, 153, 156, 177, 184; Blue and Green Water People, 21, 28; Havasupai lands, 25, 120, 123, 131, 150, 152; Nation of the Willows, 20
Hawaiians: 184
Hesperus, town of: 56
Hidden Pool camp: *see* Agua Escondida
Hobble Creek: 105
Hochi Spring: 154
Hogans: 152
Hopi Indians: 15–22, 24, 25–27, 29, 30, 33, 34, 42, 55, 69, 72, 74, 78, 103, 125, 129, 133, 150, 154, 156, 158–61, 165, 166, 170, 172, 177, 184, 185; ceremonials, 17, 20, 21; Hopi mesas and pueblos (*see also* specific mesa or pueblo names), 17–20, 24, 25, 34, 35, 107, 133, 150, 153–56, 158, 159, 168, 185, 190; jewelry making, 128; "Moquis" or "Moquinos," 19, 20, 79, 137, 149, 154; Oraibis, 20, 154, 155, 165; Tanos, 156, 158, 160; Walpis, 156; weaving, 10
Hopi Reservation: 154
Horse Creek: 97
Horse Lake: 50
Horsefly Creek: 69
Horseshoe Bend: 92
Hot Waters: *see* Rio de Aguas Calientes
Hotchkiss, town of: 74
Houck, Arizona: 162
House Rock Valley: 138

House Rock Wash: 137
Howell Mesa: 154
Hualapai Indians: 27, 133
Huascari (extinct Paiute band): 126
Hubbard Creek: 75
Humboldt, Alexander: *see* von Humboldt, Baron Alexander
Humboldt River: 191
Hunting Knife: *see* Arroyo del Belduque
Hurricane, Utah: 128
Hurricane Cliffs: 128–31, 148
Hurricane Wash: 130

Ice Age: 41, 48, 70
Idaho: 89, 97, 108, 189, 191
Ignacio, town of: 54
Illinois River: 186
Imperial Valley: 11
Incline of the Departed: *see* Cuesta de las Ánimas
Indian Canyon: 95
Indian ruins: 55, 58–60, 68, 94, 192
Indian treaties: 95
Indies: 10, 178, 183, 184
Inquisition: 5, 136, 140
Inscription Rock: 163
Invincible Armada: 5
Isleta Pueblo: 34, 169–71, 188

Jamajabas: *see* Mojave Indians
Janos presidio: 188
Japan: 22
Japan Current: 4
Jefferson, Thomas: 189, 193
Jémez Indians: 42
Jémez Mountains: 42
Jémez Pueblo: 42, 100, 188
Jenkins, Myra Ellen: 193
Jews: 5
Jicarilla Apache Reservation: 50
Jicarilla Apaches: *see* Apache Indians

207

208

209